STRAIGHT EDGE

STRAIGHT

CLEAN-LIVING YOUTH, HARDCORE PUNK, AND SOCIAL CHANGE

ROSS HAENFLER

RUTGERS UNIVERSITY PRESS
NEW BRUNSWICK, NEW JERSEY, AND LONDON

Third paperback printing, 2007

Library of Congress Cataloging-in-Publication Data

Haenfler, Ross.
　　Straight edge : clean-living youth, hardcore punk, and social change / Ross Haenfler.
　　　　p.　cm.
　　Includes bibliographical references and index.
　　ISBN-13: 978-0-8135-3851-8 (hardcover : alk. paper)
　　ISBN-13: 978-0-8135-3852-5 (pbk. : alk. paper)
　　　1. Youth—United States.　2. Straight-edge culture—United States.　3. Subculture—United States.　4. Straight-edge (Music)—United States.　5. Hardcore (Music)—United States.
　　6. Punk culture—United States.　I. Title.

HQ796.H214 2006
306'.10973—dc22

2005028099

A British Cataloging-in-Publication record for this book is available from the British Library.

Book design by Adam B. Bohannon

Manufactured in the United States of America

*To the positive straight edge kids
who strive for a more just, peaceful,
and sustainable world*

CONTENTS

When I became straight edge in 1989, never in my wildest dreams did I imagine I would be writing a book about the movement fifteen years later. I am very happy to have the opportunity and thank you for reading my work. This book is not a comprehensive history of straight edge, though I do delve into the movement's background a bit. It is also not an exposé about scene "celebrities," who, for the most part, will remain as anonymous as my other participants. This book is my sociological account of the seven years I spent with the Denver/Boulder straight edge kids, as well as my visits to other scenes around the country. I hope that I have represented their stories well. I also hope that my analysis of their stories helps readers understand other youth movements. Straight edge is interesting in and of itself, but I have attempted to apply my conclusions beyond the boundaries of this one movement.

I have tried to describe straight edge in a general way that reflects the core of the movement. However, there is simply no way to capture every nuance of every local scene in every time period, let alone the experiences of every individual straight edge kid. If you are a straight edge reader, I hope you find some of your experiences reflected in this book—but you will undoubtedly discover some differences as well. The scenes in Boston, Los Angeles, Salt Lake City, New York, Cleveland, and other locations all have their own local idiosyncrasies. Likewise, straight edge in 2006 is different from straight edge in 1996, 1986, or 1981. Nevertheless, there is some continuity, and themes such as gender relationships and social change persist over time.

At age thirty-one, I am still straight edge, though I am much less involved in the scene than I once was. I care deeply about the movement and still believe in its potential to be a positive force in youth culture. This book and the research that led up to it are thus very personal. Readers will discover, however, that I raise critical questions about the scene, examining straight edge as I observed it, including its shortcomings as well as strengths. Any movement has its positive and negative aspects; my task here is, to the best of my ability, to present and analyze my observations as I experienced them in the field. I hope that my straight edge readers will take any questions I raise as opportunities to reflect upon what the movement has meant and what it might be in the future, and I hope that readers less familiar with straight edge will recognize the positive impact it has had in the lives of tens of thousands of kids.

This project would not have been possible without the help of many excellent friends and colleagues. I owe a huge debt of gratitude to Patti Adler for training me in the arts of ethnographic research. She and her husband, Peter, are great mentors and friends. Adi Hovav is a fantastic editor whose input greatly improved this work. Several of my Denver friends deserve special mention for their encouragement and loyalty, especially Collin Ahrens, Jimmy Beam, Mike Medina, and Matt Ramirez of Touch Clothing. Long discussions with Duncan Barlow also provided many valuable insights.

I also thank the many musicians who have inspired me, through both their music and their actions, among them: 7 Seconds, Bane, the Beastie Boys, Boy Sets Fire, Chuck D, Sage Francis, Fugazi, Good Clean Fun, Ian MacKaye, Insted, the Mutiny, Outspoken, Henry Rollins, Stretch Armstrong, Trial, Vitamin X, and Youth of Today. Whoever thinks music can't motivate us to excel and stay true to our ideals hasn't heard my soundtrack.

Finally, I thank my family and friends for their unconditional love: my mother, Ruth; brother Brad; father Duane; stepmother Carolyn; my grandparents; and my lifelong friends Nate Miller, Brett Johnson, and Ellis Jones. Last, but not least, I'm grateful for the support of my wonderful partner, Jennifer Snook, whose love is truly a blessing in my life. Let's GO!

STRAIGHT EDGE

STRAIGHT EDGE 101

In early 1989 I attended my first punk rock show with my best friend, Nate, and experienced a night that changed my life forever. The venue was an old cinderblock building at the county fairgrounds, and the bands included the Skrods, from Minnesota; PhantasmOrgasm, from Denver; and locals Painful X-tremities and Limbic Salad. The music was loud and harsh, the dancing was rough, but the entire evening was infused with a positive, supportive attitude. Nate and I "moshed" around the dance floor with the rest of the misfits, relishing every minute. When we fell, the other punks scooped us up, patted us on the back, and happily continued their flailing, stomping rotation around the mosh pit. These kids wore their hair in multicolored, crazy patterns, passed out flyers about vegetarianism and women's rights, and made shopping at the Salvation Army a virtue. For the first time in my life, I felt like I truly belonged.

Scattered among the punks in the crowd were a number of youths with large X's applied to their hands with black magic marker. I had also recently noticed that a friend of mine wore X's every day to the Spanish class we shared. Eventually, I came to understand the meaning: these kids were *straight edge*. They abstained from alcohol, drugs, tobacco, and even what they called "promiscuous" sex—hardly your typical punk rockers. They seemed fun, interesting, creative, engaged in the world, and they actually made it cool not to use drugs and alcohol. I was fifteen years old, and I had found a home.

The story of this research begins earlier, however, with a series of experiences that led to my involvement with the straight edge movement. In 1986 I was in the eighth grade at Dakota Junior High, a school in downtown Rapid City, South Dakota, where I grew up. Dakota served a diverse student body, including wealthy doctors' kids, children of the working poor, and Native American youth. Dakota housed a variety of cliques: metalheads with their torn jean jackets, long hair, and Iron Maiden t-shirts; athletes, wearing expensive shoes and dressing like Don Johnson on *Miami Vice;* 'preps,' with their Guess Jeans (rolled up over the ankles), big jewelry, and gelled hair; and of course the regular assortment of nerds, band geeks, vo-tech kids, and skaters. I was caught between them all, accepted in most groups but feeling at home in none of them. I had tried being a prep, but affording the expensive clothes so necessary to fit in with that crowd proved difficult. I had a bit more success as a metalhead, but my involvement with sports and home in a middle class neighborhood left me a few steps outside the inner circle. Despite their differences, each of the cliques held one thing in common: they all began experimenting with alcohol early.

Abstaining from drugs wasn't a problem for me; Nancy Reagan's "Just Say No" campaign left me terrified of becoming a burned-out addict. By high school, however, I had already experimented with alcohol for several years. My peers and I began drinking sporadically in the sixth and seventh grades. We would steal from parents' liquor cabinets, beg older siblings for booze, and bribe legal-age strangers to buy it for us. Getting alcohol was never easy, but the booze-seeking adventure was part of drinking's appeal. We were rarely caught, although I had a near miss at a school dance when the guidance counselor noticed me stumbling around the gymnasium; several friends and I had polished off a case of cheap beer out on the football field before entering. Even as I choked down the beer a part of me wondered what compelled me to drink something so foul tasting. But the desire to be accepted won out, and I drank until I threw up.

My luck did not hold during a second incident some months later. Two of my friends succeeded in filching a variety of hard liquors from their parents. Since my mother was out that night, six of us sat on my deck drinking a mixture of bourbon, vodka, and rum. After we had drunk our fill, we roamed the neighborhood, sneaking through yards and down side-walk alleys between backyard fences. Though a few of us were old enough to drive (the legal age in South Dakota was fourteen), none of us had cars, so we often walked the streets at night. Little did we know that our friend John, a star football player, had drunk considerably more than the rest of us. As we walked between two wooden fences, he suddenly went berserk, running back and forth between them and throwing himself at the fences as hard as he could. Somehow his pants had come down and were inside out over his shoes, causing him to stumble and trip as he yelled incoher-ently at the top of his lungs. The scene may have been funny were it not past midnight and had he not been about to seriously injure himself or one of us as he swung his fists. My friends and I tackled him, pinning his muscular frame to the ground and covering his mouth to avoid detection by the neighbors. Since my house was nearby, we dragged John, kicking and screaming, to my basement, his pants still dragging behind him. Once inside, two of us held him down and tried to console him while my friend Brian used a scissors to cut off his pants. I remember looking into his eyes and saying over and over again, "It's OK, John, it's Ross" while he continued to yell and lash out in drunken fury, not recognizing me. It took three of us to hold John down until he passed out, as my ten-year-old brother Brad looked on in horrified confusion. I defied my mother's rule against friends spending the night when she wasn't home and we all went to sleep, exhausted and traumatized by the whole evening.

The next morning two of my friends returned and retrieved John, who was still drunk, and took him to another part of the neighborhood as I delivered newspapers on my route. I made it home, lied to my mom, telling her the guys didn't have a ride home last night, and went back to bed. That morning, the police found John drunk in a yard and called his mother, a single parent like mine. After a tear-filled explanation, the next day, John, Brian, and I had a date with the school liaison police officer who had found out about the affair from other students. He gave us a lackluster speech about the dangers of alcohol and wrote us each a warning ticket. On the way out, he said with a wink, "If you're going to drink, you should at least have the sense not to let a bunch of giggly girls know about it. They tell everybody." My doubts about drinking continued to grow.

By ninth grade, obtaining and drinking alcohol became one of our biggest priorities. Those with ready access to liquor were held in high esteem, and drinking great quantities of alcohol was a surefire way to climb the social ladder. If you wanted to fit in, wanted to be "cool," you *had* to drink. I felt like there was no alternative, so I didn't question. Feeling like I was always on the border between the popular clique and everyone else, I was ready to do almost anything to avoid falling out of the inner circle completely. If that meant drinking until I was sick, so be it.

By tenth grade, keg parties in the woods outside of town became commonplace. Each weekend, an older-looking student with a fake ID would purchase a keg of beer, and carloads of kids would gather in the McDonald's parking lot before cruising deep into the forest to drink. Standing under enormous ponderosa pine trees, revelers bought a cup for a few bucks, got drunk, and drove the winding roads home. Always a bit of a cautious introvert, I increasingly felt this lifestyle wasn't for me. Shortly after attending that first punk show, for the rest of my high school life and beyond, I abstained from alcohol, drugs, and tobacco and began calling myself straight edge.

Drinking, for my fellow straight edge (sXe)[1] punks and me, became associated with popular kids and jocks, groups that did not appeal to us. Though some of my former friends chided and mocked me, and a few pressured me to resume drinking, my new social circle provided more than enough positive reinforcement and comfort to prevent me from ever turning back. Coming to grips with my own family's history of persistent alcohol use, and sometimes abuse, only strengthened my resolve never to touch alcohol again.

My regard for punks, and sXers[2] in particular, grew as I learned that my new friends were among the most politically active at my high school. They constituted the majority in groups like Amnesty International and Students Against Violating the Earth (SAVE), and were later a large part of local organizing against the 1991 Persian Gulf War. These groups inaugurated me into the activist world and challenged me to examine racism, sexism, and classism. Vegetarianism and animal rights had infused the scene by this time, prompting many of us to politely ask the lunch ladies at school to "please hold the hamburger. I'll just have the bun, lettuce, and tomato." Punk made the possibility of a better world a reality for me, and sXe seemed the purest form of punk—true freedom, no outside control, challenging some of the deepest-seated norms of youth culture. It was very idealistic and heady stuff for a teenager.

Even during my earliest involvement with sXe, I never wore X's on my hands. Like some of the participants in this study, I was suspicious of any sort of label and was unsure that I agreed with every aspect of sXe. I thought outsiders could easily interpret the group's message as judgmental and intolerant. I even grew my hair out long and kept wearing my Metallica and Iron Maiden t-shirts, fashion statements much more suited to the heavy metal scene. Although I agreed with sXe's message I was conscious of its weaknesses and contradictions and always felt that sXe had to be a means to a greater end, whether that was activism, art, or self-actualization.

After graduation, I left for the University of South Dakota in the fall of 1992. Located in a sparsely populated rural area surrounded by corn and wheat fields, USD offered little in the way of punk rock entertainment. Like high school, keg parties were the social events of choice, only now alcohol was even more readily available. I knew no other sXers, but I refused to drink. Occasionally I went to fraternity parties (when I could get in; few allowed nonmember men inside), but mostly I socialized with other misfits and a few friends from high school. By the end of my first semester, I had a steady girlfriend. She smoked cigarettes and sometimes drank beer, but gave both up immediately when our relationship began. Her background in the punk scene and her Alcohol and Drug Abuse Studies major made us a good match. We wore shirts with sayings like "It's OK not to drink" and "Sober" around campus, hoping that others would reconsider the beer culture we disliked.

Whenever I could, I would drive to punk shows in nearby cities, but these events were few and far between. As my studies, playing on the university soccer team, cartooning for the campus newspaper, and my new relationship kept me increasingly busy, sXe receded to the background in my life. Never once during my college years did I drink, smoke, or use drugs, but the sXe *identity* simply didn't feel as relevant as it had previously been. Other identities came to the forefront of my consciousness: student, activist, artist, boyfriend. As I grew further away from the sXe scene, I lost touch with the current trends and music. The movement's core values stayed with me, but without others who shared the identity, claiming sXe seemed rather passé.

In 1996, I graduated from USD with degrees in sociology and psychology and, at age twenty-two, began graduate school. My youthful involvement in the Midwest sXe scene grew into a sociological interest in this largely unstudied movement. I moved to Boulder, Colorado, to begin graduate training at the University of Colorado (CU). Boulder is a predominantly white university town of approximately 95,000 people and the university a large research institution with 30,000 students. Soon after arriving, I sought out the local Denver hardcore scene and began attending shows.

I went to my first Denver show in the late fall of 1996 at a rundown former movie theater in one of the city's poorer neighborhoods. Kids began mingling outside well before the doors opened, showing each other their new tattoos and jokingly practicing their dance moves in slow motion. A Los Angeles band called Downset was the headliner, but sXe kids were there to see Earth Crisis, a metal-influenced vegan sXe band that would transform the sXe scene in the mid-nineties. I went to the show by myself, but quickly sought out kids who had thick X's marked across their hands. My personal involvement and knowledge of sXe enabled me to gain entrée into the local scene very quickly. By using their vernacular, self-identifying as sXe, and consciously dressing the part (see Warren 1988) of an sXer by wearing a shirt with the slogan "It's OK not to drink," I immediately connected with other youth, particularly a small "crew" of guys from another nearby city. Each of them bore either an sXe tattoo or a shirt with an sXe message. The only thing that made me suspect was my very long hair (remnant of my metal days), still generally a fashion faux pas in the clean-cut hardcore world.

I quickly learned that I had a lot of catching up to do. Whole trends had developed within the movement in the four years since I had been actively involved, which proved beneficial for my work as I was able to approach the setting with a relatively fresh perspective. Earth Crisis, a band from Syracuse, New York, brought a militant cry for veganism and animal rights to the scene and had become a national voice for sXe. They and other musicians were borrowing heavily from the extreme metal genre. Sports jerseys, camouflage pants, visors, stainless steel body jewelry, tattoos, bleached spiked hair, and the occasional sweater vest (!) had largely replaced Krishna beads, shorts, hooded sweatshirts, t-shirts, and shaved or crewcut heads as the styles of choice. "Windmilling," "speed skating," "picking up change," "floor punching," and kung-fu spin kicks had supplanted circle pit dancing long before.[3] By 1996, sXe had almost become fashionable, something the outcasts who started the movement and the sXe punks I had grown up with would never have imagined.

I had never been much of a record collector, so I was fairly illiterate on the more obscure details of the history of sXe. I had never set up shows, been in a band, or created a 'zine (fan magazine), other roles central to the sXe scene. So although I had firsthand experience with the movement and some knowledge of its history, I was relatively naïve at the time I sought entry into the Denver scene. I knew enough to "pass" (Goffman 1974) and even to gain members' trust, but I felt disconnected and realized that I had to rediscover sXe. This was fortunate. I believe my naiveté enabled me to set aside some of the preconceived notions I may otherwise have brought to the setting, as everything seemed relatively fresh and new.

This book, based upon seven years of field research among the Denver/Boulder sXers, will take you into the lives of members of the sXe scene, showing that there is much more to sXe than hardcore music, living drug free, and what you may have seen on MTV, *20/20*, and *America's Most Wanted*. Scholars have written books about hippies, punks, skinheads, goths, rockers, and other youth subcultures and movements (for example Hebdige 1979; Brake 1985; Leblanc 1999; Wooden and Blazak 2001; Kaplan and Lööw 2002), yet until recently researchers have given little notice to sXe, despite the movement's twenty-five-year existence.[4] In the course of describing and explaining the sXe culture, I will address the numerous questions that emerged to guide my research. Where are the boundaries between subcultures and social movements? How do young men and women challenge stereotypical gender roles, and do they succeed? Is sXe a cool, hip version of the DARE program, or is it a middle class street gang that preys upon fraternity brothers, as some law enforcement agencies suggest? What happens to members of subcultures as they grow older in the scene? How do movements create and maintain boundaries designating who does and does not belong? What are the impacts of commercialization, the media, and the Internet on youth scenes? I'll start with a brief history of straight edge, outline the movement's major eras, and discuss the methods that guided my research.

A Brief History of Straight Edge

I'm a person just like you / But I've got better things to do / Than sit around and fuck my head / Hang out with the living dead / Snort white shit up my nose / Pass out at the shows / I don't even think about speed / That's something I just don't need / I've got the straight edge

I'm a person just like you / But I've got better things to do / Than sit around and smoke dope / 'Cause I know that I can cope / I laugh at the thought of eating 'ludes / Laugh at the thought of sniffing glue / Always gonna keep in touch / Never want to use a crutch / I've got the straight edge.

—"Straight Edge" by Minor Threat, 1981

These lyrics, from seminal hardcore band Minor Threat, launched a movement that over the span of more than two decades has convinced thousands of young people to give up (or never start) using drugs, alcohol, and tobacco products. Popular media, mainstream culture, and even social scientists have often stereotyped youth as hedonistic, sexually promiscuous, and mired in substance abuse. Youth substance use has been socially constructed as a serious social problem and periodic drug scares reinforce the image of youth as "in crisis" (see Goode 1993). However, sXe promoted a drug- and alcohol-free, sexually responsible lifestyle that appealed to thousands of youth around the world. Their conservative lifestyle combined with progressive punk ideals and harsh music sharply contrasted the conventional image of youth gone wild.

Straight edge emerged on the East Coast of the United States from the punk subculture of the early 1980s. Club owners in Washington, D.C., like many places, were unwilling to allow underage kids into shows[5] (the legal drinking age then was eighteen). Clubs made a significant portion of their profits from alcohol sales and were therefore more inclined to cater to adults. Owners also wanted to avoid being caught and fined—and possibly having their liquor license revoked—for harboring underage drinkers. The fact that alcohol prevented minors from experiencing the punk scene was intolerable to many kids. Luckily, a D.C. law barred music establishments from refusing to admit minors. To accommodate eager underage fans, clubs marked underage D.C. punks' hands with large X's

1. Cover to the 1980 Teen Idles' *Minor Disturbance* record, one of the earliest examples of a punk with X's on his hands.

as a signal to club workers not to serve them alcohol. The X, however, quickly became a badge of defiance. Youth transformed the X from a stigma (that is, not having access to the "privilege" of drinking) to a symbol of pride, as if to say, "not only *can't* we drink, we don't *want* to drink." The kids, including youth legally allowed to drink, began marking their own hands. The practice was popularized by the cover of D.C. band the Teen Idles' 1980 *Minor Disturbance 7"* record that showed a punk with crossed fists, each bearing a large X.

Though sXe has its roots in kids' practical desires to see the bands they loved, the movement arose primarily as a response to the punk scene's nihilistic tendencies, including drug and alcohol abuse, casual sex, violence, and self-destructive "live fast, die young" attitudes. The youths who would form the nascent sXe scene appreciated punk's "question everything" mentality, raw energy, aggressive style, and do-it-yourself attitude but were not attracted to the scene's hedonism and "no future" mantra. Straight edge's founding members adopted a "clean living" ideology, abstaining from alcohol, tobacco, illegal drugs, and promiscuous sex. Early sXe youth viewed punk's self-indulgent rebellion as no rebellion at all, suggesting that in many ways punks reinforced mainstream culture's intoxicated lifestyle in a mohawked, leather-jacketed guise. For many sXe kids, being clean and sober was the ultimate expression of the punk ethos, an act of resistance that defied both mainstream adult and youth cultures. Being "straight" gave youth an "edge" over their counterparts, as Minor Threat singer Ian MacKaye explained: "OK, fine, you take drugs, you drink, whatever. . . . But obviously I have the edge on you because I'm sober; I'm in control of what I'm doing" (Azerrad 2001:136).

Straight edgers credit Minor Threat, a D.C. band featuring former members of the Teen Idles, for creating the movement's foundation.[6] Their 1981 song "Straight Edge" gave the movement its name, and the chorus of 1983's "Out of Step" furnished its credo: "I Don't Drink, Don't Smoke, Don't Fuck—At least I can fucking think!" MacKaye, considered by many to be the closest thing to a founder that sXe has, had no intention of starting a social movement: "I guess the movement had sort of started, but in my mind I wasn't interested in it being a movement. It ran conversely to my initial idea that it was a concert of individuals, as opposed to a movement" (Lahicky 1997:102). Being a punk meant being an *individual;* adopting any sort of label or following any creed ran contrary to individual expression. Nevertheless, sXe quickly spread across the United States, blossoming in Boston with bands like Society System Decontrol (SSD) and Department of Youth Services (DYS); in Reno, Nevada, with 7 Seconds; and Los Angeles with Uniform Choice. Punk kids who were formerly ridiculed for not using alcohol and drugs now had a community that not only accepted sobriety but also championed clean living.

Straight edge remains nearly inseparable from the hardcore music scene. Indeed, throughout the book I will refer to the hardcore scene, which includes sXe and non-sXe kids alike. Hardcore is a broad genre but began generally as a faster version of punk.[7] During the 1990s the two scenes became increasingly distinct, with their own styles and fashions. Where punk encouraged flamboyant clothes and bizarre haircuts, hardcore favored a more clean-cut, straitlaced look. "There was a quantum difference between early punk and hardcore—it was something like the difference between bebop and hard bop in jazz, or the leap from Chuck Berry's affable rock & roll to Jimi Hendrix's freaky electrocution of the blues. It was all about the intensity of the delivery" (Azerrad 2001:130). Straight edge bands serve as the primary shapers of the group's ideology and collective identity. Hardcore shows are still the most important place for sXers to congregate, share ideas, and build solidarity.

Since its inception, the movement has expanded around the globe, counting tens of thousands of young people among its members. A 2000 Commitment Records boxed collection of sXe 7-inch records called *More Than the X on Our Hands: A Worldwide Straight Edge Compilation* features bands from forty-one different countries, including Chile, Italy, the Czech Republic, Singapore, Columbia, South Africa, the Philippines, Israel, South Korea, Malaysia, Russia, Guatemala, and Sweden. Hardcore and sXe bands from the United States have toured the world since the mid-eighties, sharing their styles and ideologies with fans from Europe to Japan to South America.

The basic tenets of sXe are quite simple: members abstain, completely, from drug, alcohol, and tobacco use and usually reserve sexual activity for caring relationships, rejecting casual sex. These sXe "rules" are absolute; there are no exceptions and a single lapse means an adherent loses any claim to the sXe identity. Abstaining means many things to sXers, including resistance, self actualization, and social transformation. Members commit to a lifetime of clean-living and, despite the group's lack of formal leadership and structure, sXers zealously stay "true" to their identities.

Like all youth movements, sXe was a product of the times and culture that it both resisted and grew out of. The rise of the new Christian right in the late 1970s and early 1980s contributed to a more conservative national climate that influenced youth values (Liebman and Wuthnow 1983). Fundamentalism gained appeal among populations who felt they were losing control of their ways of life (Hunter 1987). Straight edge's unyielding, black-and-white strictures on behavior were similar to fundamentalist religion's rigid, clear-cut beliefs (Marty and Appleby 1993). In particular, sXe's emphasis on clean living, sexual purity, lifetime commitment, and meaningful community was reminiscent of youth evangelical movements, while the focus on self-control suggested puritanical roots. In addition to these conservative influences, sXe was, in many ways, a continuation of New Left middle-class radicalism oriented toward "issues of a moral or humanitarian nature," a radicalism whose payoff is "in the emotional satisfaction derived from expressing personal values in action" (Parkin 1968:41). The movement's core values reflect this curious blend of middle-class conservative and progressive influences.

Straight edge attracts a variety of young men and women, but in the United States the typical sXer is a white, middle class male or female, aged approximately fifteen to twenty-five (Irwin 1999; Atkinson 2003). Some scenes are more diverse. At times the Los Angeles scene has had a strong Chicano sXe/hardcore movement centered around bands such as

None for All and Downset. Straight edgers may or may not clearly distinguish themselves from their peers by wearing large Xs on their clothing, bookbags, or on each hand before attending punk concerts. Some are easily identifiable while others blend perfectly into the surrounding culture.

Straight Edge Trends

Like other youth movements, sXe has a long and complex history. The movement changed over time, adopting new styles and behaviors and absorbing and reacting to other social trends and musical styles (see the timeline of straight edge bands at the back of the book). Each era of sXe history produced adherents with similar attitudes and interests. The following descriptions, in roughly chronological order, are merely caricatures or loose archetypes; it is often difficult to pigeonhole most sXers into one category or another. Furthermore, younger sXers may adopt a persona based upon a previous archetype: for example, a nineteen-year-old who becomes sXe in 2006 may align her or himself with the youth crew style that was popular two decades earlier.

Old School

Old school hardcore emerged in the early days of punk rock at the beginning of the 1980s, before the two scenes separated. Bands such as Black Flag, Bad Brains, Circle Jerks, and the Dead Kennedys toured the country playing their more aggressive brand of punk rock. Though these bands were initially labeled "hardcore punk," today's hardcore scene did not coalesce until the mid-1980s. The style of dress was often typically punk: short hair or shaved heads with the occasional mohawk, jeans and band t-shirts, bandanas, and spiked belts and wristbands. Common lyrical themes included friendship, standing out from society, and voicing opinions and concerns about the world. Minor Threat (D.C.), Verbal Assault (RI), SSD (MA), 7 Seconds (NV), and Uniform Choice (CA) were sXe stalwarts of the old school era, and Warzone (NY), Cause for Alarm (NY), Agnostic Front (NY), and Negative Approach (MI) also had an impact. Hardcore was very fast and relatively simple, and the singer shouted more than sang. Gradually, an underground network of musicians and fans developed, writing each other letters, sending each other tapes, and promoting each other's bands. This era saw the rise of the rivalry between Boston and New York kids, battles with Nazi skinheads, and the initial split of hardcore from punk.

Some sXers still identify with the old school era, keeping the connection between sXe, punk, and hardcore alive. They might wear dirty jeans with bands' logos hand-sewn into the thighs, a patch-covered jean jacket with spikes, or a full beard, a rarity among sXers. They associate with punk rockers who reflect punk's original ideals such as individualism, disdain for work and school, and live-for-the-moment attitudes, yet are ardently sXe and often vegetarian. Old school sXers are just as likely to play in a punk as a hardcore band. Like many individuals aligned with old school punk, these sXers disdain what they see as the judgmental, cliquish nature of many sXers. Some claim to be "punk first, sXe second" and for them hardcore music and sXe *are* punk rock. Many old school sXers collect a variety of records, attend shows of every punk sub-genre, love circle pits, and have little tolerance for kids who only support sXe bands or only go to hardcore shows. As strong supporters of underground, "Do It Yourself" (DIY) music, though, they despise "corporate punk rock," typified by bands such as Sum 41 and Blink 182.

Youth Crew

The youth crew era of approximately 1986–1991 helped spread sXe around the United States and the world, bringing new energy and urgency to the movement. Most of the first wave of sXers drifted from the lifestyle and distanced themselves from the hardcore scene, but not before inspiring a new generation of kids. New York's Youth of Today was the main inspiration behind this era, with charismatic singer Ray Cappo seeking to unite the scene into an sXe *movement*. It is their song "Youth Crew" which gives this era its name.

Kids of the youth crew era often took on a more clean-cut image than their old-school predecessors; their carefully cut short hair, running shoes, shorts, and t-shirts sometimes evoked comparisons to jocks. Indeed, many sXers at the time were or had been athletes, and kids emphasized the healthy aspects of a clean lifestyle as much as the social challenge it posed. Champion™ brand hooded sweatshirts were common, as were high-top basketball shoes and short sleeved shirts worn over long sleeves. Bands from this era, such as Bold (NY), Gorilla Biscuits (NY), Turning Point (MA), Side By Side (NY), No for an Answer (CA) and Insted (CA), were still popular in the 2000s, years after they had broken up. (Both Insted and Bold played reunion shows in 2004-2005.) Youth crew preached positivity, personal responsibility, loyalty, sXe pride, and fun. Revelation Records was the premier sXe label of the time, releasing many

2. A girl stage dives as fans sing along with youth crew era band Bold, playing a reunion show. Reunion shows were especially common in the 2000s, much to the delight of younger fans who never had the chance to see bands that had broken up in the early nineties or before. Photo by Todd Pollock.

classic sXe recordings that now sell for hundreds of dollars on Internet auction sites.

It was also during this time that vegetarianism gained a significant hold in the sXe scene, as Youth of Today recorded the animal rights anthem "No More" in 1988:

> Meat eating flesh eating think about it / So callous to this crime we commit / Always stuffing our face with no sympathy / What a selfish, hardened society so / No More / Just looking out for myself / When the price paid is the life of something else / No More / I won't participate.

Their West Coast counterparts, Insted, spread the vegetarian message with their song "Feel Their Pain" on the *We'll Make the Difference* record:

> Hear my words—Feel their pain / Eating their flesh—You have nothing to gain / A moral opposition / To the murder of animals / It's

my philosophy / To take life is criminal / The smiling clown / For the billions served / Represents to me / Bloodshed undeserved

Bands also increasingly questioned casual sexual encounters in their lyrics, such as Youth of Today's "Modern Love Story" and "What Goes Around." Themes of personal empowerment and living a meaningful life were common.

Though the shows were intense, youth crew had a certain light-heartedness that appealed to many youth, especially kids from the suburbs. Some kids today look upon many of this era's lyrics as cheesy or simplistic and joke that sXe was a hardcore manifestation of the Boy Scout Oath. Some sXe kids today have never even heard of the youth crew bands that laid the groundwork for the movement's growth in the 1990s. Still, many kids new to the sXe scene eventually discover and enjoy this music, and the era still has a tremendous influence, as evidenced by the ongoing "youth crew revival" bands.

Today's youth crew kids retain the close-cropped hair, hoodies, and cargo shorts of their earlier heroes. Many wear vintage band t-shirts bought at shows or on the Internet. Their favorite bands include youth crew legends such as Gorilla Biscuits, Floorpunch (NJ), Bold, Chain of Strength (CA), and, of course, Youth of Today. Many older sXers (aged thirty plus) came of age during this era, which still holds a special place in their hearts. They often collect all kinds of punk and hardcore records and some are sXe historians, able to discuss the history of nearly every band, its music and members. Most reflect the positivity of the bands they love and many are vegetarian. It is fairly common to find older youth crew kids wearing the "X" Swatch, a watch with a white face and black X.

Though youth crew music was temporarily drowned out by more metal-influenced music in the 1990s and 2000s, periodic revivals have kept the sound and style alive. The music remains fast, featuring short songs without the growling vocals or intricate guitar work of metal. Floorpunch, Ten Yard Fight (MA), and Ensign (NJ) spurred new interest in youth crew sXe in the mid and late 1990s, and D.C. area bands Good Clean Fun, Count Me Out, and Down to Nothing carry on the tradition. Seattle youth crew style group Champion is perhaps the most popular sXe band in 2005.

Emo-Influenced/Politically Correct

As youth crew kids matured, many of them became increasingly aware of social issues such as sexism, homelessness, government corruption, and inequality. Wanting to break away from the perceived simplicity of old school and youth crew, musicians of this era added more melody and complexity to their music while still keeping the intensity and urgency of previous bands. "Emo" music, short for "emotional," has grown alongside hardcore and punk, becoming especially popular in the late 1990s and after (Greenwald 2003) and influencing a variety of hardcore bands. Emo has its roots in bands such as Rites of Spring, Sunny Day Real Estate, and Jawbreaker, but is now such a broad category it is difficult to define. Emo lyrics express feelings of "nostalgia," "romantic bitterness," and "general poetic desperation" (ibid.:12-13). Early-nineties hardcore and sXe bands with a variety of styles like By the Grace of God (KY), Four Walls Falling (PA), Forced Down (CA), Mouthpiece (RI), and Outspoken (CA) addressed issues of power, repression, and relationships. Like oldschool, this genre traces back, once again, to the Washington, D.C. scene where mid-80s bands such as Rites of Spring, Embrace, Faith, Fugazi and others played melodic, emotionally charged music. It was not uncommon to see sXers from this era with longer hair than their youth crew counterparts. They wore long-sleeved shirts, running shoes, beaded necklaces, and the oversize pants more common in hip hop circles.

Also known as the "Politically Correct," or PC, era, this was a period when many sXers took an interest in social issues, emotions, and self-actualization. Songs and discussions about sexual assault were common and the "Chicks Up Front" posse helped women stake out their space in the scene. Trial (WA), for example, actively promoted Native American rights, including championing the cause of imprisoned American Indian activist Leonard Peltier. It was also at this time that Krishnacore emerged, as Ray Cappo and John Porcelly ("Porcell") of Youth of Today became interested in the teachings of His Divine Grace AC Bhaktivedanta Swami Prabhupada, who popularized Krishna Consciousness in the United States. Equal Vision Records released records by Hare Krishna hardcore bands including 108, Refuse to Fall, and Cappo and Porcell's group, Shelter. Shelter and 108 toured extensively, sharing vegetarian meals and Krishna teachings with their fans.[8]

Today's PC sXe kids might wear sweaters, jeans, and sneakers; a spiked belt could be the only thing that makes them stand out from the rest of the young, alternative crowd. Buddy Holly style glasses have been a staple of this genre for years and carrier bags covered in buttons are not uncommon. These fans are somewhat less likely to sport X's and tattoos than are the old school, youth crew, and metal kids. Many of these sXers take issues of sexism, racism, and homophobia very seriously. Some get involved with activism, martial arts, or spiritual interests, while others pursue higher education. When hardcore turned toward metal with its concurrent increase in hypermasculine behavior, many PC sXers became disillusioned with the scene and what they saw as a stagnant musical style. Many have become fans (or members) of indie rock bands, holding onto sXe values while having less involvement with the hardcore scene.

The Victory Era and Metalcore

Beginning in the late 1980s, a few youth crew bands such as Judge, Integrity, and Chorus of Disapproval (CA), delved into a heavier sound. Victory Records artists Strife (CA), Earth Crisis (NY), and Snapcase (NY) paved the way for a more metal-influenced hardcore in the 1990s. Their April 1996 "California Takeover," in which all three bands played shows together at Los Angeles's Whiskey A Go-Go and Corona's Showcase Theater, marked a resurgence of sXe pride. Earth Crisis also ushered in vegan-sXe,[9] increasing the scene's focus on animal rights and opposition to environmental destruction. The style reflected hip-hop and athletic fashion, as baggy pants and sports jerseys became the norm. The bands of this era continued with the intense social criticism of the emo era, taking on issues of racism, environmental destruction, hunger, and human and animal rights. Strife and Earth Crisis were among the most political—and adamantly sXe—bands ever. While the youth crew kids sported a clean cut, athletic look, even more metal-era males were large and muscular. Dancing became an acrobatic affair as kids leaped, punched, and kicked through the air. By the mid-1990s, the number of sXe kids swelled, although it seemed many were part of the scene more for the fashion and dancing than because they were committed to the original sXe principles. Nevertheless, thousands of kids adopted a strict vegan lifestyle, refusing to eat all animal products (often including honey); wear any kind of suede, leather, or wool; and support companies that tested products on animals. Influenced by the rhetoric of Earth Crisis and Unconquered (NV), sXe kids of this kind were very outspoken about sXe, although as they aged they often became less opinionated.

Today hardcore and metal have fused into a hybrid genre often called metalcore. Many bands are still influenced by Earth Crisis, though Throwdown (CA) has made a strong impact on the scene. Hatebreed (CT), Unearth (MA), and Poison the Well (FL) are extremely popular non-sXe bands with these kids. As metal-influenced sXe grew, the style of dress shifted to large military-style cargo pants, basketball jerseys bearing band (instead of sports team) names, expensive New Balance running shoes, and large, stainless-steel hoop earrings through "stretched" ears. Kids alternated between camouflage hats and bandanas, folded hippie style, over gelled, stylish haircuts. Most metalcore kids have several tattoos and many have relatively little sense of sXe's roots. Some don't care about Minor Threat, Youth of Today, or any of the other pioneers of the movement and dislike old school and youth crew style music in general. At shows, they enjoy dancing very hard and several times I witnessed kids leaping over the front of the crowd, crawling over people's heads to sing along with the band.

Straight Edge after 2000

As Victory stalwarts Strife[10] and Earth Crisis broke up, youth crew revivalists Ten Yard Fight and Floorpunch went their separate ways, and indie rock and emo music exploded even more into the mainstream, sXe once again receded into the margins of subcultural life. Many sXers began growing out and dying their hair black and wearing expensive jeans to match their indie rock counterparts' disheveled look. "Fashioncore," a rather derogatory label describing preppy sXers in the nineties, was resurrected in a new form; instead of sweater vests and bleached hair, contemporary trendsetters wore ultra-tight black T-shirts and form-fitting jeans, adopting a somewhat effeminate look popularized by bands such as Eighteen Visions, From Autumn to Ashes, and Atreyu. Tattoos virtually became an obsession. While pockets of militancy remained, without a nationally recognized band leading the way, the movement maintained a quieter presence in the underground scene.

Hardcore has always had some mainstream commercial appeal. Some bands managed to eke out a meager living from their musical earnings. Strife and Earth Crisis had both played one of heavy metal's biggest events, Ozzfest.[11] By 2002, even more hardcore bands were receiving mainstream attention, earning radio airplay and slots on MTV 2. Hatebreed placed a song on the *XXX* (Triple X; no connection to sXe) movie soundtrack, and H2O (NY) continued to tour, as they appealed to both the hardcore and punk scenes. Victory and Revelation Records expanded, signing a variety of indie, emo, and hardcore bands. As hardcore edges its way into more mainstream youth culture, the future of sXe as an oppositional subculture remains to be seen.

Researching the Straight Edge Scene

Throughout the course of my research, I used many methods to gather and record information, from examining song lyrics to face-to-face interviews. I assumed several roles and explored various settings to discover how sXers understood and lived their beliefs. The intimate connection between sXe and hardcore music meant I spent a lot of time attending hardcore shows. Before revealing just how I went about conducting my research, I must try to convey the atmosphere at a show.

Describing a good hardcore show is like trying to explain the feeling of skydiving, meeting your hero, or standing in the Sistine Chapel; there is simply no adequate way to explain the experience to those who have not been there. Every music scene has something magical that makes it a beautiful experience for its fans. Bluegrass touches people's yearnings for a rural, simpler past and encourages everyone to sing and play along. Hip hop's energy can have an entire crowd bobbing their heads and pogo-ing up and down to the beat. The atmosphere in a great jazz club creates a mood unlike any other setting. Hardcore's gift is an urgent, physical intensity that to outsiders might look like a riot. "Patrick,"[12] a twenty-five-year-old tattoo artist from the East Coast, compared a good show to an intense religious experience:

> If you can go to show and feel like you're on top of the world when you leave, like you've just had a religious experience . . . how could you beat that?! [laughs] I just feel like there's very, very few things—especially in today's world—that can give people like a sense of self-worth and positivity. People talk about going to raves and just having this unreal experience, with the music and the lights going. Get some of those kids to a good hardcore show and see what happens. There is nothing in the world that is like that, goin' to a show like that and seeing a hundred kids piled on top of each other with the band just inches away from where they are and frickin' microphones in there—this huge melting pot of energy. Stick a fork in it. [laughs] There's no other scene that's like that. Even in the punk rock scene, there's not that sense of togetherness so much, or like strength that you can get from the hardcore scene. . . . Literally we got out of a Boy Sets Fire show and were like "That was like going to church." That was like having your faith revived. Your strength renewed.

I recall being at metalcore band Unearth's show in early 2003 where most of the core members of the Denver scene sat cross-legged on the floor just before the band's set began, forming an irregular circle in the middle of the pit. Just as the guitarists struck their first notes, the kids leapt up and pushed the rest of the audience to the walls, creating a large, open dance area which immediately filled with flailing, kicking kids. In the space of two seconds the room went from quiet, casual interaction to

3. Often the distance between band and audience completely disintegrates, with kids mobbing the singer and screaming into the microphone. For many kids, this is the ultimate hardcore experience: sharing the intensity of the music with the musicians. Photo by Amanda Raney.

a frenzy of swinging arms and stomping feet. Unearth played abrasive, fast, and most of all, *loud* music for nearly an hour, leaving the room simultaneously exhilarated and exhausted. In the eyes of hardcore kids, the best show is one in which both the band and audience "go off," losing control, jumping, and screaming together in a melee of tangled bodies. A great show carries a tense feeling in the air as if a fight or injury could happen at any moment, yet usually neither occurs. When a kid falls down, other kids, friends or strangers, ideally pick up their fallen comrade, who quickly leaps back into the fray.

Many readers may be familiar with "slam-dancing" or "moshing," both of which have been mainstays in the heavy metal and punk rock scenes for decades. Slam dancing, most popular at metal concerts, usually involves two or more burly, long-haired men running head on at each other, colliding shoulder to shoulder, bouncing apart, then repeating the motion until all involved are sweaty, sore, and grinning from ear to ear. Moshing, or "circle-pit" dancing, is most common at punk shows and involves kids running, skipping, and jumping in a large circle, randomly colliding with other moshers as stage-divers launch into the crowd from the stage. Hardcore kids frown upon slam dancing as ignorant, ungraceful, or silly. They have a more favorable attitude toward circle-pits, as many have roots in the punk scene, though a hardcore show is generally much more intense than a typical punk show.[13] Hardcore includes an exhibitionist element that slamming and moshing do not. The center of the dance floor remains relatively open, allowing a few individuals at a time take the floor, demonstrate their skills, and exit, permitting the next group to participate. (Breakdancing in hip-hop scenes follows similar patterns of "exhibition dancing.") Meanwhile, other kids crawl over one another to scream along with the singer.

As the band approaches a song's bridge, called a "breakdown" in hardcore music, the kids wait in anticipation. Hardcore bands, particularly those with a heavy metal influence such as Unearth, put slow, crunching riffs in the bridge. The kids reserve their most outstanding dance moves for the breakdown, windmilling, floor punching, and kung-fu kicking their way from one side of the pit to the other. Others practice "headwalking," stepping on the heads and shoulders of their fellows as they carve a precarious path to the stage.

An uninitiated observer might have difficulty telling the difference between hardcore dancing and fighting.[14] While it may be difficult for outsiders to comprehend how a hardcore show could possibly be fun, participants generally have a fantastic time, despite the bumps and bruises they carry home with them. In fact, the occasional shiner, fat lip, or bruised shin usually makes for a good story and serves as a badge of honor: "I survived the insanity of the mosh pit!" Moshers describe the experience as a safe, relatively harmless "release" of emotion, aggression, and frustration. Though outsiders may view moshing as violent, dangerous, or antisocial, for insiders it is a fun, communal, and essential element of what sets hardcore apart from other musical genres. This is the setting in which I conducted much of my research.

My Place in the Scene

Since I joined the sXe punk scene, I have attended over three hundred hardcore punk shows, maintained the lifestyle, and associated with sXers on a regular basis. The data I present come from over fifteen years of observing the sXe movement in a variety of roles. From the fall of 1996 to the summer of 2004 I participated in the Denver scene as a complete member (Adler & Adler 1987), attending shows, sXe parties, movies, and pot lucks; contributing artwork to a local fan magazine; and occasionally participating in a local animal rights group. I developed diverse relationships over the course of my research, leading to other roles in addition to those of researcher and fan. I was primarily a friend, but as I grew older I wrote letters of recommendation for sXers, helped them find jobs, gave advice, and even taught several sXers in my classes. People tell me I became known as one of the more positive people in the scene, serving as a peacekeeper at shows and sometimes informally mentoring younger kids. Kids repeatedly asked for my perspective about social issues and internal scene disputes. Several temporarily homeless sXe kids lived with me in my trailer home and others stopped by for an occasional meal. Likewise, when I needed help the Denver sXers were always there for me.

Though my involvement with sXe began elsewhere, when I was quite young, over the course of this research I grew older than most members of the Denver scene. Since sXe is primarily a youth movement, relatively few "adults" over twenty-five are active in the scene, making me somewhat of an anomaly. My age during this research, from twenty-two to twenty-nine, made me young enough to fit into their culture rather easily, yet old enough to have been involved with sXe during the youth crew peak of 1988–1989. Therefore my age was more of an asset than a hindrance. My experiences, dedication to the sXe lifestyle, and longevity in the movement intrigued some of the younger adherents, motivating them to seek me out for conversation.

Research Settings

I gathered data primarily through longitudinal participant observation (Agar 1996) with sXers from 1996 to 2005, conducting my research in a variety of settings. My contact with the Denver/Boulder group occurred primarily at hardcore shows and social events at sXers' houses. (Throughout the book, when I refer to Denver I include the metropolitan area, including Boulder and the surrounding suburbs.) In an effort to expand my knowledge of sXe beyond my primary friendship circle, I sought informants outside of the local scene, including individuals from other cities, members of touring out-of-state bands who played in the area, and individuals around the country I contacted via email. I also spent several days in New York City, Los Angeles, Memphis, Boston, and Connecticut to experience the scenes there. I was fortunate in that many of my Denver participants were originally from the East Coast and could highlight similarities and differences between that scene and the local scene. A few regional idiosyncrasies aside, the basic sXe ideology was remarkably consistent around the United States.

Every underground culture has a "scene" (Irwin 1977); kids speak of the "hip-hop scene," the "rave scene," and the "punk scene." Scenes exist at several levels and the term holds a variety of meanings. Generally, scene refers to a subcultural identity, overlapping networks of people that hold similar interests and beliefs and follow similar styles. It also signifies a specific genre of music; within the larger punk scene exist many sub-groups: the "indie rock," "pop-punk," and "crust" scenes, for example. Scene can also refer to geographical location, including cities (for instance the "Boston scene," the "Salt Lake City scene," or the "Louisville scene"), states ("California scene"), regions ("West Coast scene"), countries ("U.S. scene"), or the world (the worldwide punk scene). Local sXe scenes gained reputations based upon the bands they produced, how many kids would come out to shows, and how fans behaved at the shows. Boston, for example, had a reputation as a scene that produced many good bands, turned out lots of kids for shows, and regularly attracted a fairly tough, hard-dancing fan-base. Salt Lake City earned a reputation as an especially radical and sometimes violent scene during the mid- to late-1990s. Denver was known as a small, tight-knit scene that perhaps traded the intensity and numbers of a larger scene for a closer, more family-oriented feel.

"Support your local scene" was a common rallying cry at all levels: the scene should be nurtured and supported; kids should go to as many shows as possible; the scene deserves loyalty. The scene was a manifestation of the sXe collective conscience. Kids asked themselves what they were doing for the scene, how they could contribute, and how it needed to be changed. A "scenester" was someone who rarely missed a show, had heard all of the latest bands, and who may be involved in booking shows, playing music, or publishing a 'zine. While well-known and often well-liked, scenesters sometimes also had a negative reputation; to some kids, they seemed to glory in the bands they knew, the connections they made, the tattoos they had, and the clothes they wore. Viewed as overly interested in cultivating a "hardcore" image, some scenesters were more concerned with being "seen" than with contributing to the "scene." Hardcore kids joked about earning "scene points" for a variety of feats: wearing a *really* old band shirt, finding an especially rare record, chatting with a "famous" band-member online, or crawling over the heads of people at a show to sing along during a crucial chorus. Individuals built reputations not only upon their longevity in the scene and what they contributed but also on their attitude. Many sXers felt the most "true" individuals to the scene were self-effacing, modest people not out to make money or exploit the scene in any way. They gave their time and commitment for the kids and their participation was its own reward.

4. Dutch band Vitamin X plays a show at the "Junkyard" in Denver, an auto shop run by a lo-cal punk. Photo by Ross Haenfler.

I attended shows at a variety of small music clubs and bars. Typical clubs were usually rundown buildings on the fringes of downtown metro areas. However, Veterans of Foreign Wars halls, college campuses, and basements served just as well. Once I attended a show at a warehouse that was only accessible through a gap in a chain link fence at the back alley. In Denver, old movie theaters hosted many shows. The most interesting place I regularly saw bands was a garage called the Junkyard, literally located in a junkyard owned by an older punk mechanic. Kids moshed in the midst of rebuilt transmissions, dismantled engines, and the shells of wrecked cars. The stage at a show, if there was one, was often only one foot off the floor, and ideally there was no barrier between the band and the crowd, enabling the singer to hold the mic out to audience members who wished to sing along.[15] Off to one side, bands' "roadies," usually just friends along for the trip, set up the "merch" (merchandise) tables, hawking CDs, vinyl records (both 12″ and 7″), short- and long-sleeved t-shirts (often duct-taped to the wall for display), hooded sweatshirts, stickers, windbreakers, 'zines, and posters. Merch took on an almost sacred meaning; a shirt from a particularly spectacular show helped recall memories of the event. Regular show-goers felt obligated to "support the bands" and bands hoped they would sell enough items to buy gas and food until the next stop on the tour. Particularly dedicated kids would buy merch from a band even if they weren't really excited about the music. Most hardcore bands made little or no money and some arrived home from tour in the hole. Therefore, kids viewed buying merch not only as an exchange of money for goods they wanted, but as a duty to keep the scene alive. The Internet, and particularly the online auction site eBay™, brought the underground merch trade to new heights as older kids sold their collections online. Rare records and shirts sometimes commanded hundreds of dollars at auction. Record collecting was a hallowed pastime. Many punk and hardcore kids revered their records and spent years (and thousands of dollars) filling in the gaps in their collections. The most dedicated collectors coveted colored vinyl, limited editions, "splits" (records with a different band on each side), "comps" (compilations of a variety of bands), and cover variations.

Usually between fifty and two hundred youth attended a typical show, although "fests,"[16] weekend-long shows, often with over thirty bands, attracted many more. Generally there were one or two "headlining" bands, usually from out of town, and another one or two local bands. The local bands made little (if any) money from the shows they played but agreed to play to gain fans, have fun, and support the scene.[17] Local members of the scene booked bands, promoted the shows, and secured venues at little or no profit to themselves. Bands often set up their own tours across the country, contacting kids through an underground word-of-mouth network or connecting via the Internet. Kids volunteered to work the door, taking the $4–$10 cover charge and marking people's hands with a felt pen or stamp. After the show, the band slept on someone's floor until they hit the road the next day, piling into a crowded rented van in which they had probably built a sleeping loft. The DIY ethic, prominent in the punk and hardcore scenes, reflected young punks' attempts to avoid the capitalist, profit-driven music world by promoting their bands, shows, and records themselves or through small companies, thereby avoiding "selling out" (O'Hara 1999). By the mid-1990s, a variety of hardcore entrepreneurs owned record labels,[18] record stores, promotion companies, and mail order catalogs, making the scene a bit more professional. Promoters took over venues and larger record labels signed bands.

Data Gathering and Analysis

In Denver, my friendships grew to include approximately seventy-five sXers in the local metro area and another thirty sXe and non-sXe acquaintances associated with the larger Colorado hardcore scene. The sXers I studied were mostly, but not exclusively, area high school or university students from middle-class backgrounds. To supplement my participant-observation, I conducted unstructured, in-depth interviews with twenty-five sXe men and twelve women between the ages of seventeen and thirty-five. I began by contacting my closest associates in the scene and eventually worked my way to acquaintances and youth with whom I had less contact. All of the interviewees were quite willing to participate. Even those I did not know well were eager to tell their stories. In order to learn from a variety of individuals, I selected sXers with differing levels of involvement in the scene, including new and old adherents and individuals who had made the movement central or peripheral to their lives. I conducted in-depth interviews at sXers' homes or at public places free from disturbances, recording and later transcribing each session. Each session began with the participant reading and signing an informed consent document. Though I organized the sessions around particular themes, I left the interviews sufficiently unstructured for individuals to share exactly what sXe meant to them. Interviews averaged approximately seventy minutes in length and at times turned into conversations rather than question-and-answer sessions. I sometimes asked for referrals in a snowball fashion (Biernacki & Waldorf 1981), although I knew most participants well enough to approach them on my own. For additional perspective, I interviewed six former sXers still associated with the scene but no longer committed to the movement. This variety of participants allowed me to continually cross-check reports and seek out evidence disconfirming my findings (Stewart 1998; Campbell 1975; see also Douglas 1976). My own involvement with sXe made me an "auto-ethnographer" (Hayano 1979); my insider status was invaluable to my work but I had to maintain constant vigilance against potential bias.

Throughout my research, I referred to principles I had learned from feminist methodologists. Feminist ethnography emphasizes, for example, "identification, trust, empathy, and nonexploitive relationships" (Punch 1986:89), which I intentionally incorporated into my research relationships. It was essential to me to make my participants more than objects of study. I wanted to involve them in the research and get to know them on a personal level. Telling their stories was also important to me—sXe was a frequently misunderstood youth movement and I welcomed the opportunity to give adherents the chance to explain what sXe meant to them. At the end of each interview, I offered participants the opportunity to ask *me* questions. Though relatively few sXers did so, providing the opportunity was important to me in order to maintain a relationship beyond a merely professional one (Reinharz 1992). When I did answer questions, it often elicited additional meaningful dialogue from the interviewee as well. Although my questions directed the interview, several interviewees indicated afterwards that they felt the session was more like a conversation. Participants regularly commented that sharing their stories was an empowering experience and that the interview had made them reconsider sXe in new and meaningful ways.

Interviewing young sXe women produced its own set of challenges. Some of the data I sought required that I ask female sXers about potentially awkward topics, such as their beliefs regarding sex, female oppression, what I saw as their marginalized position in the scene, and what they thought about sXe men. I had constructed a very nonthreatening and in many ways nonmasculine role in the setting by refusing to act "tough," wearing shirts with antisexist slogans, and trying to make women feel welcome in the scene. I had excellent rapport with almost all sXers, including sXe women. Several commented that they felt very comfortable speaking with me, and it seemed the women were especially eager to tell their stories, probably as a result of their marginalization in the scene. However, I sometimes had the feeling that had I been a woman my female participants would have shared different and possibly more nuanced information. I took care to create a safe space, but I cannot be completely sure how my gender affected my interviews: "Living within a society, or visiting one as a fieldworker, presupposes a gendered interaction, a gendered conversation, and a gendered interpretation" (Warren 1988:10). Alternatively, I think it is possible that young women felt *more* comfortable sharing certain information with me than they would have with a woman researcher. Many women participants seemed appreciative that a man would listen to their frustrations with both women in the scene and the masculine character of sXe.

In addition to participant observation, casual conversation, and interview data, I examined a variety of other sources, including newspaper stories, music lyrics, web pages, band videos/DVDs, and sXe publications. Straight edgers built community and shared ideas through small, homemade fan magazines, or 'zines. Individuals or small groups produced 'zines filled with artwork, stories, record and concert reviews, band interviews, and columns on a wide variety of subjects, including police brutality, animal rights, homelessness, and the movement to free journalist and former Black Panther Mumia Abu-Jamal from prison. 'Zines, like concerts, were generally DIY: that is, kids created them at home, distributed them, and rarely made any money from them (in fact, 'zines often cost the producers a great deal of money).

In the mid- to late 1990s, websites and email list-servs became the latest forum for sXe discourse. Dozens of web pages offered the movement philosophy and many more profiled the latest sXe bands. Various list-servs and chat boards kept hundreds of sXers from across the country in daily contact. Periodically, I scanned the major sXe online bulletin boards to compare Denver with scenes elsewhere. I did not analyze 'zine or website data in a systematic way. Rather, I used the data to develop new lines of inquiry in my participant observation and interview research. Finally, I videotaped twenty shows and later reviewed the video, paying particular attention to dancing, gender representations and ratios, clothing style and t-shirt slogans, band-audience interaction, and messages promoted by the bands. This proved quite useful as I could review specific attributes of bands and crowds that would have been difficult to record during the show.

To record and organize my data, I took brief notes at shows and other events which I immediately afterwards expanded into full field notes on the computer. Using headings and subheadings, I coded data according to particular topics of interest, beginning the process of organizing data into useful and interesting categories (Charmaz 1983). Throughout my research, I sought patterns and emerging typologies of data (Lofland and Lofland 1995). Reexamining the coded field notes and transcribed interviews led me to analyze several themes, described in the chapters that follow. I continually refined these themes as I gathered more data through emergent, inductive analysis (Glaser and Strauss 1967; Becker and Geer 1960).

Methodological Concerns

Although for the most part my research in the Denver scene went smoothly, I was conscious of several methodological concerns during the course of this study. As my work progressed, I especially had to confront the issues of growing older in a youth setting and managing my own ethical boundaries.

Youthful Sociologist Grows Older in the Scene

My young age was an asset throughout much of my research. Had I been much older, I do not think I would have had access to sXers in the variety of contexts that I did. Though presumably people of any age could attend a show or conduct an interview, I was able to join sXers at home, in school, at work, and in a vast array of social situations that an older researcher would have found problematic at best. Younger researchers have a distinct advantage when studying youth subcultures. Initially my age increased the likelihood I could gather "authentic" data from my young participants, as they did not view me as an authority figure potentially monitoring their behavior (Eder and Corsaro 1999). My appreciation of sXe music and fashion enabled me to blend in where older researchers might have been suspect.

Aging in the scene brought challenges I hadn't anticipated. Many of the friends who originally welcomed me into the movement in 1988 had moved on by the time I finished this study. As my work in Denver progressed I became increasingly conscious of my age. I was always one of the oldest people at shows; only a handful of Denver sXers were my age or older. As the gap between our ages widened, I felt less comfortable in the setting; my current life experiences simply differed from most sXers' circumstances. Although I had no difficulty maintaining a drug-free lifestyle, my increasing involvement in the more "adult" world of academia began to draw me away from the scene. I managed my feelings of disconnection by befriending a few sXers closer to my age and focusing slightly more on interviews, rather than participant observation, toward the very end of my work.

As I aged, the potential that sXe youth would see me as an authority figure became another issue I had to address. By the end of the study, few people had been involved in the Denver scene longer than I had. I worried that this would produce a level of respect for me among the sXers that might have influenced their interactions around me.[19] Although such respect felt good and affirmed my hope that I had created meaningful relationships with sXers, I worried about the effect it could have on my research. As my work progressed and I grew older within the scene, I began to more consciously "manage" my identity in the field (Hammersley and Atkinson 1995). I tried to be as unassuming as possible, downplaying my age and experiences, and cultivated a rather neutral presentation of self (Goffman 1959). I also increased my vigilance for deviations from my original findings.

At times, balancing my researcher and member roles taxed my emotional strength. Coffey (1999:1) writes that "fieldwork is personal, emotional and identity *work*" (emphasis in original). "Fieldwork can be recast as a process where the self is central" (ibid.:24), particularly when researching as a complete member of the setting. As I studied a movement that had been so meaningful to me as a youth, I discovered the "dark side" of sXe that failed to live up to the group's high standards. Such is the danger for any researcher who chooses to study her or his own group. Some sXers' judgmental attitudes, occasional infighting and gossip, rare episodes of violence, and the fact that many members would eventually drop the sXe identity all "disenchanted" my notions of what sXe had been, causing me to reflect upon my own commitment to the group. Observing and recording the discrepancies between ideology and action enabled me to maintain a critical outlook throughout my research to offset my personal involvement. However, it also made me question who *I* was and why I chose to continue membership in a group that did not always live up to my ideals. Discussions with colleagues and older sXers, many of whom experienced similar feelings of ambivalence (see Chapter Eight) helped me persevere through challenging periods of my work.

Moments of Truth: Where Do You Stand

Ethnographers face ethical decisions in nearly every moment of their research (Van Maanen 1983). As Punch (1994) points out, our research will rarely, if ever, turn out like we expect it to and mine was no exception. Various individuals, groups, and organizations pull our loyalties in a variety of directions, creating difficult choices throughout the research process. Far from being resolved, ethical debates among ethnographers rage on, producing a continuum of beliefs regarding acceptable ethnographer behavior and loyalties. I often kept certain feelings and opinions to myself, not wanting to have too much influence on the scene. Several times throughout the course of my study I had to decide whether or not to intervene in events that could alter the character of the setting. In particular, I became known as someone who disliked fighting and would break up confrontations if at all possible. Ethically, it was difficult for me to watch someone I knew suffer physical assault. My training in nonviolent intervention prompted me to attempt to de-escalate potentially violent situations. Though I did my best to maintain a relatively neutral role in the setting, my loyalty to my friends/participants prompted me to become involved in their lives. The Denver sXers were fiercely loyal to one another and, as an adopted member, to me. Any number of them would have risked harm to defend me from virtually any aggressor. I felt I had to offer the same in return. Fortunately, I never faced a situation where I felt I had no choice but to fight, although a few confrontations came very close to pushing me in that direction.

As I have described, shows in the underground hardcore scene are extremely intense experiences, visually, audibly, and even physically. The aggressive music and hard dancing of testosterone-fueled young men sometimes sparked physical confrontations between participants. Fights were rare in Denver, remarkably so given hardcore's hypermasculine atmosphere. Generally, fights began when one youth, often new to the scene, would shove or run into another, crossing the line between dancing and violence. This unspoken line was difficult to identify, but readily understood by scene regulars. Incidental contact was generally accepted, but if someone perceived a shove or bump as intentional, a confrontation was likely to ensue. People generally tried to avoid fighting, both as a matter of principle and because too many fights might shut down the few precious venues available for shows. Sometimes, however, men brought their personal grudges to shows.

Such confrontations put me in a delicate position, potentially jeopardizing my research role and creating ethical dilemmas. An especially precarious example involved Norman, a nineteen-year-old former sXer, who decided to throw a "sellout" party where former sXers could celebrate selling out. For reasons I never understood, he continually made fun of and degraded sXe, despite still having many sXe friends. Several sXers told him they thought the party was disrespectful, but Norman believed it was all in good fun and planned to go ahead. Word spread and a few sXers from a group called Courage Crew (see chapter 6) took special offense. Shortly thereafter, I noticed Jackson, a football player, student, and soldier with tattoos covering his huge physique, and Clint, a young military man, also covered in tattoos, watching Norman at a show. I sensed trouble and, since I knew all of the parties involved, prepared to intervene if necessary. Jackson grabbed Norman and I tried to break it up, but before I could accomplish anything he took Norman by the throat and punched him repeatedly in the face. As I struggled to pull Jackson away, Clint threw me onto the floor, pinned me down, and cocked his fist back, prepared to punch me if I moved. By this time, Norman had fled the building. Two of my friends, Sid and Andy, pulled Clint off of me. When the band finished its set, I confronted Jackson, telling him what he did was disgusting and an awful and damaging reflection on sXe. He mocked me and then refused to talk with me.

Many of the Denver kids were suspicious of Courage Crew at best and hated them at worst. I had previously played the middle ground, neither accepting nor condemning the group, careful to avoid gossip that might later come back to damage my relationships in the setting. I also genuinely liked several of the members. However, in staying neutral I may have sacrificed an opportunity to learn more about Courage Crew in depth, and, though less likely, other sXers might have thought I was sympathetic to the group. The Norman incident threatened to temporarily divide the scene and placed me solidly in the "anti-Courage Crew" faction. Although intervening cost me any relationship I might have had with Jackson and Clint, I managed to salvage my relationships with two other Courage Crew members. The situation, though uncomfortable for months, eventually died down.

From then on, I wondered if certain members of Courage Crew held a grudge against me. Everything I had heard from kids around the country was that Courage Crew kids were exactly the wrong enemies to make and I wondered if they would physically attack me. Generally, my view of Courage Crew was less critical than the views of other members of the Denver scene, and I didn't believe they would go out of their way to hurt anyone. However, it was not uncommon for someone holding a grudge to "accidentally" punch, kick, or shove his adversary while dancing. The attack was then incongruous enough that the aggressor could shrug it off as "just dancing." I was sure that my other friends would do their best to make sure I didn't get hurt, and I felt like I had good rapport with the two Courage Crew members, but the entire situation made me uneasy for months. The irony that the most threatened I had ever been at a show came at the hands of other sXers left me dispirited. I attempted, almost a year later, to approach Jackson and Clint, but they were still uninterested in speaking with me.

Overview

Studying sXe has been an exciting, fun, challenging, and sometimes frustrating journey that has changed me as a person. I have done my best to present sXe from all angles, whenever possible letting the kids speak for themselves. As I work my way through the following chapters, I explore sXe as a subculture and a social movement. I discuss sXe tolerance and militancy as well as how the movement offers alternatives for both young men and women. I end with chapters on "older" sXers and the impact of commercialization and the Internet on the scene. I have never been in a band, put on a show, or released a record—this book is my contribution to the scene. I hope it adds a piece to our ongoing discussion of what it means to be sXe and where the movement might go in the future.

STRAIGHT EDGE CORE VALUES

In 1991 I saw Krishnacore band Shelter play in my hometown of Rapid City, SD. For a bunch of punk rock kids in a small Midwestern city this was an especially big event. Shelter was the newest project of singer Ray Cappo and guitarist Porcell, both formerly of Youth of Today and two of the most recognized names in sXe. The band emerged with tulasi bead necklaces and little ponytails (sikha), launching into their set with reckless abandon. Ray repeatedly leaped off the low stage and into the crowd, at times crawling over top the kids supporting him, while Porcell jumped up and down, an intense grimace across his face. For many of us in the crowd the show was like a dream come true—our heroes had arrived! These guys were *so cool*. Not only did they not drink, use drugs, eat meat, or have sex, they adopted a religion that many people consider to be a *cult*! Shelter's entire lifestyle seemed like a way of resisting parents, society, and the "cool" kids at school. It was like they were giving the entire "normal" world the middle finger and laughing all the way to enlightenment.

Most youth subcultures claim to offer a path of resistance to the mainstream, adult, or "straight" world, and sXe is no different. As Katherine, a twenty-two-year-old working class woman from the East Coast, said, sXe is about "being yourself" in a world constantly pushing you to conform, "accepting that you're different and being different and not trying to be what everybody wants you to be and what MTV says is cool." Straight edge is unusual among youth movements in that its members seek self-actualization and a more positive world through refusing drugs and alcohol. The group combines conservative and progressive values to create a distinct form of resistance to dominant *and* youth cultures, resisting and reproducing aspects of both through its core values. Early subculture research focused primarily on the style, as opposed to the substance, of youth resistance, arguing that youth movements inadvertently reinforce the mainstream society they oppose. Later research questioned the very idea of bounded, definable subcultures. In this chapter, I re-examine the question of whether subcultures offer meaningful resistance by examining sXe core values.

XXX

Studying Youth Subcultures

A subculture is a social subgroup distinguished from mainstream culture/dominant society by its own norms, values, rules, and, especially in youth subcultures, its own music and style (Bennett 2001). The term "youth subculture" connotes "a pattern of values, beliefs, symbols, behaviors, and activities that a group of young people are seen to share" (Baron 1989; see also Brake 1980; Frith 1985). These subcultures are made up of youth dissatisfied with the mainstream adult world who seek to carve out their own niche. They offer disadvantaged youth symbolic resistance to oppression, an alternative lifestyle, a "cultural space" through which to challenge dominant values, meaningful leisure time, and solutions to existential dilemmas (Brake 1985).

Subcultural studies developed in sociology from what eventually became known as the Chicago School (for instance Whyte 1943; Gordon 1947; Becker 1963). Countering psychological explanations for juvenile delinquency, early theorists conceived of subcultures as deviant groups that emerged in response to social problems, rather than as a result of individual failings. Subcultures are not necessarily groups of "bad kids" but instead are primarily working-class kids reacting to poverty, joblessness, and oppression (Mungham and Pearson 1976).[1] They emerge in resistance to dominant culture, challenging blocked economic opportunities, lack of social mobility, alienation, adult authority, and the "banality of suburban life" (Wooden and Blazak 2001:20). Adherents seek to "solve" these problems by joining together to empower themselves, celebrating the very deviance the "straight" world finds so disconcerting (Cohen 1955). They have their own style, vernacular, and rituals that serve to separate them from the larger society and resist what they deem to be an unfulfilling world.

Resistance has been a core theme among both subcultural participants and the scholars who study them (Hall and Jefferson 1976). Early subcultural theorists associated with Birmingham University's Centre for Contemporary Cultural Studies (CCCS) concentrated on the ways youths symbolically resisted mainstream or "hegemonic" society through style, including clothing, demeanor, and vernacular (Hebdige 1979; Hall and Jefferson 1976). Style is a symbolic form of resistance to dominant social relations. Subcultures resisted dominant society through "rituals" (Hall and Jefferson 1976), and stylistic "signs" embodied youth's rejection of the "adult" world (Hebdige 1979:17). Subcultures infused everything with meaning. Thus one could interpret the mods' scooter gangs as an attempt to win back space from encroaching "rockers," early punks' garish makeup as a jab at society's emphasis on physical beauty, and hippies' "free love" ideology as a challenge to what they saw as the stifling conformity of the 1950s. Subcultural style, according to these theories, holds many layered meanings, but it is primarily a symbolic form of resistance that in actuality changes social relations very little. Still, CCCS theorists leave the impression of heroic, or at least sympathetic, youth doing their best to fight the overpowering, oppressive system.

Scholars have given a great deal of attention to the question of whether these youth subcultures resist or *reinforce* dominant values and social structure (Hebdige 1979; Willis 1977; Brake 1985; Clark, et al. 1975). The researchers of the CCCS emphasized that while subcultural style was a form of resistance to subordination, ultimately their resistance merely reinforced class relations (Cohen 1980; Willis 1977). Therefore any such resistance was illusory; it gave subculture members a feeling of resistance while not significantly changing social or political relations (Clarke et al. 1975). In fact, according to this view, subcultures often inadvertently reinforced, rather than subverted, mainstream values, recasting dominant relationships in a subversive style (see Young and Craig 1997). For example, instead of engaging in collective action to challenge class oppression, punks sniffed glue, dyed their hair, and donned spiked leather jackets. Far from thwarting the existing class structure, punks' actions actually ensured their *downward* mobility, reinforcing the Birmingham Centre's theme that "subcultural empowerment is empowerment without a future" (Gelder and Thornton 1997:87).[2] Likewise, while offering resistance to some social norms a group might reinforce others, as is often the case with gender roles. Young and Craig (1997), for example, report that skinheads' sexist attitudes mirrored the sexism inherent in society.

Later work paints an even more pessimistic picture of subcultures' potential to affect society. "Club culture," "post-subculture," "neo-tribal," and "scene" theories call into question the very concept of stable, coherent subcultures, let alone the idea of subcultural resistance (Thornton 1995; Muggleton 2000; Bennett 1999). These approaches challenge the CCCS ideal of the "heroic" subculture opposing the "hegemonic" system (Muggleton and Weinzierl 2003). Rather, they argue that youth culture is fluid, heterogeneous, and postmodern, focused more on style, taste, and personal fulfillment than on politics and social change.

If resistance is defined only in terms either of fashion or of the potential to overturn the social class structure, the outlook from a participants' point of view is indeed grim. My analysis of sXe core values shows that resistance is much more complex than previously thought and that while subcultures are indeed fluid, members nonetheless maintain boundaries and a sense of belonging to a distinct group.

Straight Edge Core Values

Resistance in a time of mass self-destruction / Makes the few who walk the straight edge / A growing force of change / Committed, though gripped by the plague of a nation / Consumed by its intoxication and confined by crippling greed / In my rage / I walk the path of true change / Commitment sworn in the name / Of those who will walk the straight edge / Convictions held to my grave.

—"Force of Change" by Strife, 1997

Throughout sXe's history, trends in the movement have come and gone almost as quickly as have sXers. Identifying a core set of principles that spans time and geography is difficult because values change, each scene has its own flavor, and even individuals within the same scene have different interpretations of sXe. Straight edgers recognize that sXe means something different to each person, assuming the identity and, as with any group, individual members' level of dedication varies. However, while individuals are free to follow the philosophy in various ways, often adding their own interpretations, there is a set of fundamental values that underlays much of the movement: positivity/clean living, lifetime commitment to the movement and its values, reserving sex for caring relationships, self actualization, spreading the subculture's message, and involvement in progressive causes.

T-shirt slogans, song lyrics, tattoos, and other symbols constantly remind sXers of their mission and dedication: "It's OK Not to Drink," "True Till Death," and "One Life Drug Free" are among the more popular messages. The "X," sXe's universal symbol, emerged in the early 1980s, when music club owners marked the hands of underage concert-goers with X's to ensure that bartenders would not serve them alcohol (see Lahickey 1997:99; Wood 1999). As I mentioned in the introduction, soon the kids intentionally marked their own hands, both to signal club workers of their intentions not to drink and, more importantly, to make a statement of pride and defiance out of not drinking. The movement appropriated the X, a symbol meant to be negative, transforming its meaning into discipline and commitment to a drug-free lifestyle.[3] Youth wear X's on their backpacks, shirts, and necklaces; they tattoo them on their bodies; and draw them on their school folders, skateboards, cars and other possessions. The X unites youth around the world, communicating a common set of values and experiences. Straight edgers find strength, camaraderie, loyalty, and encouragement in their sXe friends, valuing them above all else. The community in Boulder was very tight-knit. Shows, frequent potlucks, movie nights, parties, hanging out at popular campus

5. Mike Medina, of Denver sXe band the Mutiny, "Xes up" before a show. Photo by Ross Haenfler.

locations, involvement in local animal rights activism, and even the occasional sleep-over kept members in regular contact. Many sXe youth live together. With the advent of email and the Internet, sXe kids communicate via a 'virtual community' around the country and sometimes the globe (see Williams 2003). A powerful sense of community, based in large part upon the hardcore music scene and symbolized by the visual avatar of the X, is the glue that has held the sXe movement and its values together for twenty years.

Positive, Clean Living

Through the clouds I see the light / My conscience tells me what's wrong and right / Morals goals deep inside / A bunch of feelings I just can't hide / But that's me. . . . The way "I" live / My outlook on life is Positive

—"Positive Outlook" by Youth of Today, 1986

The foundation underlying the sXe identity is positive, clean living. Straight edge is, as Darrell Irwin (1999) suggests, fundamentally about subverting the drug scene and creating an alternative, drug-free environment. Clean living is the key precursor to a positive life. Many sXers even shun caffeine and medicinal drugs, and a majority are committed vegetarians or vegans.

Positive living holds different meanings for various members, including questioning and resisting society's norms, having a positive outlook on life, being an individual, treating people with respect and dignity, and taking action to make the world a better place. Straight edgers claim that one can not fully question dominant society while under the influence of drugs, and that once one questions social convention, substance use, eating meat, and promiscuous sex are no longer appealing. Therefore clean living and positivity are inseparable; they reinforce one another and constitute the foundation for all other sXe values. Joe, an eighteen-year-old high school senior and skateboarder, explained how the "positivity" he gains from sXe shapes his life:

> To me, I guess what I've gotten from [sXe] is living a more positive lifestyle. Striving to be more positive in the way you live. Just being more positive around people. Because where I was at when I found it was really [laughs] I was really negative myself. I was negative around people and influenced them to be negative. I was surrounded by negativity. Then I found this and it was like something really positive to be a part of. Also, like the ethics, drug free, alcohol free, no promiscuous sex. It's just saying no to things that are such a challenge for people my age, growing up at that time. It's a big thing for some people to say "No."

Refusing drugs and alcohol has a variety of meanings for individual sXers, including purification, control, and breaking abusive family patterns. Purification literally means being free from toxins that threaten one's health and potentially ruin lives. Popular t-shirt slogans proclaim "Purification—vegan straight edge" and "Straight edge—my commitment against society's poisons." Straight edgers believe that drugs and alcohol influence people to do things they would normally not do, such as have casual sex, fight, and harm themselves. By labeling themselves as more "authentic" than their peers who use alcohol and drugs, sXers create an easy way to distinguish themselves. They experience a feeling of uniqueness, self-confidence—and sometimes superiority—by rejecting the stereotypical teenage life. Refusing alcohol and drugs symbolizes refusing the "popular" clique altogether. It is also a rejection of the perceived nihilism of other groups, such as punks, hippies, and skinheads.

The movement provides young people with a way to feel more in control of their lives. Many youth experience peer pressure to drink alcohol, smoke cigarettes, or try illegal drugs.[4] For some, this pressure creates feelings of helplessness and lack of control; acceptance often hinges on substance use. Straight edgers report that the group gives them a way to feel accepted without using and helps them maintain control over their personal situations. Matthew, a seventeen-year-old high school student and Christian, claims the sXe identity in part to resist both peer pressure and drug addiction in his own family:

> Everyone in my school smoked weed. It was just kind of a common thing. If you didn't do it, you weren't anyone's real friend. There was *nobody* that didn't do it and didn't hang out with kids. That was just kind of the way it went. Myself, I started smoking marijuana when I was in sixth grade. I had my first cigarette when I was in fourth grade. So I kind of knew the path I was heading down because I'd seen a lot of my family members head down that path. Like my dad, especially. He had gone through some pretty horrible drug abuse and stuff. I just kind of realized I was going the same way. That just wasn't what I wanted to do.

Breaking family patterns of abuse is a common theme among sXers. Maggie, a twenty-three-year-old community college student and a veteran of the Denver scene, claimed she became involved in sXe as an act of resistance against her family history:

> My brother, his whole adolescence he was a partier. He would do any kind of drug and it really messed up my family. It had a lot to do with my father. He left when I was two. My mom doesn't really tell me all the reasons, but I know he was a coke addict. He died when I was nine because he had AIDS from dirty needles. That really affected my family, you know. Then my brother heading on the same path. I was like, "Wow, I don't want to be like that and mess it up even more for our family." That had a lot to do with it. . . . I don't wanna mess up my family like my brother did. There were a lot of crappy days growing up just because of him.

Likewise, Gus, a twenty-three-year-old working his way through community college, became sXe in reaction to his cousin's drug abuse. He did not want to put his family through a similar situation:

> My cousin was into heroin. Just watching him, my mom, and my aunt . . . he started doing serious drugs when my grandmother died, 'cause they were really close. He started doing serious drugs 'cause

he couldn't handle it. Just having to watch my mom and my aunt pull him off that stuff—they had to lock him in a room. He would just scream and want more. It was terrible. Just having to visualize that, I knew I never wanted to be any part of it. He's the cousin I look up to the most. He taught me a lot that I know. He's like a brother to me. Every single time I go out there, he always tells me "I'm really proud of you for being who you are. A lot of people see what happened to me, but they still don't learn. You took my bad example and turned it into a good thing."

Many sXers celebrate the fact that they would never wake up after a night of binge drinking wondering what had happened the previous evening. Adherents report that sXe allows them to have a "clear" mind and be free to make choices without artificial influence (see Wood 1999). Walter, a reserved twenty-one-year-old university student and aspiring lawyer, explained:

> I don't make any stupid decisions. . . . I like to have complete control of my mind, my body, my soul. I like to be the driver of my body, not some foreign substance that has a tendency to control other people. I get a sense of pride from telling other people "I don't need that stuff. It might be for you but I don't need that stuff." And people are like, "Whoa! I respect that. That's cool."

Shannon, a twenty-two-year-old English major at CU, claimed sXe helps her be "true" to her self and maintain an "authentic" experience of life:

> I guess I want to remember my life. [laughs] I don't want . . . I meet people and they've been drinking and then they don't remember you. What's the purpose of that? I just think that you need to experience life . . . I don't know. It just bothers me to even think about not remembering the previous night. I think that it's important to experience life with a clear head and act with . . . be true to yourself. A lot of people argue that you're still yourself when you're drinking, but I don't know. I don't necessarily agree with that. [laughs]

In addition to the personalized meanings the identity holds for adherents, sXers view their abstinence as a collective challenge. The group offers a visible means of separating oneself from most youth and taking a collective stand against youth culture and other youth subcultures.

Furthermore, for many, positivity and refusing drugs and alcohol are symbolic of a larger resistance to other social problems including racism, sexism, and greed. Abstinence is the personal manifestation of a larger progressive commitment to challenge, as one sXer put it, the "ills of society."

Straight Edge—It's for Life

You said it shouldn't be taken too seriously / You said it was just your personal ideas and opinions / You said it was only meant to relate directly to your life / What about my life? / Has the edge gone dull? / Well maybe now that you've grown dull and old / We'll pick up where you left off / To you it was just music / But to us it was so much more / When we put our heads together we'll prove we've got the edge that can never dull / True till death / Has the edge gone dull?

—"True Till Death" by Chain of Strength, 1989

Straight edgers make a lifetime commitment to positive, clean living. They treat their abstinence and adoption of the sXe identity as a sacred vow, calling it an "oath," "pledge," or "promise." Members make few exceptions to this rule. Ron, an easy-going twenty-year-old musician and ex-football player, said, "If you just sip a beer, or take a drag off of a cigarette, you can never call yourself straight edge again. There's no slipping up in straight edge." Youth crew era band Chain of Strength's song "True Till Death" (1989) remained an anthem for many sXers a decade after it was published, chastising former sXers for giving up the lifestyle and celebrating adherents who stayed "true." Despite their vehement insistence they would "stay true" forever, relatively few sXers maintain the identity beyond their early- to mid-twenties. Many perpetuate the values and rarely use alcohol or drugs, but "adult" responsibilities and relationships infringe upon their involvement in the scene. When formerly sXe individuals began drinking, smoking, or using drugs, adherents claim they had "sold out" or "lost the edge." While at times losing the edge causes great conflict, I observed that more often the youths' bonds of friendship superseded resentment and disappointment and they remained friends. However, a former sXer's sXe friends often express deep regret and refuse to allow the transgressor to claim the identity ever again. Brent, an outspoken twenty-two-year-old vegan, said:

There is a strain on the friendship. It's harder to be open with someone who has sold out. What are they gonna do next? Can I trust this person with my emotions and my feelings? Why should I when I valued them in the past and they turned their back on me? Why should I continue to patronize them as friends? . . . It's frustrating to see people who you think are your friends make such heavy decisions without consulting you. . . . It's not a betrayal like turning around. It's just that you feel abandoned. . . . It's demoralizing.

Kate, a twenty-two-year-old animal rights activist and student originally from the East Coast, explained her frustration with sellouts:

> It was hard for me at first because I think when people do that it takes away the power of sXe. When people are like, "I'm sXe" and then the next day they're not. It—not delegitimizes completely—in a way it takes away some of the legitimacy of the movement. . . . It definitely upset me a little bit. How can you go from claiming sXe one day and the next day just forget about it completely? That was the main thing; I just didn't understand it.

Some "sellouts" incessantly mock their remaining sXe friends, often with a good-natured humor, but sometimes with subtle rancor. Luke, a twenty-seven-year-old sXe tattoo artist, held himself to strict standards and, like many sXers, felt disappointed by sellouts:

> I feel stabbed in the back because I don't think people take the commitment seriously enough. I always meet kids, and they're like I'm gonna be sXe. Well, it's not a five minute decision. It's something you want to think about because it's a serious commitment. To me, it's pretty much . . . to me it's an extremely serious commitment. So I feel like it's a stab in the back, because it's something that I've spent, now it's like twelve years, trying to make better. I'm trying to make sXe as positive as I can. For them to just spit in the face of it by saying, "Yeah, I tried it, it's stupid, whatever." It's one thing to try and go drug free, but sXe is like a serious commitment. People think that claiming sXe and being drug free is simultaneous. No, it's not. Being sXe is like an outspoken lifestyle, whereas being drug free, there's millions of Americans who do it. Maybe they do it for religion, maybe they do it 'cause they used to be abusers. I just see weakness when I see people sell out. I don't like that, it bugs me. . . . Being sXe *is* a commitment for life. That's a *huge* difference, I think. One of them there's no barriers. Anyone can walk up and say "I'm drug free." Not everyone can say they're sXe. Unless they know that they're down for life.

However, sellouts who disparaged their former movement especially angered him and other sXers as well:

> It is hard to be friends with sellouts sometimes, because they almost want to rub it in your face. In my experience, they always want to talk shit on sXe: "Fuck that, it's stupid, it's a gang." I'm like, "Hey, it didn't work for you. If you are going to walk away from it, fine. No hard feelings. I'm not going to be your friend, you're not going to be my friend, but don't talk trash on it either. Don't try and justify your weakness by picking apart something that to me is one of the best ways to live."

When particularly outspoken or well-known members of the scene sell out, sXers speak as if another hero has fallen. When members of especially popular or outspoken sXe bands sell out many sXers respond first with disbelief, then with profound disappointment. A very small minority of individuals base friendship on adherence to the movement and almost practice "shunning," the religious equivalent of casting someone out. It is this type of action, despite its rarity, that contributes to outsiders' conceptions of sXe as a judgmental, dogmatic group. Straight edge youth are less likely to socialize regularly with people who use simply because of the incompatibility of the lifestyles. Straight edgers only occasionally openly criticize friends who have sold out, but during interviews participants expressed to me a deeper frustration and sense of betrayal than they would ever publicly show.

Murry, raised in an alcoholic family and already heavily tattooed at age nineteen, compared the sXe vow to vows of matrimony: "It's true till death. Once you put the X on your hand, it's not like a wedding ring. You can always take a wedding ring off, but you can't wash the ink from your hands." Murry proceeded to show me a tattoo on his chest depicting a heart with "True Till Death" written across it.

Many sXe youth have similar tattoos to signify the permanence of their commitment and "[to promote] their message of personal pacification and control" (Atkinson 2003:200). In fact, tattoos (sXe or not) are almost ubiquitous in the Denver scene, for both men and women. Joe received a tattoo shortly after his eighteenth birthday. While he was interested in tattoos in general, he wanted his first one to be especially meaningful, so he chose an sXe theme to demonstrate his commitment to the movement:

> It shows that this is a *serious* commitment. It's not like a joke. 'Cause I've seen people say, "Yeah, I'll be sXe." But it's like two weeks

later they don't care. It just shows that this is something I take seriously. If other people think it's a joke, fine, whatever. But this is something that's serious for me.

The "XXX" across the inside of the wrists is common, as are large Old English style "Drug Free," "True Till Death," or "Vegan Straight Edge" on the stomach or chest. A few sXers have the triple X tattooed on the inside of their bottom lip. A number of well-known sXe tattoo artists work around the country. In Denver alone, three sXers are accomplished tattoo artists. They would often offer sXe kids discounted prices, especially if the tattoo was sXe related, and many sXers would only have a sXe tattoo done by an sXe artist.

The sXe scene has significant crossover with the body modification subculture. Some sXers attend tattoo/body modification conventions. They often sport multiple piercings, including the nose, eyebrow, nipple, tongue, and genitals. Stainless steel hoops through "stretched" ears are the most common and a few sXers have enormous "plugs."[5]

Reserving Sex for Caring Relationships

You laugh because it's funny / You laugh because it's true / You never really think about it, do you? / A union for the body / With nothing for the mind / You'll scrape and beg to get it, inside! / Yet still you call them lovers / When they're not even friends / and when they won't submit to you, love ends! / It's done without commitment / I say it isn't right / It's casual treatment of the act, that / Takes lives! / How could you possibly think that it was safe? / With self induced diseases all over the place / Casual sex has taken thousands of lives / The sense of being used is warping people's minds!

—"You Laugh" by No for an Answer, 1988

Reserving sex for caring relationships is an extension of the positive, clean lifestyle. Many sXers view casual sex as yet another pitfall of dominant society, their counterparts in other youth subcultures, and their more mainstream peers. It carries the possibility of sexually transmitted diseases and feelings of degradation and shame. Whereas hippies viewed liberated sex as revolutionary, punks saw it as just another pleasure, and skinheads valued sex as a supreme expression of masculinity, sXers see abstinence from promiscuous sex as a powerful form of resistance. Rejecting the casualness of many youth sexual encounters, they believe that sexual relationships entail much more than physical pleasure. They are particularly critical of the image of the predatory, insatiable male, searching for sex wherever he can get it. Ian MacKaye explained the "Don't Fuck" lyric in the Minor Threat song "Out of Step" as rejecting "conquestual" sex (Azerrad 2001:139). Kent, a twenty-one-year-old CU student with several colorful tattoos, said, "My personal views have to do with self-respect, with knowing that I'm going to make love with someone I'm really into, not a piece of meat." Kyle, a twenty-three-year-old senior at CU, whose girlfriend had recently slept with another man, said:

> For me, I like monogamy. If I care about a girl, I'll have sex with her. But it has to be a true feeling. Mostly love. That's why this last girl really kind of hurt me. It's the first girl I ever really thought I loved. So that was just devastating. I don't believe in sleeping around. . . . I won't sleep around with a bunch of people just for health's sake. A good positive influence. [Sex] doesn't mean anything if you don't care about a person.

Respect for one's body and health were also concerns for Walter, who said:

> For me it's just choosing how I want to treat my body. It's not something I'm just going to throw around. I'm not going to smoke or use drugs. My body is something that I honor. It's something we should respect. I think sex, if you're gonna do it you should do it, but you shouldn't throw your body around and do it with as many people as you want. If you love your body so much as to not do those things to your body you should have enough respect to treat women and sex how they deserve to be treated.

Though sXe values regarding sexuality appear puritanical, sXers are neither antisex nor homophobic as a group. Sex is not considered wrong or "dirty" as in some traditionally puritanical views, and numerous sXers and sXe bands take a strong stance against homophobia.[6] Sex can be a positive element of a caring relationship. Believing that sex entails power and emotional vulnerability, sXers strive to minimize potentially negative experiences by rejecting casual sex. Kevin, a twenty-seven-year-old martial artist who had dropped out of high school, said, "Sex should be on an emotional level. It's an addiction like everything else. My first understanding of sXe was to not be addicted." Maggie said:

> I had one friend and she was sXe and she had a lot of sex with a lot of people. She got pregnant. After that . . . well it was like right be-

fore she stopped being sXe . . . but she started drinking and stuff. She got pregnant and it pretty much just ruined her life. But I think sXe, it has a comment on [sex]: "Don't ruin your life for something because it gives you pleasure."

There is no direct religious basis for sXe views on sex. In fact, many of the sXers I associated with grew up with no formal religious involvement, and very few were presently involved in organized religion. While a few sXers connect their sXe and Christian identities, the group advocates no form of religion and most adherents are deeply suspicious or critical of organized faiths, a remnant of their punk roots.

Most sXers also believe that objectifying women is pervasive and wrong. Basically, sXe rejects the stereotypical image of high school males. A local sXe band (five male members) decried sexual abuse and rape during their set: "This song is the most important song we play. It's about the millions of women who have suffered rape. One out of four women will be the victim of a sexual assault in her lifetime. We've got to make it stop."

The movement's 'rule' against promiscuous sex is more difficult for members to enforce and thus there is greater variation in belief regarding sex than substance use. Several of my participants, both males and females aged 21–23, had consciously decided to postpone sex because they had not found someone with whom they felt an intimate emotional attachment. Most of the young women believed not drinking reduced their risk of being sexually assaulted or otherwise put in a compromising situation. Jenny, an eighteen-year-old college student, activist, and musician, said:

Like I said, it's all about control over your own body, over your own life. It's about reclaiming, claiming your dignity and self-respect. Saying "I'm not going to put this stuff into my body. I'm not going to have you inside of my body if I don't want you in there." It all just very much ties together. I like sXe because it allows me to make very rational, intelligent decisions. That's one of the decisions I think it's really important to think through very carefully. I'm not against premarital sex at all. But personally, I've got to be in love.

Some adherents insist that sex should be reserved for married couples, while a few believe sXe places no strictures on sexual activity. Only one young man, with relatively little connection to the Denver scene, had a reputation as a "player." A few sXe men are little different from the hypermasculine stereotype the movement seeks to reject. But most insist that sex between strangers or near-strangers is potentially destructive, emotionally and possibly physically, and that positivity demands that sex should be part of an emotional relationship based on trust. Matthew, the seventeen-year-old Christian who abstained from sex entirely and wished he was still a virgin, said:

> It's emotionally damaging. There's a lot of things that can come from it. Pregnancy, abortion, things that are just too emotional to deal with. Friendships are destroyed through it. Then you get around to STDs and stuff like that, horrible things you'd be stuck with for life. It's just safer to abstain. . . . Sex is almost a commitment to someone. A lot of times people have sex with someone and never talk to them again. You see that with people a lot. Emotionally, that's hard on someone to have that connection with someone for that short amount of time and then to be totally cut off. That's heartache there, that's anger, sadness. There's so many things emotional that can come from that.

Emotional concerns were also central to Patrick, a twenty-five-year-old tattoo artist:

> Sex, in general, should be a thing that's carried on between two people that care a lot for each other and have a lot of respect for each other. I'm definitely adamant about saying that I don't think sex is the ultimate expression of love, 'cause I don't. I think that you can definitely separate sex and love relatively easily. I think there's nothing wrong with two adults having sex consensually with very little emotional attachment. I don't think there's anything wrong with that, just as long as everybody's on the same emotional page, where there's really no risk of people's feelings getting hurt, somebody taking advantage of somebody else. You can really reduce sex into just like a completely selfish act. You're just basically taking something from somebody. You're just using somebody for the fact that they're there; they're a warm body. Its takes two people to have sex. You could just basically say, like, "She was just there." That whole thing like "I'm just trying to get mine." I think it's important as far as this lifestyle goes to keep in mind all those things. Realize that sex doesn't have to be the most important thing between two people. But it also shouldn't be something that's taken so lightly. It should be something that's carried out with respect above anything else.

Self-Actualization

Straightedge—the discipline / The key to self-liberation is abstinence from the destructive escapism of intoxication / I separate from the poison—a mindlessness I've always abhorred / Usage will only increase the pain—a truth I constantly see ignored / The pollutants that kill the body breed apathy within the mind / The substances that once brought release in the end will always confine.

—"The Discipline" by Earth Crisis, 1995

Straight edgers claim that resisting social standards and expectations allows them to follow their own, more meaningful, path in life, toward greater self-actualization. Like punks, they abhor conformity and insist on being "true to themselves." Similarly to hippies, sXers believe that as children we have incredible potential that is "slowly crushed and destroyed by a standardized society and mechanical teaching" (Berger 1967:19). Subcultures, like social movements, engage in conflict over cultural reproduction; they are often especially concerned with quality of life, self-realization, and identity formation (Habermas 1984–1987; Buechler 1995). Straight edgers believe toxins such as drugs and alcohol inhibit people from reaching their full potential, stifling creativity and encouraging laziness (Azerrad 2001:137). Alec, thirty, formerly a member of several influential sXe bands, believed alcohol and drugs served to pacify a discontented populace. He saw sXe as an avenue out of an unfulfilling cultural pattern:

> I realized that everybody around me was so screwed up and miserable. [Straight edge] was like one thing . . . it seemed like the most punk rock thing I could do. At an early age I developed a theory that it was OK to drink alcohol because alcohol subdued people so they didn't realize how miserable their lives were and how terrible their jobs were. So it's like they go out and have 'Miller Time.' So I got really into sXe.

Likewise, Ray Cappo wrote, "I wanted to use music as a medium to spread a message of truth and self-betterment based on inner reflection and pure living" (Cappo 1993:iii).

This view sharply contrasts with the hip version of self-actualization through dope (Davis 1968). For sXers, drugs of any kind inhibit rather than enable self-discovery; sXers believe people are less genuine and true to themselves while high. A clear, focused mind helps them achieve their highest goals. Kate, the animal rights activist, said, "If you have a clear mind you're more likely to be aware of who you are and what things around you really are rather than what somebody might want you to think they are. A little bit more of an honest life, being true to yourself." Elizabeth, a twenty-six-year-old high school counselor with a masters degree who had been sXe and vegetarian for many years, said:

> You're not screwed up on drugs and alcohol and you can make conscientious decisions about things. You're not letting some drug or alcohol subdue your emotions and thoughts. You're not desensitizing yourself to your life. And if you're not desensitizing your life, then yeah, you're gonna feel more things. The more you feel, the more you move, the more that you grow. . . . I truly believe [sXers] are living and feeling and growing, and it's all natural growth. It's not put off. That's a unique characteristic.

Like adherents of previous subcultures, sXers construct a view of the world as mediocre and unfulfilling, but they also believe that society encourages people to medicate themselves with crutches such as drugs, alcohol, and sex to forget their unhappiness. Straight edgers felt the punks', skinheads', and hippies' associations with these things blunted their opportunities to offer meaningful resistance. Substances and social pressures cloud clear thought and individual expression. Claiming that many people use substances as a means of escaping their problems, the movement encourages members to avoid escapism, confront problems with a clear mind, and create their own positive, fulfilling lives. Brent emphatically insisted that self-realization did not require drugs:

> There are ways to open your mind without drinking and smoking. . . . You definitely don't have to take mushrooms and sit out in the desert to have a spiritual awakening or a catharsis of any sort. People don't accept that. People think you're uptight. . . . There is a spiritual absence in the world I know right now, in America. To be money-driven is the goal. It's one of the emptiest, least fulfilling ways to live your life. . . . The way people relieve themselves of the burdens of their spiritual emptiness is through drugs and alcohol. The way people see escape is sometimes even through a shorter lifespan, through smoking. To be sXe and to understand and believe that means you have opened the door for yourself to find out

why we're really on this earth, or what I want to get out of a relationship with a person, or what I want my kids to think of me down
the line.

Straight edgers rarely speak openly about self-actualization and they
would likely scoff at anything that suggested mysticism or enlightenment
(which they would connect with hippies and therefore drugs). Nevertheless, for many, underlying the ideology is an almost spiritual quest for a
genuine self, a "truth." Some connect sXe to other very personal identities: "queer-edge," feminism, and activism, for example. Mark, a quiet
sixteen-year-old new to the scene, claimed sXe as a personally liberating
protest against his upbringing: "Straight edge to me, yeah, it's a commitment to myself, but to me it's also a protest. I don't want to give my kids
the same life I had from my father."

Spreading the Message

We started out to have some fun / It's amazing what we have become / Now
we're not going to stop today / No matter what may stand in the way / We're
not going to give up, and just do what we're told / We'd rather take a different
path, follow a different road / Time that we all did our part, you all know what
I mean / Together we have made a change—we've changed the scene / Look at
all the things we've done / But the real fight has just begun / We have a chance
to set it right / Now it's up to all of us to fight.
   —"Today the Scene, Tomorrow the World" by Good Clean Fun, 2001

Straight edge resistance transcends members' simple abstinence. Straight
edgers often actively encourage other young people to become drug and
alcohol free. Some hippies believed their "ultimate social mission was to
'turn the world on'—i.e. Make everyone aware of the potential virtues of
LSD for ushering in an era of universal peace, freedom, brotherhood and
love" (Davis 1968:157). Likewise, many sXers undertake a mission to
convince their peers that resisting drugs, rather than using them, will
help create a better world. A minority of sXers, labeled "militant" or
"hardline" by other sXers, are very outspoken, donning X's and sXe messages at nearly all times and confronting their peers who use drugs. There
is an ongoing tension within the movement over how much members
should promote their lifestyle. At one extreme is the "live and let live" faction—who believe that individuals should make their own choices and
sXers should keep their opinions to themselves. On the other side is the

more militant branch, often comprised of new adherents, who believe sXers' duty lies in demonstrating to users the possibilities of a drug-free lifestyle. Most sXers maintain that their example is enough. Jenny, the student-activist, said:

> I wanna show people there's a community out there; that it doesn't make you a fucking dork to be sXe. There are other people out there who are really, really into it. There's a whole group of people you can belong to. You don't have to belong to just them obviously. I just think it can be a really positive thing for people. I go to a dorm where you walk down every fucking hall and the smell of pot knocks you upside the head. I just think that in that case it's really important to get your message out there. . . . I think the best political, social, personal statement you can make is to live by example. That's definitely what I try to do.

Cory, an artist and veteran of the scene at age twenty-one, explained why sXers should set an example for others:

> It's all about calling yourself straight edge. You could be drug free and you can not drink and not smoke and go to parties and do whatever, but you're not helping out. There's a pendulum in society and it's tilted one way so far, and sitting in the middle of the pendulum isn't going to help it swing back. There needs to be more straight edgers on the other side to help even it out, at the least.

Thus while adherents maintain that sXe is a personal lifestyle choice rather than a movement directed toward others, many members "wear their politics on their sleeve" in a not-so-subtle attempt to encourage others to follow their path. The youth crew band Insted's song "Voice Your Opinion" begins with the lyrics, "Nothing is ever accomplished / When your thoughts are bottled up inside / Let your many ideas flow / Don't let them sit and hide." Kyle, the twenty-three-year-old student from a working-class background said:

> I like to show people there's another way to live. I like to say "You can go out to the parties, you can go out to a bar and you don't *have* to drink to have a good time. You don't *have* to drink to loosen up. You can be a goof and be sober. You just have to be happy with where you're at in life." I guess to me the whole drinking and drug use is a way to hide from your problems. It's a way to not deal with them

right at that time. . . . One big goal is I like to influence everybody I meet. If I can change one person's mind that I meet, it's a great feeling. I was able to convince my mom and her boyfriend/fiancée to cut back a lot. They were bad. That was kind of neat, just seeing people change. My sister has followed my footsteps. She's like nineteen and she won't touch anything either. It's kind of neat to have people look up to you and use you for respect.

Straight edge resistance also targets the corporate interests of alcohol and tobacco companies, which, adherents claim, profit from peoples' addictions and suffering. Kate, who clearly connects sXe with her activism, said, "By rejecting Miller Lite and Coors, they have less control over me and my life because I'm not giving them my money, I'm not supporting them." Brent, the outspoken vegan, said:

Each individual in society is connected to one another. When you hurt yourself, you're hurting your society. You're leading by example, your kids will see what you're doing and they'll pick it up. . . . Resisting temptation, resisting what's thrown at you day after day, by your peers, by your parents, by their generation, by business people, by what's hip and cool on MTV. Resistance is huge. That's why sXe is a movement. . . . It's all connected: resisting drugs, resisting rampant consumerism, resisting voting Democrat when you can vote third party.

By focusing their message on their families, subcultural peers, mainstream youth, and the larger society, sXers create a multi-layered model of resistance that individuals can customize to fit their own styles. Some are very outspoken and active in a number of causes. Others spread their values through their example alone.

Involvement in Social Change

Because I stand in this defiance / I wear the mark of those / Who choose to refuse / Self-destructive points of view / And with each day spent in self-perseverance / My voice is strong, against what's wrong /Forcing it to end / Forcing it to an end / Standing in this defiance, and wearing the mark of those / We choose to refuse, our system's defective views / And with each day spent, in our self-perseverance / Our voices strong, against what's wrong / We're forcing it to end/ We're forcing it to an end

—"To an End" by Strife, 1997

Like members of other subcultures, sXers often become involved in a variety of social causes. The sXe youth I associated with insisted that working for social change was not a prerequisite of sXe. Indeed, only a few belonged to the substantial Boulder activist community. However, many viewed their involvement in social change as a logical progression from clean living that led them to embrace progressive concerns and become directly involved at some level. Clean living and positivity lead to clear thinking, which in turn create a desire to resist and self-actualize. This entire process opens them up to the world's problems and their concerns grow. Karl Buechner, singer of the very popular vegan sXe band Earth Crisis,[7] explained (Sersen 1999):

> The reasoning behind [sXe] is to have a clear mind and to use that clear mind to reach out to other people and do what you can to start thinking about fairness, thinking about how to make things more just in society and the world as a whole. . . . It's about freedom. It's about using that freedom, that clarity of mind that we have, as a vehicle for progression, to make ourselves more peaceful people. And by making ourselves more peaceful people we make the world a more just place.

As Earth Crisis toured the country, Karl often encouraged crowds of youth to think of sXe as a means to a greater end. While their primary messages promoted veganism, animal rights, and abstinence, some songs discussed world hunger and poverty (for example "Filthy Hands to Famished Mouths") while others warned of world domination and exploitation by a few elites (such as "End Begins"). I asked Karl, "Is sXe supposed to be a means to a greater end?" He replied without hesitation, "*Absolutely.* For me, one of my goals is to be as peaceful as I can and alleviate some of the suffering around me that I see in the world. Through sobriety I think I have a lot more control over my own life and a lot of distractions are eliminated." In a similar vein, Kevin, the martial artist, believed that sXe was fundamentally about becoming a strong person in every aspect of life. Strength includes rejecting stereotypes and prejudices:

> Technically, according to the "rules," you can be homophobic and racist and fuckin' sexist and shit like that and still technically be sXe. You're not drinking, you're not smoking, you're not doing drugs. But I don't personally, on a personal level, I wouldn't consider that person sXe. Because they're weak. I don't think you can be sXe and weak.

Again, in contrast to the hippies, punks, and skinheads, sXers, see a clear, drug-free mind as pivotal to developing a consciousness of resistance. The movement provides a general opening up to or expansion of social awareness. Kent, the rather quiet young man with many tattoos, said:

> I would never have even considered being vegetarian or vegan if it wasn't for sXe. Once you go sXe, I don't really think you're supposed to stop there. It's supposed to open you up to more possibilities. . . . It just makes me think differently. It makes you not so complacent.

In the mid- to late-1980s, sXe became increasingly concerned with animal rights and environmental causes. Influential leaders in bands called for an end to cruelty against animals and a general awareness of eco-destruction. At least three out of four Denver sXers are vegetarian and many adopt completely cruelty-free, or vegan, lifestyles. Veganism had become such a significant part of sXe by the late 1990s that many sXers gave it equal importance to living drug and alcohol free. Many sXe vegans self-identify as "vegan straight edge" and some bands identify as "vegan straight edge" rather than simply straight edge. Veganism, while still widely practiced, has declined somewhat after 2000. Among the approximately seventy sXers I associated with regularly, only fifteen ate meat. Several individuals had "Vegan" tattooed on their bodies. Others led or actively participated in the campus Animal Defense organization. Essentially, the movement frames (see Snow et al. 1986) animal rights as a logical extension of the "positivity" underpinning the entire lifestyle, much like reserving sex for caring relationships and self-actualization. Brian, an extremely positive, twenty-one-year-old CU student and musician, explained vegetarianism's connection to sXe: "sXe kids open their minds a lot more. They're more conscious of what's around them. . . . Some people think it's healthier and other people like me are more on the animal liberation thing." Elizabeth, the older veteran, said:

> If you are conscientious and care about the environment or the world, which perhaps more sXe people are than your average population, then [animal rights is] just going to be a factor. You're going to consider "how can I make the world a better place?" Well, being vegetarian is another place you can start. . . . I'm glad it's usually a part of the sXe scene because it just goes along with awareness and choices. What kind of things are you doing to yourself and how is that impacting the world and the environment? The big, corporate-owned beef lots and cutting down the rainforests . . . the

most impactful thing you can do for the environment is to stop eating meat.

Like many sXers, Eric, a twenty-one-year-old student and scenester visiting from Boston, traced a direct connection between listening to sXe
music and becoming vegan:

> I think sXe and the whole sXe scene opens a lot of kids' eyes to other
> movements and activities they can do. Listening to hardcore music
> and being sXe, I listened to Earth Crisis. By listening to Earth Crisis,
> they opened my eyes to veganism. I got disgusted by this hamburger
> I had in my cafeteria at college and it made me be sick of meat. So I
> educated myself more on what veganism was about and I had always
> known about it from hardcore and being sXe and listening to Earth
> Crisis. When you're sixteen you listen to the CDs your friends listen
> to and the stuff you're about because that's what it's about. So I
> knew about veganism from listening to the idea that one hand feeds
> another, one thing feeds into another. By being sXe, by being hard-
> core, by listening to Earth Crisis it taught me about veganism. So
> when I finally became vegetarian and wanted to become vegan, I had
> already known about it by being sXe. I think kids can get involved in
> other [causes] by being sXe to begin with.

Some sXe youth get involved in social justice causes such as homelessness, human rights, and women's rights. They organize benefit concerts
to raise money for local homeless shelters, sometimes including in the
price of admission to shows a canned good for the local food pantry or a
donation to a women's shelter. I observed several sXers participating in
local protests against the World Bank and International Monetary Fund
in conjunction with the large 1999–2000 protests in Seattle and Washington, D.C. and others took part in a campus antisweatshop campaign.
In the insert for their *Through the Darkes Days* CD, the Seattle-based sXe
band Trial encouraged listeners to take responsibility for their involvement in a corporate/consumer culture:

> While human and animal life are oppressed, disrespected and de-
> stroyed by corporate terrorism the world over, the dollars of our con-
> sumer culture provide fuel for the fire. We must be more responsible
> for ourselves and for our actions, identifying as best we can what we
> are supporting with our purchasing power. Each can set limits of his

or her own morality, recognizing and accepting that there is no one pure or correct lifestyle, and within that framework strive towards ahimsa: a way of life which causes the least possible amount of harm.

Similar to progressive punks, some sXe youth print 'zines on prisoners' rights, fighting neo-Nazism, challenging police brutality, and championing various human rights and environmental issues. Alec used his music to raise awareness for many causes: "We wanted to be a catalyst for people to have ideas and speak their mind and get involved. [Our singer] really started getting into women's issues." He explained how his band tried to involve kids:

When we would play, we would request that all the promoters . . . say like the show was six bucks. The show is six dollars and we told the promoter when we were setting up the shows, to make it five dollars and a canned good or a shirt, then you take that to the homeless shelter. A lot of people didn't know why we did that. We're like, "Well, what it does is it gets everybody involved." The band's involved, the promoter has to be involved, and the kids are involved. Whether or not they care, they're helping. We even tried to do that in Europe when we toured there.

Minneapolis sXe band the Real Enemy claimed their band had a political purpose as well (www.tchc.org/enemy/, viewed 2/22/2000):

We are also a political band and consider straight edge to be an important weapon. All of our actions are political and affect others. Think about that. There are many other subjects in this world than just straight edge and animal rights. Everything ties together. There are more important things to talk about as well. We can't limit ourselves to songs about friends and being stabbed in the back or singing about violent retribution that will never take place.

Many sXe women disdain more traditional female roles and appreciate the scene as a space where they feel less pressure to live up to gender expectations and the movement encourages men to reject certain hypermasculine traits and challenge sexism on a personal level (see chapters five and six). Many bands write songs against sexism and some young sXe men demonstrate an exceptional understanding of gender oppression given their age and experience. However, despite the movement's claims of community

6. Kevin Seconds, singer of 7 Seconds, has inspired punk and hardcore kids for over twenty-five years with positive lyrics in songs such as "Not Just Boys' Fun." Photo by Todd Pollock.

and inclusivity, some sXe women feel isolated and unwelcome in the scene. Men significantly outnumber women, often creating a "boys club" mentality exemplified by the masculine call for "brotherhood."

Straight edgers strive to live out their values in everyday life instead of engaging in more conventional "political" protest (such as picketing, civil disobedience, petitioning). Rather than challenge tobacco, beer, or beef companies directly, for example, an sXer refuses their products and might boycott Kraft (parent company of cigarette manufacturer Phillip Morris), adopt a vegetarian lifestyle, or wear a shirt to school reading, "It's OK not to drink. Straight Edge" or "Go Vegan!" In sXe and other youth movements, the personal is political. By The Grace of God's CD, *Perspective,* included a message encouraging listeners to make the personal choice to support local businesses:

> In an attempt to make our world livable, we must all educate ourselves on the products we consume. We as a people have the power to refuse global powers. We as a people have the power to support local economy. We as a people have the buying power to end the lo-

cal economy meltdown. Educate yourself, Educate your friends, Educate your community. Convenience kills towns, not companies.

In the post-2000 sXe era, political concerns seem to be slightly overshadowed by the growing popularity and commercial opportunities of hardcore music and style. Yet many sXers continue to extend their sXe commitment beyond simple abstinence.

Conclusion

Straight edge is more to many adherents than just music, more than posing at a show: yet determining just what sXe *is* beyond the style and music is difficult. Indeed, outlining the core foundations of any youth movement is a challenging undertaking. Straight edgers are a very diverse group whose members interpret and live the movement's core values in a multitude of ways. In many ways, subcultures are individualistic, heterogeneous entities (Muggleton 2000; Grossberg 1992; Rose 1994). I have done my best to outline sXe ideals that span time and place, but sXe is fluid and values change. Some sXe scenes greatly encourage involvement in social change while others do not. For some sXers, reserving sex for caring relationships has fallen by the wayside; for others it is central to their lives. There is no one, all-encompassing sXe. Nevertheless, the values I have outlined capture the enduring themes present in some way throughout sXe's twenty-five year history. While not every sXer lives up to each of these ideals, most refer to these guidelines, using them as a "subcultural frame of reference" (Wood 1999).

Some years ago, a popular sXe t-shirt slogan read: "If you don't stand for something, you'll fall for anything." Straight edgers (and youth in general) are ever wary of "rules" and "molds" that give a clear definition of their group. The whole notion of rules runs counter to youth movements' celebration of the individual—no one wants to feel like the cookie-cutter stereotype of the alterna-scene flavor-of-the-month. Yet if sXe can be anything it will quickly become nothing. Through all of its changes and incarnations, sXe has held onto one central value: clean living is a positive personal choice, a meaningful alternative to a youth culture that pushes young people to drink, smoke, and even do drugs.

CHAPTER 3

STRAIGHT EDGE AS A SOCIAL MOVEMENT

I first met Jenny at a student activist meeting shortly after the terrorist attacks of September 11, 2001, when word had spread that the United States would begin bombing in Afghanistan. Jenny stood out from the other students—she had dyed her hair maroon and was wearing a studded leather belt, horn-rimmed glasses, tight pants, a bandana, and Chuck Taylor All-Star shoes. I immediately pegged her as part of an alternative music subculture—probably emo/indie rock, maybe punk, and possibly hardcore. The meeting broke into smaller affinity groups and I made sure I joined Jenny's group. As we went around the circle introducing ourselves, Jenny explained her interests in activism and added, almost as an afterthought, "I'm also part of the sXe movement." Her passion for social change was immediately evident and her positive attitude made her a natural leader. At the Junkyard, some time later, Jenny told me how she considered sXe central to her activism:

> I think every element of my life philosophy is very much interconnected. They all sort of fit together like puzzle pieces. The connection I make between sXe and political activism is sort of that whole attitude like you see something wrong, fix it. I don't like the things that drugs and drinking bring about in society so I fix it by fixing myself.
> When I see other problems in society as well, I have the same drive to fix it by doing everything that I can do. It's all about claiming power, saying, "All right, I'm in charge of my life. I can do as much good as I want to do."

Jenny had sung in her own hardcore band, printed her own 'zines, and been involved in a number of social change efforts from a young age. I was struck by how adamantly she believed that sXe was a *movement*, rather than solely a subculture especially given her experience in groups we more typically think of as social movements.

When most people imagine a social movement, they think of Vietnam protestors clogging the Washington Mall, feminists lobbying for equal rights, student sitins during the Civil Rights era, or some other organization of activists marching the streets with huge signs demanding political change. Labor unions, AIDS activists, pro-life and pro-choice demonstrators, environmentalists, gay marriage advocates and opponents, and human rights organizations are among the nearly countless movements struggling to influence the political process. Such groups have had an undeniable social and political impact, pressing the government for voting rights, health care, and labor and environmental standards, among other things. But what about groups that pursue change yet have little in the way of *formal organization,* whose members do not necessarily consider themselves *activists,* and that are not challenging the *government or other institutions?* What about self-help movements? People who compost, recycle, buy organic food, and eat primarily vegetarian diets? Conservative Christians and other religious groups? Members of the "simple living" movement? Anarchists? People who boycott chain stores and support local businesses? Young people who pledge to remain virgins until marriage? Such groups claim a significant number of followers who have a sense of being part of a larger identity, but are they *movements, in the sociological sense?*

I have always been interested in how ordinary people work for social change in their daily lives and I find it intriguing that many sXers interpret their lifestyle as a movement making a cultural challenge. They believe their cause is more than a personal lifestyle choice—they want to *change* the culture around them. Joel, activist and singer for Memphis band That Was Then, encouraged kids to make the connection between hardcore and social change: "All this screaming and jumping around doesn't mean anything unless it changes who you are in the rest of the world out there." Some, like Jenny, even tie their more traditional activism to sXe. A Swedish sXe website addressed the question *"What is the political impact of sXe?"*:

> Though sXe is not inherently political, politics are a logical extension of an sXe lifestyle. Once you have regained control over your life, the desire to help others and to make a positive contribution to your culture, society, community by addressing issues of social justice is a very natural thing to do. Many sXe'ers join organizations like Greenpeace, Amnesty International, and SADD (Students Against Drunk Drivers). They also encourage friends to give up drugs, alcohol, and smoking. [www.straight-edge.net/sXe.html, viewed 1/21/99]

Straight edge, as the previous chapter demonstrated, has much in common with other youth subcultures and therefore fits the definition of subculture fairly well. While it is useful to analyze sXe as a subculture, it is also clear that sXe shares many features of *new social movements*. Straddling the conceptual boundary between subculture and movement, sXe provides an ideal opportunity to rethink not only subcultural resistance but also movement theory, as well as a significant opportunity to combine subcultural and social movements studies (Martin 2002).

Non-structured, culture-based social movements may ultimately mount equally significant social challenges as do more formal, organized, bureaucratic movements.

Studying Social Movements

Social movements are typically distinguished from subcultures by their more formal structure, lesser emphasis on style, and focus on political change. Movements are organized, last for a specific period of time, and typically work for change from outside the political system (McAdam and Snow 1997:xviii). In a half-century of research on social movements, scholars have created four paradigms explaining how social movements emerge and why people participate in them: strain theory, resource mobilization theory, political opportunity theory, and a number of theories loosely called new social movement theory. The underlying premise of strain theories, the dominant perspective of the 1950s, is simple: discontented individuals form groups to challenge their suffering (strain) and press for change. Marginalized groups of alienated, relatively unorganized people protest to contest their marginalization (Kornhauser 1959; Turner and Killian 1957; Smelser 1962). People who compare their lives to a reference group that seems better off experience "relative deprivation," a feeling that they have not received their due (Merton 1968; Morrison 1971). If their path to the desired goal is blocked, discontented individuals may form a movement.

Beginning in the 1960s, a new generation of theorists thoroughly critiqued strain theory, developing another paradigm known as resource mobilization theory (Zald and Ash 1966; Oberschall 1973; McCarthy and Zald 1977). Strain, they argued, is not enough to explain movement emergence; people are always under strain, they always have grievances, yet they engage in collective action relatively rarely. Rather, movements emerge when people strategically organize around a particular complaint. Resource mobilization theorists claimed that movement participants are neither irrational nor isolated; rather protesters carefully recruit new participants, conduct research, systematically plan strategy, and execute challenges. Movement organizations, such as environmental and human rights groups, share many characteristics and needs with a variety of other conventional organizations, such as businesses, churches, and civic groups; they have offices, solicit support (money, resources, volunteers), and use their resources to promote their political agenda in a calculated, rational manner.

Closely tied to resource mobilization theory, political opportunity theory (also called political process theory) gained attention in the early 1980s (McAdam 1982), hypothesizing that movements emerge when political opportunities arise: "People join in social movements in response to political opportunities and then, through collective action, create new ones" (Tarrow 1994:17). An expansion of political opportunities (such as shifting political allegiances, gaining influential allies, governments weakening, conflict arising among elite groups) promotes movement emergence (McAdam 1996). Rather than emphasizing the importance of a group's internal resources, such as money or power, political opportunity theory focuses on the significance of resources *external* to the group.[1] To survive, movements must adapt to shifting political and economic conditions (Locher 2002). The resource mobilization and political opportunity paradigms dominated the discussion about social movements since the late 1970s, but in the late 1980s they fell under increased scrutiny. These theories, while useful in explaining more organized movements, are less useful when applied to diffuse movements such as sXe. Straight edge kids, for the most part, do not face significant strain or hardship; there is no sXe organization; and sXe is not engaged in the formal political process. Theorists challenging the "structural bias" in movement research (McAdam 1994:37) are turning to new social movements approaches. For instance, I discovered that a strong collective identity is the foundation of diffuse movements, providing "structure," a basis for commitment, and guidelines for participation.

Recently, some scholars have challenged the dominance of organizational and political approaches to social movements, insisting that much of the life of a movement takes place outside of formal organizational and political contexts. Not all movements revolve around a concrete, bureaucratic organization with activists engaging in political action.[2]

These new social movement critiques of resource mobilization center around the idea that ideology, identities, and culture are vital aspects of social movements (Melucci 1989, 1994; Laraña, Johnston, and Gusfield 1994; Buechler 1993, 1995, 1999). New social movement theorists have brought renewed attention to movement culture, the role of expressive action, how movements construct an ideology, the connection between individual and collective identity, and how participants interact at the micro level of movement activity. In reifying organizations, resource mobilization leaves out interaction and actors almost entirely.

New social movement theorists distinguish between older, class-based labor movements and more contemporary, identity-centered political challenges such as the civil rights movement, the women's movement, and gay and lesbian liberation (Melucci 1994). New social movements concern themselves with social reproduction (Habermas 1981), moral crusades (Eder 1985), and culturally oriented challenges (Touraine 1985). They are often reformist rather than revolutionary (Cohen 1985) and issue symbolic challenges to civil society as much as, or more than, to the state (Melucci 1985). In sum, the 'new' of new social movement theory implies not so much a temporal relationship as a difference in structural form, modes of participation, focus of change, and commitment.[3]

Even new social movement theories, however, fall short of adequately explaining decentralized movements. Despite their theoretical leanings toward less structured forms of social protest and their recognition of the importance of identity, new social movement theorists have primarily studied conventional social movement organizations, as if collective identity were simply another dimension of movement organizations and nothing more. The lack of empirical studies of diffuse, decentralized movements has produced a vision of cultural challenge, lifestyle politics, and collective identity mediated through bureaucratic organizations. In fact, the structural composition of social movements form a continuum, with one extreme being fully bureaucratized, formal social movement organizations and the other being very diffuse movements devoid of any formal structure.[4] The former tends to focus on institutional and political change while the latter emphasizes cultural and lifestyle-based change. Both qualify as movements in the sense they are collective preferences for social change. In particular, the precise role of collective identity in diffuse, culture-based movements has yet to be fully explained. Straight edge serves as an ideal type of the unstructured end of the structural continuum, a movement in which fostering a strong collective identity is especially crucial.

Structure, Commitment, Participation, Targets, and Tactics
Diffuse Structure
Minor Threat was together for about three years, and we played all over the god damn place. More and more people were coming out and you saw a lot more "Xs." I guess the movement had sort of started, but in my mind I wasn't interested in it being a movement. It ran conversely to my initial idea that it was a

concert of individuals, as opposed to a movement. . . . What I look for in life is people who I respect, living and teaching by example, and I trust that human beings can make up their minds and make the right decisions for their own lives.

—Ian MacKaye (Lahicky 1997:102–103)

The sXe movement has no headquarters, holds no meetings, and keeps no membership list. There is no charter, mission statement, newsletter, or formal set of rules. The movement recognizes no leaders, collects no dues, gathers few resources, and rarely challenges institutionalized politics. Yet sXers around the world agree on a set of fundamental principles of the movement and act accordingly. The core values of clean living, positive attitude, resistance to social pressures, and community transcend national boundaries (Haenfler 2001), despite sXe's complete lack of bureaucracy.

As the opening quote to this section indicates, Ian MacKaye did not set out to create a movement per se. Indeed, some sXers do not conceive of the group as a movement at all and are opposed to it becoming one. At the heart of sXe, punk rock, and many other youth cultures is a quest for individuality and individual expression. Members define themselves against a mainstream society which enforces conformity, crushing individual thought and action. For some sXers, being part of a collective implies sacrificing some of the individuality they seek. While they are still committed to the sXe identity (rather than simply to being drug-free), these adherents emphasize that sXe is primarily a *personal* commitment to *themselves*. An sXer involved in the early youth crew scene said, "A lot of people took [sXe] as 'true to not doing drugs' or 'true to my friends.' I never really took it that way personally. The statement for me meant 'true to yourself, true to your inner quest and discovering knowledge.'" Beth, a twenty-two-year-old who had been sXe for several years, thought of sXe more as a personal philosophy and commitment than as a movement:

Straight edge is a philosophy of being in control of your mind. Not giving in, making a promise to yourself. It's a personal commitment. It's no one else's. Not to a crew, not to a band, not to a group of friends. It's all about *you* and making a commitment to yourself. . . . Not giving up, not giving in to social acceptance.

Ever suspicious of trends, no sXer wants to feel like she or he is simply following the crowd. It is as if adherents of youth subcultures believe "we are all being different together," often failing to recognize the pressures to conform within their own group. Most sXers, however, do think of sXe as a movement, even if members hold many different interpretations of what being a movement means. A participant on an Internet message board responded to another sXer's claim that sXe was simply an individual choice and not a movement:

> Some people are just straight edge because it suits them, not because they feel there is something wrong with the world. But I guess that's the difference between you and I. I want to have an impact on society, where as you might not be interested in sharing your ideas with other people. I have no problem with that because we share the same values of being drug free. I'm not here to disagree with you. I simply think that the movement should still be a movement, and not just a claim for the sake of personal gain. But like I said, I understand your view and respect it as well. My goal isn't to cause everyone I know to be straight edge. I've said this several times before. My goal is to advocate and promote a poison free society. I'm straight edge because I chose to be. It's purely symbolic. Being drug free for yourself is one thing, but to actually go out there and stand for something is entirely different.

Kate, the student/animal rights activist, explained her thoughts on sXe as a movement:

> In a sense I think it's a movement, but it's not a typical movement the way people perceive movements. There's no president, there's no organization, there's no meetings, no sXe rallies or anything like that, but . . . you can't deny that such a large group of people choosing to live their life a certain way *and* labeling themselves and putting themselves out there is gonna have an effect on other people around them. Younger people that look up to them, stuff like that. It's almost like an unconscious movement. Not like people aren't thinking, [but] they're not thinking about being a social movement when they decide to be sXe.

Kate also claimed sXe is a movement because it helps kids go against the grain: "Most people, the norm is you go out and drink, smoke cigarettes, or you go out and do drugs sometimes. That's the normal. I see [sXe] as a movement because it's a conscious decision people are making against what's normal."

Like the virginity pledge movement, sXe is "loosely organized" and relies upon "the development of new products and cultural symbols" including music and the Internet (Bearman and Brückner 2001:860). Straight edgers use creative avenues to engage in an *active* process of constructing the sXe identity.[5] They maintain communication, structure, and continuity of values via sXe shows, 'zines, music recordings and, since the mid-1990s, websites and Internet message boards. Lacking formal avenues of communication, continuity, and diffusion of ideas (such as meetings, newsletters, or mass mailings), more "cultural" arenas hold special importance to sXe. The scene's connection to hardcore music means that sXe bands serve as the primary creators of the sXe ideology. The music preserves the movement's history, reflecting the goals and concerns of each sXe era (Wood 1999). Bands repeatedly sing about the virtues of a clean life; resisting mainstream society; supporting one's friends; staying positive; and a variety of social issues including racism, sexism, and the environment.

The notion of sXe "leaders" goes against the group's individualistic bent. While formally there are no leaders, informally leaders emerge in every scene. These are often, but not always, members of bands or kids who book shows. They are typically a bit older than the average sXer and involved enough to be respected, but humble enough to avoid being labeled scenesters. Nationally, several leaders have emerged over the years, moral entrepreneurs looked up to by masses of sXe kids. As the forerunners of sXe and significant figures in hardcore, Ian MacKaye and Kevin Seconds (of 7 Seconds) were early examples. Ray Cappo of Youth of Today ("Ray of Today") was one of the most charismatic leaders in sXe history, convincing thousands of kids to adopt vegetarian lifestyles. Karl Buechner of Earth Crisis and Rick Rodney of Strife were tremendously popular. Still, these individuals had no bureaucratic/rational/legal authority; they relied instead upon charismatic leadership (Weber 1946).

Independent, underground record companies distribute CDs and vinyl records around the world. Hardcore shows provide consistent central gathering places to celebrate and reaffirm values and share new ideas. Young punk entrepreneurs set up "distros" to sell records, patches, and 'zines. Distros, short for "distribution," serve as the outlet for disseminating the latest hardcore music. The distro owner buys records in bulk from record companies at a discounted price, marks up the price only slightly, then sits at a table during a show selling the goods as the bands play. She or he makes a little money, the record label makes a little money, and, most importantly, kids are constantly exposed to music and ideas unavailable in conventional stores.[6] 'Zines document the scene with photos and interviews with bands, in some ways substituting for a formal sXe "newsletter." Contributors discuss political concerns, review music recordings, and debate problems within the scene. Some are little more than gossip rags, but many help connect local scenes to the larger national or even global scenes. The Internet enables contemporary sXers to create a virtual community (Pileggi 1998; Helton and Staudenmeier 2002; Williams 2003) and messages boards, websites, and email have revolutionized networking, allowing greater diffusion of values and ideas.

All of these avenues of sXe expression foster a meaningful collective identity that creates an immediate connection between adherents. Members experience a bond that is difficult for them to describe, yet feels very real. Kendra, a twenty-three-year-old artist who had recently received her B.A. in fine arts, explained, "There's a bond. There's an unspoken thing when you're sXe—you don't have to explain yourself to those people, you don't have to feel weird. There's a commonality." This bond, even between strangers, leads sXers to support each other whenever they can, including opening their homes to each other, sharing resources, buying sXe recordings, setting up shows, or backing each other up in confrontations at shows. On numerous occasions, I witnessed veterans of the local scene welcome new sXe kids who had recently migrated to Denver from the East or West Coast. Such newcomers had an instant community. Andy, nineteen, a working class sXer from the east, explained the value of sXe friendship:

> The kids that don't sell out are the ones that are your friends forever. That would do *anything* for you. Like if you get thrown out of your house they'd be right there, they'd be picking you up, they'd be bringing you to work. You'd be sleeping on their floor. Friends like that you can't live without. . . . You treat 'em like they're family. They're not your friends because they're sXe, but you saw 'em at shows with an X on their hand and you went up and talked to 'em and you've been hanging out ever since. Or like nowadays, kids talk to each other online, meet each other online. You just meet people all over the world and you can basically go anywhere. . . . It's something that's never undersold. Your friends are your friends, but when you make friends when you're sXe and they're all sXe, it's a little . . . it's tighter, because your friends are just there whenever; they're not at a party. Your sXe friends are there whenever you need 'em no matter what. I would put my life into every one of my friends' hands without a problem.

Straight edge forms a loose national (even global) network of strangers who would often support one another simply based upon the fact that they self-identify as sXe. Sid, a twenty-one-year-old college dropout who was now a mohawked anarchist, said, with just a hint of exaggeration, "It's a cool feeling that I can go anywhere in the world and have a place to stay with an sXe kid. And I feel obligated to help sXe kids out, too. It's not like I wouldn't help other people out, but with sXe I feel more of an obligation." Thus despite lacking a formal structure and membership list, the sXe identity creates a basis for commitment and mutual support and encourages personal actions in line with the ideology. The sXe community fosters a special connection between sXers that they rely upon in tough times. Gus, a twenty-three-year-old singer in a local hardcore band struggling to complete his college education, held all of his friends in high esteem, but was especially committed to the sXe scene:

> As far as the sXe brotherhood thing goes, in high school I only had four sXe friends. The rest drank and were always going to parties and doing whatever the hell. I never found interest in parties. I probably went to three parties the whole time I was in high school. . . . The sXe brotherhood just gave me a reason to not *want* to participate in that 'cause then I could go out and have fun with them, clean and sober. Instead of being around a bunch of people that aren't going to remember anything about the night the next day. To me, the brotherhood in sXe is a great thing if you are sXe.

Thus despite its lack of formal structure, leaders, and membership, the sXe collective identity is very prominent for adherents, creating a basis for commitment and encouraging personal actions in line with the identity.

Commitment and Accountability

Addiction kills the mind / And leaves you dependent / Chemicals of ill intention / Mixed to break you, break your vision / Don't lose sight / With confidence to fight addiction / Take the second step / Stand among as we stand as one / Live straight edge / Until the day you die straight edge.
—"Don't Lose Sight" by Throwdown, 1999

As their professed pledge to be "sXe for life" indicates, commitment is central to sXers' lives. Sociologists have generally written about commitment in terms of commitment to an organization or group and its goals (for example Kanter 1968; Hirsch 1990). Members of movements who have a strong commitment are more likely to handle the organization's day-to-day maintenance, take on extraordinary movement tasks (including high-risk actions), and stick with the group during hostile political times or under unfavorable social conditions (Becker 1960; McAdam 1988; Taylor 1989). Activists identify with ideologies, leadership, and communities, all of which are usually grounded in identifiable organizations (Downton and Wehr 1997). The example of sXe demonstrates, however, that in focusing on participants' commitment to conventional movement organizations and tasks, researchers have overlooked the fact that many individuals have instead committed to *collective identities* that reflect personal value identities (Gecas 2000).

Though they lack a discernible organization with concrete tasks or goals, sXers often speak of their commitment to sXe, bonding primarily to the *identity* itself, rather than a particular goal, specific organization, or cause. Straight edge fosters a community of like-minded individuals which participants often frame as a brotherhood. Brian, a twenty-one-year-old university student and member of an sXe band, said,

> I think mostly sXe brotherhood [means] we have something in common right away. The instant we meet we have something in common. Right there it gives us one up on someone else. That's huge. That's a lifestyle. It's not just like, "Oh, you like hockey, too?" It's a lot more than that. That's where brotherhood comes from. So if something happens to any of my friends I'll stick up for them, I'll help them out. Like brothers.

Framing their commitment in terms of personal integrity, honor, and accountability, sXers offer very individualized explanations of commitment, showing how individual and collective identities blend. Kent, the tattooed vegan from New York, said, "It defines part of who I am. Straight edge and hardcore have done more for me than anything." Kendra, the artist, said,

> In a sense [sXe] has become my identity. It's just like saying your social security number. Kendra Derber: 123 45 6789, straight edge, white, female, 5'9", 130 pounds. It's just part of who you are. We're all labels and we're all a certain mix of something. Irish/German, English/straight edge [laughs]. It's just who I am and I never want to get rid of it. Now as an adult you think back on all your childhood experiences and now you look to the future and I just don't want to change. Not even when I'm eighty years old. I'm gonna sit there with a blaring sacred heart [tattoo] with a triple X on it. It's informed my life and the choices I've made and the individual I've become.

Although sXers feel a commitment to other sXe individuals, they are still primarily committed to the identity and the ideals it implies. When sXers move, they might not have any nearby sXe friends, yet many continue to identify as sXe and live the values through their actions. Again, commitment to the identity replaces formal movement structure. One of Luke's friends believed the true test of commitment was in how long an sXer would stay clean without the social support of the hardcore scene:

> Someone told me once, I think it was my friend Bob, and this was definitely an extreme point of view, but he said you shouldn't be considered sXe unless you had or could live like *years* without any other sXe friends. In a way, that's totally off center. But it's true. Can you . . . how many sXe kids are going to be sXe if there are not shows? How many sXe kids are going to be sXe if all their friends sold out? There's not very many unfortunately. I think people just depend on the scene.

The sXe identity holds differing levels of salience for various adherents. For many, sXe is central to their identity: that is, sXe ranks high on their hierarchy of identities and is therefore very salient (Stryker 1981). Straight edgers frequently invoke their sXe identity in a variety of situations and contexts, indicating a high level of commitment to that identity. Wearing an X means demonstrating one's values to the mainstream world and symbolizes sXe commitment (Wood 1999). For example, I observed sXers wear X's to graduation ceremonies, disclose their sXe identity to critical students in college courses, place X's in their email addresses, and wear sXe messages in a variety of situations. Straight edge bands adorn their record covers with X's and write lyrics demanding intense commitment: Bold and Earth Crisis even evoke images of crucifixion with their songs "Nailed to the X" and "Forged in the Flames" (Bold 1988; Earth Crisis 1993). Tattoos, popular with both men and women in the scene, are the most permanent symbols of sXe commitment (Helton and Staudenmeier 2002). Both my perusal of sXe websites and my observations at shows revealed a variety of sXe tattoos, ranging from "XXX" on the forearm and "STR8 EDGE" across the knuckles to "Vegan" on the stomach and "Drug Free" across the chest (see Atkinson 2003). Two male Denver sXers have enormous stylized X's across their entire backs.

Straight edge differs from most movements in that it explicitly requires a lifetime commitment from its participants. T-shirt slogans such as "Straight edge: it's for life," "One life drug free," and "Straight edge: If

7. Especially committed sXers prominently display their dedication, getting tattoos on their fingers, hands, necks, wrists, and forearms. Tattoo by Ron Perry.

you're not now, you never were" exemplify members' rhetoric about the lifelong nature of sXe. Clearly, such a promise made in the hubris of youth is difficult to enforce. The absence of formal membership "rules" (such as a written covenant) requires sXers to create informal methods of enforcing commitment and accountability. George, a twenty-two-year-old engineering major active in the punk scene, said, "There's definitely accountability. But that's part of the movement. Other movements have their phone lists. We kind of have this unspoken thing going on." Informal shaming includes labeling sXers who begin smoking or drinking "sellouts." When sXers sell out, their sXe friends often feel disappointed, though rarely to the point of abandoning the friendship. However, rather than seeming simply a personal "failing," selling out becomes a betrayal of friendship and the entire sXe identity. New Jersey sXe band Floorpunch, like many bands, equated selling out with betrayal, or stabbing a friend in the back: "Dedication is what you lack / I turn my head, pull the knife out of my back" ("No Exceptions"). The insistence that sXe be a lifetime commitment intensifies sXers' dedication to the lifestyle. Movements with high expectations of their participants often receive greater commitment

(Kanter 1968). There was no "partial" sXe; the identity demands all or nothing. One sip of beer, one drag off a cigarette means the revocation of any claims to sXe. B.K., twenty-five, a talented tattoo artist, was very accepting and tolerant of people who used and sXers who sold out. However, he still felt strongly about sXe being a one-chance opportunity:

> I'm very adamant about saying . . . if you were once sXe and you gave it up, decided it wasn't for you, you can never be sXe again. . . . If you don't stick with it or whatever, that's fine, but you have nobody to be disappointed in but yourself. Nobody else should really be disappointed. In essence, it's a big deal but it's not that big of a deal. But it's important enough that you should realize that once you make the decision to be sXe it's a decision you make for life. So when you decide *not* to be, that's also a decision you make for life. Straight edge is a vow, a commitment, for good.

The fact that many sXers sell out doesn't faze new adherents' belief that they will be sXe forever.[7] Enough sXers maintain the sXe lifestyle into their late twenties and beyond to fuel the belief that sXe *can* be for life.[8]

Participants in social movements hold strong convictions, but not everyone with strong convictions joins a movement organization. Some commit to a collective identity instead of an organized group. Commitment to a collective identity *may* lead to involvement in a social movement organization, which in turn reinforces commitment to the identity. However, commitment need not rest on membership in a formal organization.

Customized Participation

. . . You and me / We'll make the difference! . . .
—"We'll Make the Difference" by Insted, 1987

Straight edgers do not "participate" in the movement in ways scholars typically think of movement participation: strikes, picketing, signing petitions, lobbying, writing letters, joining and/or maintaining an activist organization, civil disobedience, and other common avenues of social protest. Bound loosely by a guiding collective identity and united in their commitment, sXers customize their participation to meet their own interests and needs. Commitment to a meaningful identity is fundamental to a variety of forms of participation, as McAdam and Paulsen (1993:154) point out in their study of the 1964 Mississippi Freedom

Project: "neither organizational embeddedness nor strong ties to another volunteer are themselves predictive of high-risk activism. Instead it is a strong subjective identification with a particular identity, *reinforced by organizational or individual ties,* that is especially likely to encourage participation." However, participation in less structured movements, based upon commitment to an identity, is more individualized than participation in a social movement organization as there is less guidance and oversight from movement leaders.

Straight edge is not a formal group pursuing an explicit political goal. Rather, sXers' more individualized forms of participation, taken together, amount to a collective cultural challenge. Committing to the sXe identity includes forging behavioral expectations just as committing to an organization would. Of course, in any movement, participants' levels of commitment to the collective identity vary (Stryker 1968; Snow and McAdam 2000), and it follows that adherents' behavior varies as well. The sXe collective identity encourages a continuum of behaviors, including *essential, secondary,* and *peripheral* behaviors. Everyone who claims sXe must fulfill the essential behaviors; they are prerequisites to "membership." Many adherents fulfill the secondary behaviors; doing so often indicates a higher level of commitment, but secondary behaviors are not required. Finally, the collective identity suggests a variety of possible peripheral behaviors, unnecessary to claim the identity but indicative of even greater commitment.

All sXers refuse drugs, alcohol, and tobacco products. Abstinence is *essential* to the collective identity's behavioral expectations and is the most crucial criterion of membership. *Many* sXers abstain from "promiscuous" sex (which they define as sex outside of a caring relationship), follow strict vegetarian or vegan diets, get sXe tattoos, and become involved in more formal social causes such as women's rights, animal rights, or environmentalism. These behaviors are *secondary* to the collective identity. *Some* sXers avoid caffeine, legal and/or over-the-counter medication, and mainstream jobs, connect sXe to their religion, or contribute to the scene (setting up shows, running a record label, printing a 'zine, playing in a band). Such *peripheral* manifestations of commitment are common enough to constitute a pattern, yet relatively rare compared with more central behaviors. Thus, barring the core behaviors, sXers are free to customize their commitment and participation to their individual interpretations and values, tailoring the identity to match their own biography. For many, sXe serves as a support system for personal action, and individual consciousness shifts beyond substance use. Katherine explained how identifying as sXe opened up other avenues of political involvement, a common claim among sXers:

> Once you get involved in sXe, then a lot of people get involved in something like vegetarianism, veganism, different humanitarian things. They start getting involved in political things. Then you get the political bands like Boy Sets Fire and Good Riddance, bands like that that talk about all different topics going on in the world today. I think people in the scene are more open and willing to help and try to understand what's going on. Help other people out with whatever situation is going on with them. Not to say that people who aren't involved in the scene don't care, but I think when you're involved you end up getting more exposure because of all the 'zines, and all the pamphlets and everything that's all around. The political bands talk about what they want to talk about between songs. It kind of makes you think.

Jason, twenty-seven, a musician and computer support technician from the East Coast, indicated that personalizing the collective identity was an ongoing process:

> As you grow older, you start to comb through it and you find out what really means something, why you're doing something. You come up with your own reasons, your own image of why and what it is. It starts off as something that someone has to introduce you to it, the whole scene. But then it becomes a more personal side of you.

Luke had not adopted vegetarianism or any other secondary values of sXe, yet he understood that many other kids added values to the essential sXe characteristics:

> I used this analogy once when we were in an argument in Phoenix. 'Cause Phoenix used to have a huge Christian sXe scene. They would always be like, well, it's vegan-sXe, or it's Christian-sXe. To me, sXe is the trunk of the tree. Any other thing that you bring into it, those are just the mere branches. When it comes down to it, it comes down to being sXe. If you're vegetarian, cool. If you believe in . . . there's Krishna sXe guys, there's Catholic, and there's Jewish sXe guys, too. That's cool. But those things don't have anything to do with sXe except they might have blossomed off it. . . . You make it what you want.

8. Some sXers frame their commitment as a sacred oath or vow. Tattoo by James McGrory.

While the essential behaviors are the same for everyone, the openness of the secondary and peripheral behaviors encourages different *interpretations* of sXe. Abstinence from alcohol, for example, holds a variety of meanings for participants (Haenfler 2001), including: individual freedom, corporate resistance, personal empowerment, defying family history, defying social norms regarding substance use and abuse, generally challenging a corrupt society, stepping toward enlightenment, keeping a clear mind for other pursuits, and being an example for other young people. The movement actually encourages participants to make the ideology their own, to create their own meanings. The flexibility of sXe meanings leads adherents to incorporate a variety of others' beliefs and issues into their own sXe identities. Most adherents agree, however, that sXe should be more than an abstinence movement. Kevin, the martial artist, believed that sXe provided an avenue to living a stronger life, which meant many things to him, including examining every aspect of life.

> Kids get into sXe 'cause they're looking to improve themselves and better themselves and become strong and break away from the weaknesses around them. But when they start that, it becomes a habit and it makes you look at *everything*. So these people are like "Being a carnivore is weak!" and they get into that. If you look at most sXe kids, there's like a common core of being sXe—we don't

drink, we don't smoke, we don't do drugs—but then if you look at them, there's also other things. They're vegetarian, or they're vegan, or they're political, or they're feminist, or they're gay rights, or they're militant and they work out and do 9000 bench presses a day. They're all pursuing strength in other areas. I don't think they're pursuing it because they're sXe, but I think their interest in sXe spawned an interest in becoming strong which manifests itself in different ways.

Similarly, the owners of Commitment Records, an sXe label located in the Netherlands, claimed that sXe should create in its members a general progressive outlook:

For the people involved in Commitment Records, straight edge means more than just not drinking, not smoking and not using drugs. In our eyes these are just necessary conditions to be able to strife [sic] for the really important things: creating a society, based on mutual respect, without prejudice, hate and ignorance; working for a world without the big differences in welfare which exist nowadays, a world where humans, animals and the environment have priority, and not economic growth and monetary considerations. There is no place for hardline attitudes, racism, sexism, homophobia, nationalism, Satanism and machoism (including violent dancing!) in straight edge. [www.poisonfree.com/commitment, viewed 5/30/2001]

Participation in the sXe identity continually encourages individuals to question their beliefs on a variety of subjects. Adopting the collective identity often leads to other consciousness shifts around race, class, gender, sexuality, the environment, education, and a variety of global problems. B.K., the tattoo artist, explained how sXe served as a jumping off point for further education and action:

I think it's really good that people involved in the scene can have priorities that go outside just the music, just the sXe lifestyle. That they can have a more global mind, more environmental or social thoughts. Things like vegan lifestyle, vegetarian lifestyle. Protesting this or writing about this. Getting people more aware. It definitely is a good thing. I think it makes overall a little more well-rounded person, too. Especially when people take it upon themselves to do those things. Just through a simple thing like a lifestyle to have such an impact on most of the kids involved in it—to want to get involved in other things, like animal rights. That's pretty rare and should definitely be taken with a lot of respect.

In an individualistic culture, many people live out their values as individuals connected by a collective identity. Individuals bonded by a collective identity experience a *community of meaning* that makes the personal political and gives new, politicized meaning to everyday actions. It creates an oppositional consciousness and a framework for understanding social problems that leads to a politicization of everyday life (Whittier 1997). Adherents committed to the collective identity live out a set of core values and/or behaviors, but then they are able to fit the collective identity to their individual preferences. They tailor the identity to match their interests, biographical availability, and values.[9]

Cultural Targets and Tactics

Now is the time for the kids to take a stand / For what is right, in our lives / It's up to you and me / To make a change, move forward / We won't be left behind / This is our life, our time / It's time we set things right / No excuses this time / For what's been said and done / Take control of your life / Just stand your ground / . . . You and me we can stand up / And go against the grain / This is our life and this is our time / It's time we made a change.

—"Directions of Things to Come" by Ensign, 1997

Straight edge's diffuse structure, commitment to identity, and individualized forms of participation combine to create a challenge to mainstream society that is primarily cultural, rather than political, in nature. Generally, scholars have studied movement organizations that challenge the state (McAdam and Snow 1997; Tarrow 1994), although a few have focused on more cultural movements (such as Eder, Staggenborg, and Sudderth 1995; Gamson 1996). Political challenges typically seek institutional change via the political system, although activists use many creative and unorthodox means to engage the state. Cultural challenges focus more on lifestyles, asserting and/or reclaiming an identity, and creating alternative institutions. Social movement scholars, feminists, and activists have debated (without reaching definite resolution) whether social change efforts are most effective in the cultural or political realm (for instance Cohen 1985). Theorists now see through this dichotomy and realize that movements have both cultural and political elements (Polletta 1997; Scott 1990). However, a movement may emphasize one aspect over the other.

The culture/politics debate raises interesting problems such as identifying the "enemy" and the focus of change. Some movements engage in a more generalized "resistance" rather than singling out a particular opponent. For example, it is difficult to specify the Promise Keepers' enemy. Gamson (1989:357) points out that sometimes "the enemy is invisible, abstract, disembodied, ubiquitous." Likewise, members of the American Sociological Association's Collective Behavior section discuss the possibility that movements engage a variety of *authority structures* rather than simply the state (Snow 2001). Such "extra-institutional challenges" might include creating alternative institutions (for instance, lesbian feminist bookstores; support groups), making lifestyle choices that reflect personal values (such as shopping at local businesses; pledging virginity), or promoting consciousness shifts by setting a personal example (for example wearing a "What Would Jesus Do" bracelet or "Hate is not a Family Value" t-shirt).

Straight edge is a culturally oriented challenge that creates a space for young people to feel "cool" for *not* using drugs. They interpret their individual choices as taking a stand against an alcohol-obsessed society, setting a positive example, and forging a personal form of resistance that has broader consequences. In the insert to their CD, *Through the Darkest Days,* the band Trial wrote, "We are raised to believe in false ideals: that money is necessary for happiness; that image is necessary for life; that control is necessary for love. Questioning these patterns brings on blinding defiance." Jason explained how sXe provides the foundation of a broader resistance to society:

> You think of bands like Youth of Today, there's songs like 'Take a Stand.' That's what they're talking about. They're not just talking about vegetarianism, they're not just talking about sXe, they're not just talking about one specific thing. They are talking about a whole, a broad society. . . . He was talking about "Look at us. We kind of live in hell."

Although they question society at large, many sXers focus on resisting what they perceive as a youth culture obsessed with alcohol. Sid, a twenty-one-year-old college dropout turned mohawked anarchist said, "I guess that had a lot to do with sXe because it was a rejection of the whole beer culture thing. Definitely that's what CU is all about. Especially freshman year in the dorms. It's really hard to hang out if you're not into doing that. It's just not a good place to be."

For many sXers, being part of the movement means setting a positive example, particularly for other youth. Rather than proselytizing, most sXers believe their lives demonstrated their convictions. Kent said, "The idea behind sXe is that you make a life decision. You're making a statement by doing it." Sending a message to the rest of society was also important to Kate:

> I think that sXe is a way for young people to say to adults and other young people, "Hey look, there's this huge group of people that have fun, get along, they're normal kids, they have friends, they just don't do drugs, they don't use, they don't smoke. They can have fun without it." I think that's a pretty important part of or a goal of sXe. It's an example of a positive youth movement in our society, which rarely people pay attention to.

Elizabeth, the high school counselor, explained both the collective significance of sXe and how she strove to set a positive example:

> You can be sXe on your own, but there's not a lot of significance to that. You're more powerful as a group. . . . I wanted to claim sXe because I think the more people that know about living a clean lifestyle, it gets people thinking about that as an option. Truly, some people may never hear of anybody living a drug-free or alcohol-free lifestyle by choice. . . . I know that everything I do is modeling. People see what you do and hear what you say. People are always searching for people to act according to what they say, and live in correspondence to their beliefs and ideas and thoughts. Unfortunately, that's not that common. So I know that personally I have an impact in that regard.

Some sXers are very persistent and vocal about their beliefs; a vegan sXe offshoot called "Hardline" was very outspoken and confrontational. Its popularity faded, but certain small factions of sXe and certain "crews" remained extremely vocal (see Chapter 4). Most, however, are suspicious of "preaching" about their cause. They are more likely to spread their message through t-shirt slogans, 'zines, and personal example. B.K., the tattoo artist, said, "Making people aware is an important thing, and I think most of the time it's best accomplished just through your daily interactions with people. It needs to be something that's kept very personal." Sid, the anarchist, explained further:

> It is important . . . not to push it, but to say, "I'm sXe. It's OK to be sXe. Straight edge is cool." I think it is important. It's just like anything else. I'm vegetarian, I'm vegan. It's easy, it's cool. There's nothing hard about it and it's good for X, X, and X. You lead by example. You lead by showing people you *can* have something else.

While being sXe is an individual choice and a lifestyle, individuals often interpret their personal resistance as having consequences beyond their own lives. Carrie, twenty-four, an sXer who worked for a nonprofit corporation, said:

> It's definitely taking a stand and hitting the major tobacco and so forth corporations in the only place where they really are concerned. Even if it's unintentionally political, I think that it's political. . . . Most of the kids I've known who are sXe have been pretty politically active. They are very strong-minded about specific issues. . . . It would be pretty hard for me to go to a show and listen to somebody talk about all these politics and then go, "Yeah, I agree with that, I agree with that!" and then walk into some corporate firm and work all day. I'd feel kind of like a hypocrite. I think most people would.

To be effective, diffuse movements must find ways to unite individual choices with collective action and transform them from "self-improvement to world improvement" (Helton and Staudenmeier 2002:463). Collective identity fulfills this role by giving meaning to individual participants' actions, adding an additional layer of meaning to what could be isolated, individual acts (Taylor and Whittier 1992). Calhoun (1994:28) claims, "the politics of personal identity and the politics of collective identity are . . . inextricably linked," suggesting that personal actualization and social transformation are not mutually exclusive. Straight edgers repeatedly made this connection. As Melucci (1996:115) writes, "To an increasing degree, problems of individual identity and collective action become meshed together: the solidarity of the group is inseparable from the personal quest." For example, coming out of the closet for lesbians or gay men has become more than a personally fulfilling and beneficial choice. It became a political act, a statement, an action that ultimately made the world a better place for *all* lesbians and gays. While most sXers refuse alcohol, drugs, and tobacco for individualized reasons, their collective choices add up to meaningful resistance to youth and mainstream culture. Abstinence is an individualized means to a collective end; sXers' intention is not only to live fulfilling individual lives, but also to create new possibilities for youth culture.

Conclusion

Cynics might claim that sXe has accomplished little or that it does not deserve analysis as a social movement. That attitude would reflect a narrow understanding of what movements are, what they do, and what they are capable of achieving. Movements are more than organizations raising funds, holding demonstrations, and lobbying politicians. They include identities that shape people's lives in the most personal ways, while simultaneously making a collective statement. It is difficult to gauge the cultural impact of sXe on youth culture or the larger society. As independent, punk-inspired music begins to push again into the mainstream during the late 1990s and early 2000s, sXers bring their energy, values, and DIY ethic with them. Hundreds of current and former sXers play in popular bands (such as H2O, Good Riddance, Saves the Day, Snapcase, Boy Sets Fire, Vision of Disorder, Stretch Armstrong, Ignite), produce records, run labels (Revelation, Victory, and many others) write for music magazines, and otherwise work in the music industry. Indie rock, pop punk, Christian metal, and other scenes have all felt the cultural impact of sXe. At the very least, sXe has helped make leading a drug-free lifestyle more of an option in a variety of youth settings and has brought the vegetarian and animal rights movements into the independent scene. Increasing press coverage since 1997 has exposed an entirely new generation of young people to the movement, and metalcore's growing popularity could expose even greater numbers of kids to the sXe life.

POSITIVITY VERSUS MILITANCY
STRUGGLES WITHIN THE SCENE

In July of 2001 I attended Hellfest,[1] an annual two-day hard-core music festival sponsored by Trustkill records and held in Syracuse, NY. The bill included dozens of bands, including popular sXe bands Ensign, Good Clean Fun, and Earth Crisis. Thousands of energetic fans attended the event, most from the United States but others from the U.K., Australia, and Mexico. Most were hardcore and sXe kids, though punks and metal-heads had a strong presence as well. Some had stretched ears, long dreadlocks, or pierced nipples. An outsider passing by would probably have wondered if the roadside circus freak show had come to town before locking car doors or crossing to the other side of the street. Indeed, the promoters were forced to switch venues at the last minute when some anxious Syra-cuse residents worried over the event's name. Yet, when I asked a police officer working security for his thoughts on the whole affair, he said, "This is the best concert I've worked in thirteen years." There were very few fights, no drugs or alcohol, and no disturbances in the parking lot. In many ways, the festival ex-emplified hardcore at its best.

But inside the sweltering, humid hall I did notice isolated scenes of violence and negativity amid the sweating crowd of dancers. I watched as one youth tried to apologize for running into an older, much larger kid on the dance floor. The "victim" and several of his friends beat down the youth, chasing him out of the room; apology not accepted. I also observed members of an sXe crew pa-rade around in packs with grim expressions, shirts off, displaying mus-cled, tattoo-covered frames as if to intimidate their detractors and boost their tough image. Another kid's t-shirt read "STRAIGHT EDGE—If you aren't now, you will be"[2] over a picture of an X'd up hand holding a sub-machine gun—hardly a welcoming invitation to the group.

Despite members' avowed "positivity," sXe has always had a reputa-tion, fueled in large part by the mainstream media, of intolerance toward people who use alcohol, drugs, and tobacco. Andy and Darren tried to ex-plain the reality and the perception of sXe:

Andy: Straight edge made a good and a bad [statement]. It was both sides of that. You had sXe kids that were having fun at shows being awesome, stand up dudes. Teaching the kids who really had no idea, that were like unclear about it. Then you also had the kids wearing— sXe kids—that were just kicking the shit out of everybody. You had militant sXe kids that were just fighting anybody for no reason. On the one hand you had kids actually doing something positive for the scene which actually made the scene look better. On the other hand you had the *minority* starting shit, making sXe look bad to *everybody*. Which for some reason overshadows the fact that there's so many kids doing something *right*.

Darren: cause the bad always, *always* overshadows the good. That's what people concentrate on.

Since its inception, there has been an ongoing tension within sXe between positivity and militancy. The hardcore scene as a whole has always attracted a few violent elements and at some shows you can almost expect there will be fighting. Even early bands Minor Threat, Uniform Choice, and SSD struggled to create a drug free scene while fighting to defend their beliefs from attack (Blush 2001). Throughout sXe history, various bands and individual sXers have been labeled "militant" by both external authorities and by insiders. Militancy can mean many things, from randomly attacking a smoker to simply being exceptionally outspoken in promoting the sXe lifestyle. Militancy worries parents and other adults, who are, of course, quick to condemn violence and have occasionally gone so far as to ban sXe clothing at schools or place the group under the watchful eye of police gang units. What many fail to realize is that sXers themselves wrestle with what it means to be "edge" and how one best promotes the lifestyle (or whether one should promote it at all).

Movements construct and maintain boundaries, designating who can claim the movement identity and who cannot. Straight edgers wage a constant, low-intensity battle against one another as they struggle to define the sXe collective identity. Conventional thought for most sXers is that militant kids draw unwanted attention to the group from police, give the movement a bad name, and create unnecessary tensions within the scene. Uncovering the history of the movement's internal struggles leads to insights regarding the consequences of creating an inclusive, tolerant identity verses an exclusive, militant one. Ultimately, both may have their place and the movement could come to a balance between the two.

XXX

Studying the Boundaries of Collective Identity

Social movements engage in an ongoing process of creating collective identities that attract potential supporters, delineate boundaries between insiders and outsiders, and provide meaning and context for social movement activities. Collective identity does not simply emerge through interaction; movement actors intentionally *create* the identity. A dilemma arises regarding how exclusive or inclusive to make the identity: who can claim the identity? What must adherents believe? What actions must one take to claim the identity? How will the movement "police" its identity boundaries? From a strategic standpoint, questions such as these arise for many social movements, for example:

- Can men claim a feminist identity?
- What are the consequences of whites joining movements of people of color?
- Should gay, lesbian, and bisexual movements include transgendered people?
- What real actions must someone take to claim the environmentalist identity?
- Should sympathetic and active straights have a claim on the queer identity?

Conventional wisdom suggests that movements wishing to attract and maintain a large membership must have a relatively open identity, be accepting of a variety of viewpoints, and welcome a variety of members. The temptation for movement leaders is to appeal to as many audiences as possible, framing the movement with a variety of meanings to reach a wide range of potential adherents. However, in being inclusive, a movement risks diluting its meaning and thereby lowering intensity of commitment. The more meaningful (and the more demanding) an identity is to an individual, the more likely that individual will fulfill movement actions (see Kanter 1972). Framing the movement in ways that will appeal to the greatest number of potential supporters may, in fact, water down the meaning for those who would be most supportive, thereby weakening their commitment. If almost "anything goes," that is, if many people can relatively easily claim the identity, then adherents have little incentive to *act* according to the identity's strictures.

There is a tension between two extremes: relatively closed, stringent collective identities (such as cults, Nazis) and identities open to greater interpretation (for instance environmentalists, New Agers). Successful movements must balance inclusion and meaning and accept the benefits and limitations of each. Perhaps the greater commitment garnered from more closed/exclusive identities outweighs the greater numbers of people attracted by open identities. In part, mobilization becomes a process of mobilizing *meaning* for a core constituency.

Creating a collective identity involves active, ongoing decisions about who 'we' are and who 'we' are not (Taylor and Whittier 1992). Thus, social movements necessarily exclude people on the basis of collective identity claims. Establishing boundaries is a constant and difficult process that often creates friction.[3] Just as participants often contest frames within their movement (Benford 1993), collective identity is frequently under dispute, as various member factions argue their positions in planning meetings, at conferences, and over email. Sometimes the disputes create symbolic boundaries for the public's benefit (Gamson 1997); thus sXers might condemn militant sXers to the public (to improve sXe's image) while being friendly to the militants outside public view.[4] At other times, different generations come into conflict when the younger cohort brings different ideas to the movement (Whittier 1997), as when new sXers' views clash with the old school. Despite these struggles, collective identity has the power to build solidarity, and activists must manage identity boundaries to promote unity and action:

> In political systems that distribute rights and resources to groups with discernible boundaries, activists are smart to be vigilant about those boundaries; in cultural systems that devalue so many identities, a movement with clarity about who belongs can better provide its designated members with the strength and pride to revalue their identities. (Gamson 1997:179)

Participation depends upon creating a collective identity that includes enough people's experiences to form a movement yet is exclusive enough to be meaningful (see Friedman and McAdam 1992). The more individual and collective identities link, the greater participants' commitment to the cause (Gamson 1991).

Within sXe, one general faction envisions a relatively inclusive, accepting identity based upon personal choice. Being straight edge is less central to this group's sense of personal identity; it is one identity among many. Another believes the movement should be more active in trying to convince other kids to live drug- and alcohol-free lives and that sXers should outwardly demonstrate their pride. For them, sXe is more than a personal choice: it is an imperative for larger social change. The former group tends to be more tolerant of a variety of lifestyles, leaving the sXe identity open to much interpretation (beyond the core values). The latter constituency is more militant in its attitudes, placing the sXe identity at the center of their lives and actively (sometimes aggressively) promoting the sXe lifestyle.

From Tolerance to Militancy and Back Again

I'm through with tolerance / No more acceptance of your crimes / I don't care about your "freedom" / 'Cos your actions restrict mine.

—"I, The Jury" by Vegan Reich, 1990

Throughout sXe's history, an ongoing rift between tolerant, easygoing sXers (typically self-identified as "posi" or "positive" kids) and more militant, contentious adherents has created heated discussion, hard feelings, and sometimes physical confrontations (see Atkinson 2003). Though the less assuming, more tolerant sXers have always outnumbered their counterparts, the militant thread has been especially prominent at various points in the sXe timeline.

Tolerance and Positivity

The youth crew and, especially, the emo/politically correct eras ushered in a relatively positive, proactive atmosphere. Certainly, youth crew had its share of arrogance, intolerance, aggressive dancing, and masculine posing, but many members were geeky punks looking for a place to fit in. In general, the Denver scene characterizes this openness, as Katherine attested: "The hardcore scene in general is very accepting to whatever you believe in." Maggie, the progressive non-traditional college student, is ardently sXe but recognizes the lifestyle is not for everyone and that sXe is only one aspect of her life: "Straight edge to me is just another part of me, another part of what I believe." Though there are no definitive lines between tolerant and militant sXers, tolerant sXers generally fit the following profile:

- Believe sXe is one's personal choice. Envision straight edge as a loose movement, but are more focused on the individual.
- Less inclined to advertise their beliefs. Typically wore X's less often.

- Aside from being disappointed, don't really care if kids sell out. The individual is championed over the group, so individual choices are respected. Recognize and generally accept that not every sXe kid will be down for life.
- Less committed to style requirements in sXe. Anyone welcome, whether they look like a punk, computer geek, or a nu-metal kid. (Younger sXers, however, tend to be more rigid in their style.)
- Tend to have a greater variety of friends than their more militant peers.
- Beyond core values, are relatively open to individual interpretations of sXe. Though vegetarianism is often promoted it is not *pushed*.
- Less inclined toward hypermasculinity and hard dancing. Tend to be more careful about not hitting others in the pit.

Despite their rigid beliefs about alcohol, most sXers keep an open mind about drinking. Justin, a twenty-two-year-old sXer visiting Denver from the East Coast, said:

> In high school, my weekends consisted of sitting around with my friends watching them drink forties. And watch them smoke cigarettes. I didn't care. I'm just open-minded about it. It doesn't bother me. The only time it bothers me is when people close to me get completely wasted and have no self-control. That's the only time it bothers me. Otherwise, I don't care. I'll go out with my friends.

Though many are too young to patronize bars, tolerant sXers over twenty-one sometimes join their non-sXe friends for a night out. Kyle, the positive university student, said:

> I like to go out to bars. I like to go out with all my friends I've known my whole life. Whenever I ask sXe friends if they want to go out, either they're too young or they just don't care to go. I like to see everything. I'm not going to say because I don't drink I won't go out to a bar. Bars can be kind of fun.

Some sXers secretly believe sell-outs should be given one more chance. Megan, twenty-one and sXe for five years, felt disappointed when someone sold out, but believes some people deserve a second opportunity:

> RH: Straight edge is kind of this all or nothing type thing. If you really mess up once . . .

Megan: I disagree with that completely. I think everybody deserves another chance. Especially like . . . if you've *never* touched anything. I think everybody should experiment at one point in their lives, I really do. Just so that these values are stronger.

RH: Do you have any idea *why* that's so important to the movement?

Megan: I honestly think it's insecurity. They don't want to be equal to somebody who has . . . left the scene and dissed it like that.

Katherine agreed, though she saw limits: "Second round sXe, I don't see it as a big deal. But once you're like third, fourth, whatever, I don't think you can call yourself sXe anymore. . . . After the second time, you're all done. There isn't a turning back." Matthew held that the notion of "you can only be sXe once" was an important aspect of sXe, but acknowledged that there could be exceptions:

I think that kind of adds to the extreme of it. It kind of makes it sound a little bit stronger. But I see no problem if someone's trying to get their life straight and they want to be sXe. I think that they should wait to call themselves that before they make a commitment. I've known people that called themselves sXe then one night got drunk. They told me about it, they're like "It's really dumb. I can't believe I did it." I don't believe in not slipping up. This person has not had a drink since. He told me about it. I don't see a reason for there to be all or nothing.

Therefore, while sXe projects a rigid, unyielding identity to the public, within the movement members might be more flexible.[5] In any case, very, very few individuals who give up the sXe identity attempt to claim it again.

Turn toward Militancy

The advent of the mid-1990s Victory era infused renewed energy and passion to the scene. As Strife, Snapcase, and Earth Crisis brought a metal edge to their music, the movement's numbers swelled with new members who had little connection to late-eighties and early-nineties positivity. Even the name Victory evokes struggle and dominance, whereas the primary record label releasing sXe music during the youth crew era was Revelation, implying a search for knowledge or a spiritual quest. The already hard dancing at shows became even more physically intense. Hardcore in general increasingly adopted a brutal, metal-influenced sound as bands such as Converge, Integrity, Cave In, Vision of Disorder, Hatebreed, Candiria, and Disembodied rose to prominence.

"Militant" signifies someone who is dedicated and outspoken, but also believed to be narrow-minded, judgmental, and potentially violent. For most sXers, the term is derogatory. In general, the characteristics of militant sXers include the following:

- Less tolerant of drinking and drug use and therefore less likely to associate with people who use.
- More outward pride in being sXe. Straight edge is a more prominent part of their identities.
- More outspoken. Wore sXe messages often, regularly X'd up, prominent sXe tattoos.
- More judgmental of sell-outs. More likely to mock and dissociate themselves from former sXers.
- More likely to wear the sXe "uniform" of the time (such as camouflage pants, bandana, athletic shoes), or a t-shirt with a message like "Keep smoking. I want you to die" or "Kill Your Local Drug Dealer."[6]
- More hypermasculine. Enjoy hard dancing at shows, for example. Dancing a very macho thing; some feel women don't belong in the pit.
- More likely to be homophobic. Essentially, in some ways they resemble the aggro skinheads present in the early punk scene.
- More likely to avoid over-the-counter medication and/or caffeine.
- Often, but not always, have a greater focus on animal rights.
- Maintain rigid boundaries around the sXe identity. For example, an individual must be *invited* to join a crew.

Earth Crisis is alternatively credited or blamed for much of the mid-1990s resurgence in sXe pride and militancy. Their early releases, *All Out War* (1992) and *Firestorm* (1993) jump-started the trend toward veganism and an ever-greater awareness of social injustice. The anthem "Firestorm" inspired a host of new sXe recruits, capturing the rage and disgust many sXers felt toward drug dealers who prey upon the weak and the corrupt politicians and law enforcement that seemed incapable of protecting innocent people. My introduction to the Denver scene was a 1996 Earth Crisis show in a run-down former movie theater, hundreds of kids literally climbing over one another to sing along to this song, X'd hands pointed in the air. Having been largely absent from the sXe scene for several years, I had no idea the movement had undergone such a transformation. The band's passionate following continued to grow until I saw them play their last show at Hellfest 2001 in their hometown of Syracuse, NY.

Even the band's style reflected images of militancy: camouflage pants and hats, bandanas, absolutely no leather or animal products. They often framed their dedication to sXe as an oath based upon honor, reminiscent of the military. The Earth Crisis (1998) song "Ultramilitance" championed environmental and animal rights activists who took their fight directly to corporations and mink farms, framing the struggle as a "war" and the activists as "rescuers." Citing the failure of legal forms of protest, the song praised direct action techniques favored by groups such as Earth First!, Animal Liberation Front, and Sea Sheppard: damaging bulldozers, freeing mink, and sinking whaling ships. Singer Karl Buechner explained the motivation behind his commitment to veganism:

> I had always been fascinated by animals and respected them. When I started to learn about what was happening to animals in slaughterhouses and with vivisection in laboratories I was horrified and wanted to make sure I wasn't doing anything that contributed to their suffering. My grandmother kind of led by example; she was vegetarian. As time went along, my friends saw how I was living. When they asked me why I would tell them exactly why I was and it obviously made sense to some of them.

Earth Crisis was the initial inspiration for many Denver kids' decision to claim sXe. After watching an episode of the news magazine *20/20* on sXe that featured the band, Maggie wanted to learn more:

> It was their radical viewpoints on *everything*. They have some cool stuff to say. I think I got a Victory Style sampler and I was like, "This band is awesome!" It had the "Firestorm" song on it. I was all about it. It was pretty much their radical viewpoints because I wanted to be as different as possible in high school.

Though the members of Earth Crisis had many characteristics of more-tolerant sXers, and most of their songs were outlets for anger as much as calls for militant action, many sXers *perceived* the band as militant and interpreted the band's message accordingly, likely missing some of the band's intended meanings.

In the mid-1990s, perhaps no other band ignited as much controversy within the sXe scene than youth-crew style One Life Crew (OLC) from Cleveland. Tolerant sXers interpreted their lyrics as xenophobic, anti-immigrant, misogynist, racist, and full of hate. It was difficult for many sXers who had never seen the band live to determine if their message was sincere or a joke. Many kids boycotted their music; others handed out anti-OLC flyers at the band's gigs. Their song "Stra-Hate Edge" (1995), a rant against sellouts, called for bringing the "HATE" back to sXe. The song kindled the "hate edge" label and, along with Courage Crew, brought the Ohio hardcore scene national attention.

Ironically, the record also included the song "Our Fight," an explicitly antiracist track claiming "Racist ways are so wrong / Blacks and whites are equally strong." The band spawned a cottage industry of opposition, including 'zines and websites, and fueled heated discussion in Internet chat-rooms. One poster wrote, "I don't understand how someone with any heart or taste in music can like them. The only appeal I can see in OLC is that they appeal to lonely privileged white boys who like to pretend like their life is hard and that the rest of the world owes them something for being a lonely and pissed off white male." While their message may have had great appeal to a minority of aggro sXe men, many in the scene wanted nothing to do with them. After one release with Victory Records the band quickly faded away, some members going on to form Pitboss 2000.

The Salt Lake City, Utah, scene emerged as the dominant face of militant sXe during the mid-1990s. Reports of violence against smokers and drinkers and connections to the Animal Liberation Front landed Salt Lake City (SLC) sXers on FOX's *America's Most Wanted* program and placed the movement on law enforcement's list of gangs. Interviews with a few of them on ABC's *20/20* displayed both tolerant and militant members. During the 2002 Winter Olympics, officials placed sXe on a list of potential domestic terrorist threats. An exchange on the *20/20* program between journalist John Quinones and Officer Brad Harmon illustrates the authorities' view of sXe:

Quinones: Are these kids as dangerous as the Bloods, the Crips? Can they be?

Harmon: I consider them every bit as dangerous. We see them carry weapons. We see them maiming people. We see them doing millions of dollars of destruction to business people around the city. In other countries, they call it terrorism. I would say it's about the same thing here.

Quinones: They sound like politically correct terrorists.

Harmon: I couldn't say it better myself.

I spoke with a variety of kids from SLC. Most were fairly typical, tolerant sXers, but a few fit the militant profile. Denver kids who were either originally from SLC or who visited to see shows almost universally despised the scene and some bands refused to play there. The notoriety of SLC sXe resonated throughout the U.S. scene. The Reno, Nevada, scene has been the latest to attract negative national attention. In March 2005 the area's regional gang unit added straight edge to its list of street gangs after a number of attacks on smokers and/or drinkers (O'Malley 2005). No doubt lyrics of bands such as Detroit's xTYRANTx (for example "I kill for straight edge" and "made for fucking war, best bring your best") help keep periodic sXe gang scares alive. Their label, Seventh Dagger, markets the band's supposed militancy: "Overtones of hatred run throughout their music, and they haven't the slightest interest in positivity."

Denver itself had few kids who strongly fit the militant sXe mold. The relatively small size of the scene encouraged a more familial atmosphere amongst sXe kids and non-sXe hardcore kids. Certainly there were conflicts and judgments, but overall few sXers were hostile to outsiders or tried to push their beliefs on others. For a time, however, several members of the Courage Crew became notable exceptions to the relatively tolerant Denver scene. At an Ignite show in March 2001, I observed an older kid, Trey, wearing a XXX shirt drinking a beer. Many of the local sXers felt disrespected; they had no problem with someone drinking a beer, but believed Trey was intentionally mocking sXe. A few sXers tried reasoning with him and one even offered to trade Trey shirts, but he wouldn't budge. As I left the club, I noticed a few kids leaning against the wall, including Jackson and Brody, two large members of the Courage Crew.[7] After talking with everyone a few minutes, I deduced that the two were waiting to confront Trey when he emerged from the club. I told them I didn't think Trey was worth it and that we should go get something to eat. I wasn't particularly interested in hanging out with Jackson and Brody, but I also did not think Trey deserved to get beaten for his actions; eventually I convinced them to leave. I have no way of knowing what would have happened if Trey had come into the street before we left, but I strongly believe the two sXers may have beaten him badly.

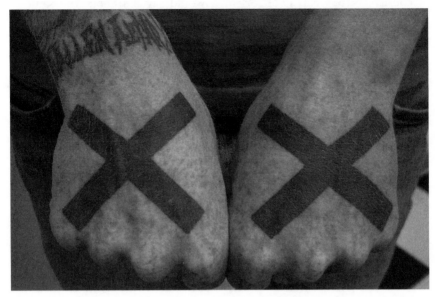

9. A member of Courage Crew with X's tattooed on his hands. Tattoo by Eric Carlson.

Many Denver sXers worried that Courage Crew would misrepresent the movement to other youth and to outsiders. Naomi, a college dropout from an affluent family, said,

> There's a lot of glitches inside of sXe. Like the Courage Crew gives the wrong name instead of showing youth a positive alternative [to drug use]. They give it a *really* wrong name. Because a lot of those kids get in a lot of fights. No matter what, violence is not the answer to anything. Aggressive as I am [giggles] fighting is not going to solve anything. Straight edge *is* a positive thing, but it all depends on who you get involved with when you become sXe.

The Positive Response

The mid- to late-1990s peak of so-called militant vegan sXe, the notoriety of sXe crews, and the Salt Lake City hysteria evoked a powerful response from the more tolerant sXers. Though the vast majority of sXers had never abandoned their positive roots, the actions of the militant few overshadowed much of the scene. Individuals and bands, in Denver and across the country, spoke out for a return to positive hardcore and scene unity. "That's not posi!" became a tongue-in-cheek retort applied to anything Denver sXers deemed negative, such as fighting, being judgmental, or talking about someone behind his or her back. Katherine explained her distaste for sXe militancy:

> I think it's pretty lame. For anything to believe in, to be militant about it is pretty lame, because everybody has their freedom of choice. They can think what they want and feel how they want. Just because somebody wants to drink once a year, doesn't make them a bad person. Even people that drink everyday, that's not a good thing and you maybe try to help them, but that doesn't make them bad people either. There's just no reason to become violent or just be an asshole about it. I feel the same way about religion and any political view that are out there now that people argue about constantly. It's their choice. If it's not hurting someone else, there's no reason why they can't make that choice.

As sXe hardcore adopted a more metal sound and tough-guy pose, Issa and Mike Phyte, veterans of the Washington, D.C., sXe hardcore scene, formed Good Clean Fun, a youth-crew style sXe band dedicated to "Putting the 'Ha' back in Hardcore." Their positive live shows,[8] lighthearted lyrics, and DIY attitude served as a popular alternative to increasingly commercial, metal-influenced bands. Their song "11th Commandment" celebrated men who resisted the hard dancing that excluded other kids: "Let's hear it for the boy who'll say / 'Get this macho tough guy shit away'." "Tough guy" was a pejorative expression usually applied to very muscular men (sXe or not) who danced especially aggressively or picked fights at shows. Most people involved with the hardcore scene despised tough guys. With "In Defense of All Life,"[9] Good Clean Fun mocked the hardline element of sXe:

> Peaceful protest doesn't get the job done / So I wake up for the rally, grab my soy milk and my gun. / Breakfast with the family, get the grub on, see what's up / Then I saw my sister had milk in her cup. / I jumped out of my chair and sprayed her with my mace, / I yelled "Vegan Power!" and I kicked her in the face. / Dad was bugging, he started to run, / But he's a meat eater so I pulled out my gun. / Shot him in the back, then I shot his wife, / That's how it's got to be in defense of all life.

At one of the many Good Clean Fun shows I attended they opened this song with the beginning chords of Earth Crisis's "Firestorm," another playful jab at sXers who took themselves too seriously. Despite his discouragement with sXe's militant turn, Issa seemed to hold a certain respect for Earth Crisis. At Hellfest 2001, he acknowledged that they had done for veganism what Youth of Today had done for vegetarianism, almost single-handedly changing the sXe scene.

Good Clean Fun were not the only band to try and counter sXe's militant image. Alec's band put the slogan "Straight Edge is a Nonviolent Movement" on the back of a compact disc they released. He explained this as an attempt to take back the scene from the hypermasculine minority:

> It was right during the hype of the "crews." We put it on the back of the Victory CD, *The Perspective*. A lot of kids made stickers and shirts out of it, which was really cool. It was like us trying to take back the movement. We were trying to be a wake up call to the smart kids that it was your scene. You own your scene.

Joey, a thirty-four-year-old former singer of a popular East Coast sXe band, explained how he formed his band in part to provide a counterbalance to the militant perception of sXe:

> The band I was in, our stand on it was kinda like, OK, there were a lot of militant, asshole sXe people out there. Like Salt Lake City, when we started the band in '97, Salt Lake City was what everyone's idea of sXe was. It was coming into the mainstream and it was beating people over the head, "I'll kill you for drinking a beer." I know a lot of people because of that dropped the label sXe. They didn't start drinking or doing drugs. They said, "I don't want to associate with sXe, I don't want to call myself sXe 'cause these assholes have *taken* what I believe in and ruined it." You know, if you believe in something, you can either let assholes have it and ruin it or you can say, "No way, I'm not going to let you assholes ruin it. I'm not going to just hand you over sXe because you decided that's what you wanted to be. 'Cause I totally believe in this. I'm gonna say, 'Hey. No. You can be sXe and be cool and try to set an example.'" I wasn't gonna let them ruin sXe for me. Just because that's the public perception of it. I'm gonna say, "No, *I'm* sXe. I'm not in a gang. I don't beat people up. . . ." We decided we want to be sXe by example, not by violence, not by a militant message, not by beating people over the head with it.

Popular punk/hardcore band H2O included both sXe and non-sXe members. During their live shows, sXe singer Toby often preached scene unity, particularly between sXers and others. The band revived the 7 Seconds song "Not Just Boys' Fun" and encouraged women to sing along.

Denver/Boulder bands were likewise critical of intolerant sXers. The singer for Mutiny, a local sXe band, spoke out against narrow-minded sXers while onstage, yet rarely advocated sXe directly in his lyrics or otherwise. As We Speak, a popular local hardcore band with two sXe singers, preached scene unity and vehemently put down any sense of sXe superiority. Only XFallenAltarX were known as an ardently sXe band, though I believe this had more to do with their Courage Crew members and the X's around their name than any real outspoken militancy from the band. In fact, Luke, a member of the band, was just as frustrated as other sXers with the negative image that Salt Lake City had given the movement. He actively tried to counter this image by setting a more positive example:

Like four or five years ago, everyone was getting flack for being sXe with Salt Lake. They were taking a lot of the blame, too. It was just negative. Everyone had something negative to say about sXe. . . . I had to live up to what some pieces of shit who had nothing better to do in their lives so they adopted sXe as their label for six months and then did a bunch of fucked up shit. Now we're all bearing the burden of it. I would just like to try and clean up that image. It's not going to be perfect, it's not going to be a bunch of altar boys. It's a bunch of young kids who have just as much pent up aggression as people who drink and smoke, but I want it to be as good as possible. Just being moral, good people. Just because you go to a show and you dance and have fun, big deal, somebody might get a bloody lip or whatever, that doesn't mean we're violent people. It just means that we're having fun together. We all know the consequences. It happens at every show in every town, there's a mosh pit. It just so happens at a sXe show or a hardcore show in general, people care about each other and they're like, "Oh man, that guy got hit, let's see if he's OK." Instead of a fight ensuing. Generally, I'd like people when they hear sXe and when I say "I'm sXe," I'd like people to not think, "Oh, they're those guys who go burn down McDonalds, they're those guys who beat up old ladies for smoking." No, it's those guys who, they might have views the general public doesn't understand, but we're still decent humans, and we're still leading decent lives. Some of us might have families, some of us have careers, some of us have goals. We're normal people, we just happen to be drug free, too.

While many sXers respond to militancy with positivity, others choose to leave the movement. Several older Denver sXers gave up the sXe label rather than be associated with the closed, tough-guy mentality they deplored. They maintained the clean-living lifestyle, but moved on to other social circles. Frustrated with less tolerant sXers, Reno, Nevada band Fall Silent sang "FUCK YOUR MOVEMENT negative edge won't last" in their song "Looking In." A written explanation under the song's lyrics explained:

Fall Silent is not a Straight Edge band, yet we are a sober one. This song is about how some kids think sXe is a neat way to start fights and to push their views about life on everyone else. This song is about my experience with it and my realization that sXe is, or should be, about being alert and aware of the world around you, and not giving in to society's tools of oppression. As soon as sXe becomes a set belief system, with rules and preachers it will be just like Christianity or any other kind of established religion. Which is not what it should become.

Despite the fact that almost no Denver sXer, when pressed, could name more than one or two "militant" or "hardline" members of the local scene, there seemed to be almost a paranoia of being associated with "negative" sXe. By the late 1990s, the media hype about Salt Lake City sXe thugs had so infected even members of the scene that some sXers seemed to be on the defensive.[10]

Balancing Point—All or Nothing with a Tolerant Edge

"Some people have given sXe a bad name by acting exactly like those who we despise. For us it's NOT about a set of rules, purity and superiority, segregation, intolerance, elitism, hatred toward others . . . sXe for us is all about being free; not letting anyone or anything control your life. We don't expect anyone else to be sXe and we don't feel better than anyone else."

—notes in Amsterdam band Vitamin X's record *See Through Their Lies*

Many sXers claim the movement would mean less to them if it were not a lifetime commitment or if it were not a one-chance opportunity. While they generally disdain militant sXe, the group's meaning, and thus part of the attraction, is tied to a degree of exclusivity.

Virtually all sXers still insist that sXe be a lifetime commitment. Even ultra-positive Good Clean Fun chastises sell-outs; their song "Coll-Edge" mocks sXers who stay sober only until arriving at college. Kyle, while generally quite tolerant, felt his dedication to sXe reflected upon his personal integrity. Though he felt the sXe label didn't mean as much to him as it once had, he still X'd up at shows and regularly wore sXe clothing, pins, and patches:

> It does mean all or nothing. Just one glass, even if it doesn't affect you, it's still . . . it's a mind thing, it's a personal thing. Even if I were to do it and nobody was around, it's a mind thing. It would make me feel terrible for saying one thing to my friends and doing another. . . . It's still important to me. It's how I live my life. It's the best label that fits me. I mean, I could just say "I don't drink," but that would just be "I don't drink." Since I stand up for that belief and tell people "You don't have to drink," I think sXe is a label that fits me. Because it is a word that means you stand up for what you believe in, you don't just *do* what you believe in.

George, the engineer active in the punk scene, shared similar views, reflecting why many adherents claimed sXe rather than simply living a drug free lifestyle:

> The label is the biggest part. It's the weirdest part, too. I'd like to think that you could still have a yearly beer—I'm not advocating it—but have a yearly beer and still be sXe. The problem with me is that I personally don't think I could call myself at all sXe, because I feel that other people would feel really betrayed if I used that word. If I at one time felt that other people were being a bad image of sXe, then I don't want to be one myself for them. So I will not call myself that. But I may have like 99.9% in common with you. It's that .1% that I will, out of respect for you, just pop out.

Matthew, the sXe kid still in high school, did not want to claim any "superiority" over non-sXers, yet he believed he was better off than many of his peers who used:

> I still like the standing up [for sXe]; I'm stronger, I'm healthier, I'm better because of this. Sometimes I don't want to think I'm better 'cause that's almost going back to what I'm trying to reject. But I think I have both those parts. I still want to show that even though I'm not doing those things I can still be a tough guy, but I can still

be kind to women and show respect to people. Not be negative all the time. That's another thing I don't want to be a part of is the whole Hot Topic scene, if you will, that's really "I hate my parents and my parents hate me and that's good." [laughs] I guess I'm still trying to be not that negative but still be who I am, a growing adolescent male.

As they grow older, many sXers become more tolerant of sell-outs and less concerned with defining or identifying with the sXe label as they are with living out the ideals (see chapter 7). Initially very critical of kids who gave up sXe, Maggie's stance softened considerably in the six years I knew her. She still felt strongly about claiming sXe and making a statement to her peers:

> I think it gives me . . . I guess kind of an identity and people to associate with. Just being drug free [non-sXe] I've noticed those people eventually, aren't. Straight edge seems more committed. To me anyway. I know to a lot of people it's not [laughs]. I guess I just kind of want to make a statement. . . . After a while, you're like an example to the young kids. If *you* can't stick with it, why would they? Why would they even start? When I see a twenty-five-year-old give it up for no reason, it's just like, "Wow . . . you're twenty-five and you can't do it anymore?" It's not hard. I don't see it as a hard thing to do. The young kids look at you and are like, "What's the point in doing it now if when I'm twenty-five I'm just going to give it up?" Or twenty-one, or eighteen, or whatever.

Other sXers take on a pragmatic view of sXe, focusing on the movement's benefits for kids who eventually sold out. If kids get *something* positive from sXe before giving it up, their involvement is beneficial. George respected the exclusivity of sXe, but was less concerned that sXe be for life:

> What bothers me the most is those who are usually most vocal about things are those that usually last the shortest. I think that a lot of people were, or maybe are still today, in this glorious thing of sXe they get caught up a little bit in. "It's either all the way or none of the way. You better be sXe for the rest of your life until you die, or else." Whereas I personally would rather have if one kid is gonna be sXe for one year . . . he starts off drinking and smoking and doing cocaine, for an extreme example . . . then he goes sXe for a year.

Then after a year he finds out sXe is not for him and he goes back to smoking. But he's lost the drinking or cocaine. To me that's a posi- tive. Sure, maybe he's not, as an ideal, sXe. We'd like him to be. *But,* he's made some progress. To me that's a win for sXe, that's a win for this culture we're trying to create.

Straight edgers understand that by claiming the sXe identity they are setting themselves up for others to perceive them as judgmental or closed- minded. Most sXers, even those in the more exclusive crews, have non- sXe friends and do not judge their friends on the basis of drug use or non-use. However, due to the actions of a relatively small minority, other youth often perceive sXers as preachy and intolerant. Some sXers pay little heed to these labels and continue to spread the sXe message by example, Xing up at shows, talking to kids about sXe, and wearing sXe shirts. Most are very conscious of walking the fine line between advertising their lifestyle and managing the stigma associated with the sXe identity. Joey, the avid thirty-four-year-old scenester, said,

I think it's sad. I don't think I'm perfect. The whole thing is like, if I have a friend who I think has a drinking problem and I say some- thing to him, then *I'm* the elitist sXe asshole and I'm only saying this 'cause I'm like sXe. It's so hard to say anything, to stand up. People think because you're sXe you think you're better than them. It's so hard sometimes.

Another older sXer found it ironic that youth complained about sXe "preaching" when alcohol and tobacco companies constantly "preach" the virtues of their products via advertising:

I find it odd that non-sXe kids will complain about sXe kids being "preachy" when these kids are constantly bombarded by alcohol and tobacco ads, when popular culture is always preaching that you have to smoke and drink to be cool. If you're worried about someone "preaching" to you, you better turn off your TV, put down your *Maxim* magazine, and hide your eyes from any billboards you come across. Straight edge is small change compared to the alcohol and tobacco in- dustries. It's a small voice going up against a juggernaut; it's David and Goliath. Yet kids don't perceive it that way. Instead of question- ing advertising, they complain that the sXe kid wearing a "Drug Free" hoodie is preaching, telling them what to do. It doesn't make sense.

In the Salt Lake City aftermath and the post-Earth Crisis sXe world, sXers are even more cautious about how they present themselves. Though still a visible presence in youth culture, sXers in the early 2000s are, on average, less outspoken, less inclined to share their convictions with their peers than they were in the previous decade.

Conclusion

Throughout this project I have struggled with how to describe and characterize "militant" sXe and, especially, violence in the sXe scene. From time to time colleagues and critics have asked me whether or not I am casting sXe in a too-positive light, leading me to question whether sXe on the whole nurtures violent, intolerant, hypermasculine men rather than "positive" alternatives. In fact, I began going to shows *looking* for violent attacks (including in the supposedly brutal Boston scene). It is tempting to see the arrogant, aggressive, moshing, shirtless, tattooed, muscle-bound tough guy as representative of sXe as a whole—he is the most spectacular example, and if he spin kicks into you or punches your friend, also the most memorable. I *have* seen sXe (and hardcore) tough guys intentionally punch or kick metal kids or other outsiders and, as I have stated throughout this book, there are intolerant, violent sXers. There are even a few gangs in the hardcore scene. However, my findings simply do not show that anywhere close to a majority of sXers have ever sought to hurt someone, based on sXe beliefs, at shows or elsewhere. Straight edge tough guys do not represent other kids standing at the back of the venue, kids dancing without attacking others, kids who don't go to many shows, most female sXers, online sXers, and older sXers who are only marginally associated with the scene. If there are 300 kids at a show and ten are thugs (keeping in mind they may or may not be sXe), is the subculture violent? What about the 98 percent of the time sXe kids don't spend at hardcore shows? They are still sXe. Are they violent? Straight edge is much more than dancing, and occasionally fighting, at hardcore shows or skirmishing with fraternity brothers. Claiming that sXe promotes attacks on innocent smokers is akin to saying that college athletics or the Air Force academy promotes rape based on a few highly publicized incidents.[11] I am certainly not excusing violence in any way; indeed, I have spoken out against it repeatedly. Nor am I trying to paint too rosy a picture of an ever-positive, peaceful sXe. However, to characterize sXe as a violent group or a gang simply does not reflect reality.

Like any scene, sXe has its share of "scene politics," internal disputes, and opposing factions. Hidden are the intense arguments *within* the scene over the meanings and goals of the movement, often leaving the public with a one-sided image of sXe. Tolerant sXers have always outnumbered their more militant counterparts. Yet tolerant sXers should be wary of dismissing the important role played by more outspoken (but not violent) sXers within the movement. The ongoing tension between tolerance and militancy may serve several useful functions, including galvanizing members, re-examining core values, and attracting a wide variety of new faces. It may be that the more exclusive and demanding a collective identity the more likely a movement will survive, because core participants/activists who most fit the identity will have high commitment and keep the movement alive.

MASCULINITY IN CONTRADICTION
THE TWO FACES OF STRAIGHT EDGE

On a wintry evening in early 2001, I did something I could have never imagined myself doing—I went to a "No Holds Barred" fighting competition, a sport that pits opponents against one another in a fight where virtually anything goes. Imagining a brutal contest with malicious fans screaming for blood, I was sure I would find the event repulsive. However, Kevin, the professional martial artist, was a contestant. My loyalty to him overcame my distaste for violence and I attended the event with a crew of a dozen or so sXe supporters. After freezing in line for what seemed an eternity, our group made it inside, wound our way through the legions of drinking fans, and staked out an sXe zone in the balcony.

In some ways, the event fulfilled my expectations. The fighting was at times brutal; one contestant was pummeled bloody before the referee stopped the fight, another "tapped out" to prevent his leg, twisted almost backward by his opponent, from snapping. The stomping, screaming fans, nearly always on their feet, seemed almost eager for a fighter to be injured, like NASCAR fans who don't *want* a crash but secretly can't wait to see one. But the event also, surprisingly, challenged my earlier preconceptions. First, even if I didn't like it, NHB fighting was indeed a *sport*, with coaches, rules, officials, and a governing body, a sport that may, for all I know, cause less serious injury to its opponents than professional football, hockey, or rugby. Second, just after the bell sounded the beginning of a match, the athletes touched hands in a sign of respect, and, after the match, they often embraced and encouraged one another. Several times, the loser even called on the crowd to cheer for the victor. This regard, while not universal, seemed to go beyond the grudging respect I'd seen boxers and other athletes offer one another. These guys really seemed to *care*. How could these men, warriors who moments ago were choking each other in submission holds, nearly dislocating shoulders, and punching each other with taped knuckles, embrace with such deep emotion? As I pondered this question, Kevin went on to win his matches, to the thunderous applause of his many fans.

I saw the contradictions in NHB reflected in the young men of the Denver scene, especially Kevin, who embodied sXe's masculine contradictions perhaps more than any other participant I encountered. He spent most of his time training for his next fight and teaching at a Brazilian Jiu-Jitsu academy. Black tattoos covered his muscular frame, including an X engulfed in flames across his entire back. Watching him coach on several occasions, it was clear to me that he was a gifted teacher, much-liked and admired by both his male and female students. He often spoke of sXe in terms of strength, honor, and discipline. Yet Kevin, more than most sXers, expressed an uncompromising, comprehensive view of sXe: intolerant of racism, homophobia, sexism, sexual conquest, and the tough-guy mentality. Like many men, he does not wholeheartedly embrace the vision of masculinity offered by our culture. But neither does he feel comfortable disengaging from every dominant notion of masculinity:

> I saw two divisions in the scene. I saw this tough-guy shit where people want to be sXe just 'cause it gives them an excuse to punch somebody in the face and not feel bad about doing it and have everybody think they're cool instead of just a total dick. They're these jock, football player assholes that just—"oh, wait a minute, we get to punch people while listening to music and beat somebody's ass because they're doing something we don't like?" That ain't me. Then there's these fuckin' little Christian, hippy, pacifist little kids that were like doing it as an extension of their Sunday school program. I didn't fuckin' belong to that either. I was like "I'm sXe and you people are off."

Kevin, like many sXers, is deeply suspicious of crews and questions the male-centered nature of sXe. He despises sexism and homophobia and ties his opposition to these oppressions directly to sXe. However, he also finds great comfort in certain expressions of hegemonic masculinity. He spoke of despising "weakness," not in the physical sense so much as the mental. Everything from drug dependency to racism to conforming to prevailing trends and fashions were signs of weakness for Kevin, who promoted "toughness" in the physical and, more importantly, the mental sense.

Kevin's case illustrates the contradictory masculinities within the sXe scene. Progressive, idealistic, anti-sexist, pacifist, animal rights activists coexist with hypermasculine, domineering "tough guys" who resemble the stereotypical "jocks"[1] they claim to resist. Youth counterculture movements often seek to undermine dominant gender roles, but in reality sometimes reinforce exactly the values they challenge (see Young and Craig 1997). Leblanc (1999:110) illustrates this contradiction in her study of punks: "In theory, punks oppose the norms and values of mainstream culture. In practice, punks adopt many of the gender codes and conventions of mainstream adolescent culture." Like punks, sXers seek to create an alternative to sexism and patriarchy and question what it means to be a man, but the pull of dominant society is difficult to overcome. Straight edge presents two general faces of masculinity, one proposing a more progressive vision of manhood, the other reflecting "hegemonic masculinity." Multiple expressions of masculinity emerge within *any* single men's movement and each faces problems of reconstructing manhood in a masculine context.

Studying Men and Contemporary Men's Movements

The majority of sXers are, and always have been, male, outnumbering women three to one. The movement is certainly open to women, and many women do participate, but the group primarily attracts young men. Although sXe is not a men's movement per se, it is undeniable that the movement is male-centered and has a decidedly masculine core. Masculinity and men's movement research provides a starting point for understanding how participants enact gender in the setting.

Since the mid-1980s, scholars have shown an increasing interest in masculinity (Brod 1987; Connell 1987, 1995; Kimmel and Mosmiller 1992; Kimmel 1996; Messner and Sabo 1990; Messner 1997). A common theme in such studies is that manhood is in crisis (Kimmel 1996)—men are struggling with the meaning of manhood in a post-industrial, post-feminist world. Based on the social constructionist and interactionist understandings of gender, manhood is, as Kimmel (1996:5) writes,

> a constantly changing collection of meanings that we construct through our relationships with ourselves, with each other, and with our world. Manhood is neither static nor timeless. Manhood is not the manifestation of an inner essence; it's socially constructed. Manhood does not bubble up to consciousness from our biological constitution; it is created in our culture.

Masculinity is not a fixed trait—the definition of manhood changes from generation to generation, culture to culture, and context to context. There is no good way to define masculinity, as there are simultaneously multiple masculinities. Men of color and gay men for example, construct different masculinities than white men and straight men and even the same man might enact varying masculinities, at work, at home, and at the gym.

While there are many possible expressions of masculinity, society values some more than others (Carrigan, Connell, and Lee 1985). Connell (1987, 1995) labels the most dominant, most valued expressions of manhood "hegemonic masculinity." "Hegemonic masculinity can be defined as the configuration of gender practice which embodies the currently accepted answer to the problem of the legitimacy of patriarchy, which guarantees (or is taken to guarantee) the dominant position of men and the subordinate position of women" (Connell 1995:77). Hegemonic masculinity values competition and hierarchy, individualism, sexual prowess, physical toughness, rationality and emotional distance, dominance, aggression, and risk-taking. It best fits heterosexual, middle class, white males; and those men who adhere most closely to the hegemonic construction of masculinity will reap the most benefits from the "patriarchal dividend," the privileges ascribed to manhood (Connell 1995). Young men, especially, feel compelled to prove their masculinity through exhibiting toughness, sexual conquest, and excessive drinking. The men's liberation movement proposed that these characteristics of patriarchy caused *men,* as well as women, a great deal of suffering (Farrell 1974, 1993; Messner 1997). Living under a constant "burden of proof," men feel overburdened and undervalued, despite their continued advantages in a patriarchal society.

The Crisis of Masculinity

Since the late nineteenth century, masculinity has been widely believed to be in "crisis." The traditional "proving grounds" of masculinity, such as the expanding frontier and control over one's work, have rapidly disappeared as women demanded rights similar to those of men, further destabilizing traditional gender roles. In the late nineteenth century, "Masculinity was widely perceived as in "crisis," as men were confused about the meanings of masculinity in a rapidly industrializing, post-bellum economy" (Messner 1997:17). In short, the societal basis of masculinity has been undermined and men are uncertain about what it means to be a man.

Messner (1997) locates the origins of the crisis of masculinity in the forces of modernization and the rise of women's movements. Modernization, including the closing of frontiers, rapid industrialization and urbanization, and the rise of bureaucracy, has separated boys from fathers and destabilized the male 'breadwinner' role (Kimmel 1996). Since the 1960s, especially, feminism has challenged dominant notions of gender. Messner (1997:xiv) posits that the masculine crisis may actually provide a chance for men to create a new, healthier masculinity:

It's actually getting harder and harder for a young male to figure out how to *be* a man. But this is not necessarily a bad thing. Young men's current fears of other men and the continued erosion of the male breadwinner role might offer a historic opportunity for men—individually and collectively—to reject narrow, limiting, and destructive definitions of masculinity and, instead, to create more peaceful and egalitarian definitions of manhood.

In a culture that glorifies masculine displays of confidence, sexual prowess, strength, and power, men increasingly feel unsure, impotent, weak, and powerless. Kimmel (1996:ix) writes, "This theme—proving manhood, manhood as a relentless test—has been and continues to be a dominant one in American life." Kimmel (1996) asserts that men have responded to their confusion and feelings of inadequacy in three primary ways: self-control, reactive exclusion, and escape. Men who felt they were losing control over their work and relationships often exercised extreme control over their personal lives; fitness, diet, alcohol consumption, and sexual appetites all became objects of self-control. Men also reacted to the crisis of masculinity with exclusion, attempting to shut women out of positions of power and influence. Finally, men sought to escape women's influence by retreating to homosocial ("male only") preserves such as men's clubs, saloons, and certain sporting events.

Gender studies have demonstrated that male privilege does come with a price. The "costs of masculinity" are many, as Messner (1997:6) reveals:

> The promise of public status and masculine privilege comes with a price tag: Often, men pay with poor health, shorter lives, emotionally shallow relationships, and less time spent with loved ones. . . . men tend to consume tobacco and alcohol at higher rates than do women, resulting in higher rates of heart disease, cirrhosis of the liver, and lung cancer.

While men's liberationists and anti-feminists have unfairly used such arguments to shift attention from women's oppression back to men (as if to say, "You think *you* have problems, look at *us*!"), it is undeniable that men suffer under patriarchy as well (Harrison, Chin, and Ficarratto 1995; Sabo 1994; Sabo and Gordon 1995). Such a realization is not meant to displace attention from women's oppression, but rather to give a more complete picture of the consequences of hegemonic masculinity for both women and men. Straight edge men felt the burdens and contradictions of the masculine crisis, and some began to acknowledge the sexist, patriarchal culture that oppressed women.

Men's Movements

In response to the crisis of masculinity, men have formed a variety of movements, across the political spectrum, some seeking to grasp onto and maintain a patriarchal image of manhood from the past, others striving to create a feminist-influenced, less rigid masculinity. During the 1990s, men's movements grew at an astounding rate. Approximately one million black men marched in Washington, D.C., in 1995 as part of the Million Man March, "calling on men to stop their self-destructiveness, stop their violence, and bond together with other men to retake responsibility for caring for and leading their families, their communities, and their nation" (Messner 1997:92).[2] Over one million Christian men filled Promise Keeper stadium events across the United States, claiming that men had lost the true meaning of manhood and faced a moral and spiritual crisis (Messner 1997).[3] The mythopoetic movement emerged in the 1980s with the goal of increasing men's self confidence, fostering male spirituality, helping men establish connection to their own and others' feelings, and questioning what it means to be a man (Harding 1992; Kupers 1993; Schwalbe 1996).[4] Like the other men's movements, profeminist men such as the National Organization of Men Against Sexism (NOMAS) wanted to change the ideal of manhood. They were the only major men's movement that took an explicitly profeminist stance, believing that men's problems emerge from inequality in social relationships (Kupers 1993:139), particularly those between men and women and straights and gays.[5] Straight and gay men must join with straight and lesbian women to transform the unhealthy relations inhibiting everyone's full potential. Like sXe, these movements often challenged the perceived destructive aspects of masculinity such as excessive drinking and other risk behaviors.

The Two Faces of Straight Edge

The sXe movement is caught between two extremes, one with profeminist leanings and one reflective of hegemonic masculinity. Like many contemporary men's movements, sXe challenges what participants see as the 'unhealthy' aspects of masculine ideals while creating and redefining the meaning of manhood. Straight edge produces multiple masculinities (some progressive, some not), contradictory and fraught with unintended

10. Pat Flynn, singer of Boston sXe band Have Heart, encourages the crowd to sing along. Most of the women at the show are standing in the back, not an uncommon scenario at a hardcore show. Photo by Todd Pollock.

consequences. Kyle, the twenty-three-year-old senior at CU, recognized the two faces of sXe masculinity:

> There's like the tough guys and the passive guys. I don't know why. I've always tried to figure that out, too. It's always stunned me. You see it everywhere. You see the guys that want to fight and you see the guys who want to break it up. There's no real in-between.

Straight edge shares many traits with men's movements. Like many men's groups, sXe seeks to redefine masculinity within a primarily masculine context—the movement encourages personal responsibility, self-control, and masculine camaraderie. Likewise, they deride the role of alcohol, drugs, and sexual conquest in dominant definitions of masculinity. Straight edgers would agree with the Promise Keepers that "A man who is secure in his position as a man has no need for alcohol, has no need to destroy his own body or other men's bodies through violence, has no need to resort to sexual promiscuity to prove himself" (Messner 1997:34). Like the participants in the Million Man March, sXers feel alcohol and drugs are poisons that damage relationships and cloud priorities. Straight edgers share important Million Man March values such as self-reliance, self-discipline, sobriety, civility, and enterprise (Boyd 1995). Similar to the mythopoets, sXe men often report a disconnection with their fathers and a desire to create better relationships than their fathers had maintained.

Responsibility and commitment are common themes in men's movements. The mythopoets urged men to take responsibility for their repressed 'wild man' inside; the Promise Keepers stress responsibility to family and God; the Million Man Marchers pledged to be responsible to their community, people, and families; profeminists take responsibility for society's sexism, homophobia, and racism. Like sXe, each movement stresses personal accountability within a context of men supporting men. Members make commitments to other men to live their versions of positive lives, believing that social change begins with personal change. Straight edge creates a sense of brotherhood among its members, similar to the Million Man March, mythopoets, and Promise Keepers, and offers a critique of hegemonic masculinity like the profeminist men. All of these movements provide a relatively safe place for men (at least heterosexual, and usually white) to congregate, share their concerns, and reinforce their values.

The Progressive Face of Straight Edge

Straight edge rhetoric promotes several profeminist ideals, such as egalitarian relationships and raised awareness about and prevention of sexual assault. Since the movement's beginnings, sXers and sXe bands have questioned a variety of oppressions, including sexism, racism, and homophobia. They have created a setting in which young people could avoid their family's patterns of addiction and have provided a context in which young women feel empowered.

Resisting Oppressions

You can never have enough lyrics about ending war, ending racism, ending sexism, etc. So as long as those things exist I will never stop singing about it!! And to those who don't like political lyrics: fuck off and go back to listening to your Phil Collins collection!!

—notes in the Vitamin X record, *See Through Their Lies*

In the Denver scene, sXe helped many very young men to question and subvert dominant notions of manhood, including sexism, the emphasis on sexual conquest, and homophobia. Joe and Isaac, sixteen and seventeen years old, respectively, were adamantly against homophobia and sexism and would often challenge their contemporaries' homophobic and sexist comments. Becoming sXe brought about a transformation for Joe in many areas of his life:

> I didn't realize how much I put women down by my actions or how I spoke to my friends about women. Just certain terms like "bitch" and just talkin' about a girl's body all the time. It just makes them an object, not really a person there in front of you. So when I took that on, I decided it *wasn't* positive to keep thinking about women like that all the time. It was something I knew needed to change.

Joe and Isaac tied their new attitudes and actions directly to their involvement with sXe. Their outspoken stance was due in large part to the mentorship of Elizabeth, the sXe high school counselor, who introduced them to sXe and served as a role model. She corrected the boys when they made sexist or homophobic comments and encouraged them to question gendered behavior, explaining how sXe meant more than simply not using alcohol and drugs. Similarly, for four years I watched Vin, a Spanish American who became sXe at age thirteen, grow into a conscientious, progressive young man who strove to treat women with utmost respect. Two Christian sXe men, Matthew, seventeen, and Jordan, nineteen, blended their pro-social Christian values with sXe core values. For them, the clear minds sXe provided them enabled them to more closely follow their faith's emphasis on compassion and justice. These are but a few examples of the many young men who, through their involvement in sXe, do their best to create a new masculinity infused with profeminist values.

In resisting the sexual conquest ideal of hegemonic masculinity, sXe men try to respect women as people rather than "pieces of meat," as one participant put it. They are particularly critical of the image of the predatory, insatiable male, searching for sex wherever he can get it. Several Denver bands consistently spoke about these issues during their sets, encouraging men in the crowd to take a stand against sexual assault.

Some women are critical of male bands for raising "women's issues" from stage; they feel only women can adequately express the frustration, pain, and rage of living in a patriarchal society. However, most sXe women appreciate the fact that men tried to take some responsibility for making the world, or at least the scene, a more egalitarian place. Carrie, the twenty-four-year-old nonprofit employee, understood that while women should have a platform in the scene to raise their concerns, equally important was men communicating with men:

> Carrie: I think that there's an honest effort being made though, definitely, by the bands. I know sometimes lots of females might have problems with men singing those songs. I personally think that it's good. I feel like if men hear it from other men it makes it easier for them to accept.

> RH: Hear what?

> Carrie: Anti-sexist thoughts. Anti-date rape songs, this sort of thing. I feel like somehow it comes across as more masculine to [take a stand against sexism and rape]. If a guy is telling you it's OK and he's in a band. Not that it should be that way but that's to an extent how it is.

Many sXe men take the sXe guidelines against using women for sex especially seriously. Kevin said,

> To this day I'm by no means celibate, however . . . in the last eight years I've had sex with three girls. . . . I'm not celibate by any means but I also don't believe in fuckin' bullshit meaningless sex. I definitely don't believe in that. So those tenets kind of took place in my life even though I didn't take it to the actual celibacy extreme. Whoever, whatever, and how many ever people that you are attracted to on an emotional level, you should be able to express that. But, it should be on an emotional level. It's not like every time your dick gets a little extra blood in it you gotta go run off and do that.

Joe's refusal to have sex with women he had only dated a short time was sometimes difficult for them to accept: "I've hung out with girlfriends or whatever that have told me they want to have sex. And I told them I *won't*. And they've got upset about that, whatever." Sex is not wrong, dirty, or sinful to sXers. Sex can be a positive element of a caring relationship. Believing that sex entails power and emotional vulnerability, as well as the possibility of sexually transmitted diseases, most sXers strive to minimize potentially negative experiences by rejecting casual sex. Furthermore, sXers believe sex could become an addiction similar to drugs or alcohol.

For a scene dominated by young males, sXe is relatively tolerant. Prominent sXe bands such as Outspoken, Good Clean Fun, and Earth Crisis challenged homophobia in their songs. The lyrics to Outspoken's "Inno-cent" imply that homophobia is a personal fault to be overcome:

Alone / He doesn't want to face the prejudice / Afraid / While the fear lies in the ignorant / All love is legitimate / It is hatred that is the enemy / An innocent man portrayed as being guilty / What crime is love between two people / The crime is hatred caused by ig-norance of difference / Have to open my eyes to see a wider range / Have to open my mind / I'm the one that needs to change / Change is unavoidable / Understanding / Ignorance breeds intolerance / Love is all powerful / Hatred is a weakness / No limits on love.

Walter, a middle-class twenty-one-year-old who eventually became a law student, explained how sXe changed his beliefs:

I've been brought up really Catholic. My family is really Catholic. Before sXe I was a little homophobic. I'm not saying that I'm not [now], but I've definitely opened up a lot more. Plus where I work, at [a hotel], there's 5 or 6 gay people that work there that I don't think . . . if I hadn't learned about this stuff through sXe, through the movement, I don't think I would be as accepting to them as I would be. I'm not knocking on the Catholic Church; I still hold a lot of the beliefs. But I think sXe has led me to look at the world with open eyes, to see things how I want to see them rather than how I've been taught to see them. So there's that. I'm not saying I'm totally cured of homophobia but I'm definitely a lot more open.

Joe explained how he risked isolation for sharing his views with his friends:

Joe: When I stopped saying slurs like fag and stuff like that, my friends were like, "What's goin' on?" My friends were like . . . I don't know, they'd just be talkin' crap, talkin' about gay people or what-ever, and I'd be like, "I don't hate gay people." And they're like, "What?! I thought you did?" And I'd say, "Well, that was before, you know. I don't now and it's not worth my energy to just sit here and hate these people. I can use my energy for better things." So they've kinda noticed that and they've kinda mellowed out about that, around me at least [grins] especially.

RH: So have you ever taken some serious shit for being sXe?

Joe: Umm . . . yeah, but kinda different, I guess. When I stopped hating gays was a big one, 'cause I have friends that are pretty homophobic. And I've been cussed out and yelled at and had them pissed off at me, 'cause of that. 'Cause I've stood up for gay people and they were talkin' shit about them. I've just been like, "I don't hate gay people." And they'll call me a fag or whatever. And I'll be like, "You know it, baby." I'll just stick it right back into their face and give them exactly what they don't want to hear. They got pretty upset about that.

I had asked Joe this question thinking he would talk about being teased for not drinking. Instead, his response shows how intimately he ties his change of heart regarding homophobia to his process of becoming sXe.

Earth Crisis, perhaps the most outspoken and influential sXe band during their peak in the mid- to late-1990s, included in their *Gomorrah's Season Ends* (1996) CD rhetoric against United States imperialism, racism, homophobia, and other oppressions. Part of their message contains radical feminist undertones intertwined with a "warfare" frame:

There is a war. One out of every four women are [sic] raped. Among those numbers are our sisters, mothers, and friends. This is a weapon. To teach men to unlearn the lessons we are taught: that women are objects to be acted upon and dominated. To teach men to channel our rage from our *Broken Foundations* into something useful instead of something destructive and deadly. To bring real justice in cases of rape and to make the streets safe for our sisters.

Another section calls for an end to homophobia and heterosexism:

There is a war. The violent attacks on gays continue. In Colorado, legislation has been passed which permits explicitly homophobic hiring practices. Same sex marriages are still not recognized. This is a weapon. To demonstrate to heterosexuals that gayness is natural and beautiful and that it is not a threat to their existence. To make being openly gay safe and to make the pain of the closet part of a mystical past. . . . This is a weapon, not only to destroy all forms of oppression, but also to celebrate the beauty of all our different cultures, races, sexualities, genders, religions, species.

The band that almost single-handedly inspired many vegan sXers to new levels of environmental concern and animal rights radicalism was also the band that understood and espoused the most comprehensive sXe-based statements calling for celebration of diversity and decrying multiple forms of oppression. Ironically, their militance and heavy, crushing music often attracted hypermasculine men at the same time their lyrics questioned white male privilege and the stereotypes defining manhood: drinking, eating meat, homophobia, and sexual conquest. The contradictions within Earth Crisis served as a metaphor for the contradictions in the entire scene.

Breaking Patterns of Abusive Masculinity

Finally, you understand / Drinking doesn't make you a man / Not me, I know what's smart / In touch, I'll always be alert / Waiting do you feel better, does it make you feel good when you drink / Now you laugh and today you're happy but it's not as funny as you think / You can do it now and still enjoy it, the people that care are all still here / But one day when you're laughing, you'll turn around and no one will be standing there.

—"No Thanks" by Uniform Choice, 1985

For many adherents, sXe is in part a reaction to bad experiences they had with their fathers' drinking, drug use, or abusiveness. Like the mythopoets, sXers react to broken relationships with their fathers by creating different ways of being masculine, trying to break the patterns they learned within their families. As Matthew and Maggie demonstrated in chapter three, many sXers defied their families' history of drug and alcohol use. Kyle explained how being sXe was in part a way to live a different masculinity than his father's:

Kyle: My father got really sick. He got Hepatitis A and C. He's an old, evil biker. Tattoos, drunk, drug addict, really mean, mean person. As soon as I found out he was sick from just being a stupid person, I decided I needed to be clean, completely and be completely opposite of what he is. Now sXe is just the easiest way to classify how I live. . . . That's what got me into never drinking or doing drugs and trying to not be a fighter, a violent person. I tried to be everything he wasn't, because everything he is is what I hate in life. I needed to, I guess, rebel against it. Usually people rebel and they follow their parents' footsteps even though they don't really think they are. I chose to rebel the complete opposite.

RH: What does it mean to you to be a man?

Kyle: Just to be a role model. For people to strive to be like you. I know what the whole society view of what being a man is, but it's not mine. I don't care to be like the head of a household, or dominant in a relationship. I just want to be the really nice, positive person that people can get along with. I think that should be the goal for a man or a woman.

Andy, the nineteen-year-old construction worker, despised the way his father had treated his family:

My father was an alcoholic and did all kinds of drugs and shit. A lot of really screwed up shit happened when I was younger and I promised myself I was never gonna be like that and [sXe] is one step further, which is to never *ever* be like that. Not even close. Which is the way to go. If I ever treat my kids the way he treated us 'cause he was drunk, I'd shoot myself. It's fucked up.

Both Kyle and Andy had been sXe for several years. Many sXers, both male and female, shared stories of fathers, brothers, and sometimes mothers who had serious substance abuse and/or aggression problems. Straight edge was part of their strategy for avoiding following the same path. Some sXers are recovering alcoholics and drug users themselves and rely upon the strong social support network in the scene to stay clean.

Not only do sXers avoid the substance abuse that engulfed their families, they attempt to resist the emotional distance so common in male relationships. Straight edge men in Denver are very openly affectionate with one another. They express their regard for each other in typical manly ways such as dog-piles, high-fives, play fighting, and wrestling. But many also give each other big hugs, openly expressed their feelings about their friendships, and call each other "brother." In this sense, sXers are somewhat similar to the mythopoets, Million Man Marchers, Promise Keepers, and profeminists for encouraging men to care for one another and openly express certain emotions taboo in most contexts. Though hardly a revolution in emotional expression, sXe does allow men to stretch beyond the confines of hegemonic masculinity.

Straight edge also empowers many adherents to question the aggressiveness and violence inherent in hegemonic masculinity. Despite the media's portrayal of sXe as a violent group, the majority of sXers took great care to avoid fighting. For every sXer willing to enforce his views with violence, there are ten who renounce violence except in self-defense, and for every member of an sXe crew there are twenty sXers who refuse to be part of such a group. Most sXers believe fighting is stupid, especially at shows where a fight might encourage the venue owner to ban hardcore shows. A few sXers even adopt a strict code of nonviolence.

In the late 1990s and early 2000s, more and more sXers were influenced by emo music. There have always been connections between emo and hardcore, as both emerged primarily in the Washington, D.C., area. Bands such as Rites of Spring and Embrace added feelings and emotions besides anger and aggression to hardcore. While emo packs an emotional punch similar to hardcore, its melodic music and sensitive lyrics attract a more mellow fan base and encourage introspection rather than militancy around any issue (Greenwald 2003). A few sXers, most of whom enjoy at least some emo music, nevertheless playfully mock emo kids as being overly sensitive crybabies who whine about lost love and rejection. Still, throughout the 1990s, many sXe hardcore youth defected to more emo scenes. Emo opens sXers up to more progressive and less rigid expressions of masculinity.

Empowering Women

Love is gone / Locked from your heart / Lust is strong / It's all you feel / Close your eyes for selfish pleasure / You broke her will / Relationship, a mountain we climbed / Fell to an immoral world / Close your mind to all commitment / You're addicted to yourself / Far too many backs you've broken / Far too many wounds to heal / When you find someone special / Ask is it for real / You touched her cheek / Cannot hold back / You broke her will / And she's never coming back.

—"Priorities" by Endpoint, 1990

Another aspect of sXe's approach to gender is the movement's efforts to involve and empower women. Straight edge differs from the nonfeminist men's movements in that it does include women. Despite their misgivings about certain aspects of sXe, every sXe woman I spoke with felt empowered by the movement. For some women, becoming sXe is part of a broader "remaking" of self, as Katherine attested: "I hit this point in my life where I just wanted to be a better person." Carrie, who had negative experiences with hard drugs both personally and within her family, felt sXe helped her achieve self-respect and control over her own life:

I feel like it's also showing I have some respect for myself. It is being in power of your situation. For a long time I wasn't in control of anything around me. I always tried really negative ways to control them. You probably don't know this but I had a really severe eating disorder when I was younger. To the point at which hospitalization had to happen. So it's really nice to look at this and say, "I can control my own life, my own surroundings and *not* have it be negative, not have it be self-destructive." That's real important to me. . . . I feel like I actually like myself, which is a really, really good thing. I feel like that was a long time coming. To an extent I *kinda* did, but never enough. Never enough to respect myself enough to actually make positive decisions in my own life. To stop doing the whole "I can't control this, and I can't control that" so I'm just destroyed and this helpless little girl or whatever. I just got really sick of that. And I got sick of hearing that, too.

Many sXe women feel they had an advantage over non-sXe women, believing the movement provided them a context to reject what they viewed as negative aspects of femininity such as passiveness, a constant concern with impressing men, competitiveness with other women, and a focus on appearance (see chapter 6). Many said that they didn't feel pressured to impress men and they enjoyed the fact that they would never end up in a compromised situation due to excessive alcohol use. Katherine said, "I know that I'm different than a lot of people my age, a lot of girls my age. I guess getting involved has made me realize who I am and what I want to be and that it's achievable. I don't have to follow anybody or think a certain way because that's how I'm supposed to think." Kendra, though critical of sXe's hypermasculine tendencies, believed sXe women had an advantage over their non-sXe counterparts:

I think as a woman and being sXe, I have the advantage. It's a unique thing for a girl to be like that. Most girls aren't that way. Girls will start smoking to impress a guy, girls will have a drink to relax to be 'OK' [sarcastically] in front of men. "I'm just gonna go out with the girls and have a cocktail." There's such a minority of women in the sXe scene. Again, it's a source of pride. I can be just as cool as a guy, even more so—I'm a girl. It's kind of sad that more girls don't do it. You don't have to smoke to be cool, you don't have to drink to be cool, you don't have to do it to relax in front of people—be loose, be wild, show your free side in front of guys. I think girls do a lot of things unconsciously to attract men. . . . I think I have an advantage. My wits are a lot sharper. I've never done anything seriously to impress a man before.

Megan, the twenty-one-year-old university student who had been sXe for five years, said,

> I could imagine it being more difficult for guys to be sXe because they're expected to drink and all that. However, girls, especially in college, tend to drink to get guys. I respect *all* the girls, too, that don't need to get drunk to get guys. I think a lot of girls in college just go to parties and get drunk to impress guys, and we don't feel like we have to at all. In fact, I think it's more respectable [not to do that].

When I interviewed women, I fully expected them to express their disgust and disappointment in sXe men who were not completely living up to their professed dedication to gender equality. Coming from a profeminist perspective myself, men's dominance of the scene was very apparent to me. Though the women certainly expressed criticisms, their positive regard for the movement and appreciation for most of the men involved surprised me, even though it is common for women of various groups to defend "their" men. Carrie believed that a majority of sXe men possessed a greater understanding of sexism than other young men:

> I think it's probably 60% that aren't [hypermasculine], that I think they've totally got the message. I think for the most part, most of the people I know here when it comes right down to it, they have quite a bit of respect for women. I would feel safe with any of them. Which to me is a big deal because I don't think I've ever been able to say that in any group of people before. I would never feel like I was in a compromised position at all.

Other sXe women, like Katherine, also feel sXe had made a significant positive impact on young men. I asked her if sXe guys were really that different from men who tried to prove their manhood through sexual conquest. Katherine said:

> The ones that I know personally and I'm really good friends with *totally reject* everything about that. I think for the most part, sXe guys have more respect toward girls. They *know* that girls aren't a sex object [sic]. They know that there's more to girls than that. That's just from people I personally know. I can't speak for all of them. But I think for the most part, sXe guys *do* reject the whole jock image, don't agree with it at all.

Most of the sXe women in Denver date sXe men. The ratio of men to women in the scene gives women ample opportunities, whereas sXe men often have to look outside the scene for companionship. Most sXers, male and female, are not opposed on principle to dating non-sXers. Maggie, who had dated several sXers, also believed these young men stood out from their peers:

> Every sXe guy I know—this could just be me—pretty much every sXe guy I know thinks a lot more highly of women and doesn't really believe in a lot of sex and stuff. They're all about having *one* girlfriend and trying to get married and start a family and stuff. Other guys are just like, "I wanna get laid. Let's go to Cancun on spring break and get laid and have a video camera of girls flashing us and we're gonna sell it." I can't really picture an sXe person doing that. They just, I don't know, they seem to be more compassionate about everything.

Even Megan, who had had some frustrating interactions with "immature" sXe men, believed that in some ways they had more respect for women:

> Megan: I think hopefully they have more respect for the girls and themselves as a whole. For their age, their wisdom is well beyond their years in that respect. They know it's not important. That's how I've looked at it. They may be outwardly incredibly immature, but I think they have better morals than their peers.
>
> RH: What are some examples of better morals?
>
> Megan: Not drinking, not giving in to that peer pressure. Again, the sexual conquest thing. They're resisting that. They don't *care* about it, necessarily. I think that brings in a respect for the women.

Some sXe men are especially reflexive about the ways in which they enact masculinity in the scene and try to disrupt the barriers to women's full participation. Like the profeminist men, they seek to bring equality to social relationships and empower women and other minorities, especially through cultural rather than explicitly political means. Alec, the musician and writer, hoped to influence people in profeminist directions via his band: "We always wanted to have a sXe band, to say, 'Hey, there's a solution. You can do this and not have to be like the stereotypical bully male or whatever.'" Sid, the anarchist, was extremely disappointed with the lack of women within the scene and believed many sXers avoided truly challenging conventional gender constructions:

> It's supposed to be like this enlightened thing. But for some reason there's like ten girls there in a room with like two-hundred guys. That's just the way it's always been. And a lot of times it just seems like it's guys who drag girls into it that don't stick around very long. It's this hypermasculine thing, this incredibly hypermasculine thing that . . . I don't know if it just turns women off, or if they don't identify with it. It's just not very accepting. The guys who are like 'extra-sXe' are the guys who can like puff their chest out and take ten hits in the pit. The toughest guys are the most revered and the most held high. It's really upsetting. I think it's truly, truly upsetting. It just shows that punk rock is not the end and sXe is not the end, 'cause look how fucked up it is. It's all these guys running around enforcing a lot of the things about the system that are fucked up. Like all this militancy and hypermasculinity that gets women raped and gets people beat up all the time. All this crap that *is* the problem. It claims to be enlightened and then it completely adopts all those things. It's fucked. It doesn't make sense at all.

Sid went on to explain how he did not feel that the exclusion of women was necessarily overt or intentional, but that it happened nonetheless. His disgust with this particular issue eventually drove him from the scene:

> There are definitely a lot of good people around, a lot of . . . I think it's especially good here, there's like a lot of sXe guys who are really into being not masculine, not really tough-guy. But there definitely is still that really large element of . . . I don't think it's misogyny or anything, it's just not creating a space for women. It's not saying it doesn't want a space. It's like society, not saying that women are bad. It's just not facilitating anything to make it better. It's just playing off all the stuff in society. I really don't know. I don't know how I feel. I haven't seen a lot of individuals treating individuals really poorly, or doing anything that's really fucked up. It's just . . . I hardly feel comfortable going to the front of a show. I'm like 180 and 6'4".

As more men like Alec and Sid questioned the aggressiveness and masculinity in the Denver scene, I observed a shift: many of the tough-guy types more prevalent from 1996 to 2000 eventually drifted out of the scene to be replaced in 2001–2003 by younger, less hypermasculine men and a cohort of dedicated young women.

The Hypermasculine Face of Straight Edge

Straight edge rhetoric encourages men to adopt profeminist ideals and, like the Promise Keepers, mythopoets, and Million Man Marchers, seeks to create a more fulfilling masculinity. Members of contemporary men's movements want "to experience mentorship, initiation, and a new kind of brotherhood" and gather "for the express purpose of figuring out what it means to be a man" (Kupers 1993:146). However, although each men's movement aims to empower men through a new masculinity, eventually creating a world of happy, healthy, loving men, doing so in isolation from women is problematic. Like the nonfeminist men's movements, sXe undermines its quest for healthy masculinity by failing to include women fully and create a cross-gender dialogue. Kimmel (1996) describes three primary ways men and men's movements have responded to the crisis of masculinity and the growth of women's movements: self-control, exclusion, and escape. Straight edge follows these patterns of hegemonic masculinity as well.

Self-Control

Life's filled with many paths / Which one should I take? / When the choice comes, I won't run / I'll be thinking straight! / Life's filled with conflicts. . . . We'll face / We'll overcome them . . . thinking straight / Experiment with your mind / You see things I can't see / Well no thanks, friend / Because now it ends when you push that shit on me! My mind is free to think and see / Strong enough to resist temptation / We've been strong for all these years / Yes, life gets rough, so we'll stand tough and confront / All our fears!

—"Thinking Straight" by Youth of Today, 1986

Since the early nineteenth century, the rapid pace of urbanization, industrialization, and other social and political changes, along with the pressures of individual success, have become overwhelming to many men, who felt disempowered in a tumultuous and uncertain world. As they experience less control in their social and political lives, men often focus on the one area they still feel they can dominate to some degree: their personal lives. A prominent theme in Promise Keeper meetings is concern about "men's feelings of having lost control" (Messner 1997:32).

Participants in the Million Man March also desired control in what often seemed a violent, disintegrating world. As Kimmel (1996:44–45) explains, in a disordered, fragmented world, men seek comfort by controlling the only thing they can, themselves:

> The drive for control, for order, stems from experiencing the world as disordered, as out of control. . . . Where many could never attain the self-made manhood of success, middle class masculinity pushed egotism to extremes of aggression, calculation, self-control and unremitting effort. The Self-Made Man was a control freak.

Men manifest the drive for self-control in many aspects of life, including sexual appetite, diet, fitness, and alcohol consumption. Control of sexual lust became especially evident at the turn of the twentieth century: "To the medical experts of the time, the willful sexual control of a body was the ultimate test of mind over matter" (ibid: 45). Sid, the anarchist, reflected on sXe's strictures against promiscuous sex, echoing this theory: "I guess [abstaining from promiscuous sex] was supposed to be about controlling your mind through sex. I think that's originally what it was supposed to be about. You can get sucked into the whole sex thing just like drugs and stuff. I can definitely see that and I recognize that." Self-control is central to the sXe ideology, and, as Alec explained, the most significant aspect of sXe men's focus on self-control is abstaining from alcohol use:

> We live in a world where we have no control. I just can't imagine surrendering any more control, even for a moment. I still feel very much the same about being sober, or sXe, whatever. I have trouble dating people who drink or use. I could never marry somebody who drank or used because my mother drank herself to death.

Drinking alcohol has long been a signifier of manhood, solidarity with other men, and resistance to female influence. It gave men feelings of strength; promoted male bonding; and became connected with a variety of events, including baptisms, elections, corn-huskings, and house-raisings (Kimmel 1996:49). Drinking is so central to masculinity that, men have often argued, female attempts to reign in men's drinking are emasculatory (Lunbeck 1994).

Like most sXers, Clay, a twenty-two-year-old university student visiting from the East Coast, experienced control as a way to resist social pressures: "I take pride in that I have self-control. I take pride in not succumbing to peer pressure. I've never, ever been susceptible to peer pressure." Straight edgers not only resist drugs and promiscuous sex, but many intentionally modify their diet to reflect their more "pure" or "positive" lifestyle by being vegan or vegetarian, and some sXe men are quite fitness conscious.

Ironically, by using abstinence to seek self-control and a more-assured sense of their place in the world, sXers are subverting significant aspects of hegemonic masculinity. For sXers drinking and sexual conquest are not signifiers of strength, power, and masculinity, but weaknesses that 'real men' should overcome. For Kevin, the martial artist, strength in all areas of life was at the center of his understanding of sXe:

> My first understanding of sXe was to not be addicted. I looked around and realized I was addicted to things, and it pissed me off. Everybody in the world, they weren't even living their own lives. They were living to satisfy addictions. They drink a beer to satisfy that addiction, they smoke a cigarette to satisfy that addiction, they hit on some stupid whore in a bar to satisfy that addiction. Their whole lives they weren't even actually living their own lives, they were just going from one moment of addiction to something to the next moment of addiction to something else. They never even lived their own lives. They were just like satisfying every urge that drove them like it was out of their hands.

(Note that although Kevin was one of the most antisexist sXers, he still uses the clearly sexist label "whore," further evidence of the contradictions in the scene.) Although abstinence serves as a foundation to sXe's profeminist face, the focus on self-control sometimes inhibits a deeper understanding of structural gender expectations.

Exclusion

I wasn't involved in straight edge because I couldn't think in those terms; because straight edge didn't involve me. The demographics of every single straight edge practitioner I knew were completely alien to me: they were almost all young white wealthy suburban boys who were athletically and musically inclined, or tried to be.

—Glynis Hull-Rochelle in *All Ages* (Lahicky 1997:73)

Analyses of contemporary men's movements often cite exclusivity as one of the major pitfalls such groups fall into while seeking to undermine hegemonic masculinity (Messner 1997; Kimmel 1996; hooks 1995). As women and other minorities sought and gained civil rights, men often reacted by grasping more firmly to their remaining privileges and intentionally limiting such groups' further access to power. The Promise Keepers, for example, insisted that God had chosen men to be the ultimate leaders within the family, thereby denying women an equal voice. Mythopoets excluded women from their gatherings to avoid women's "feminizing influence." While the profeminists included women in their growth work and incorporated a feminist perspective, the other men's groups are exclusively male. Messner (1997:xiv) expresses profeminist concerns with the exclusivity of most men's groups purportedly reshaping masculinity:

> Although they are very different in some important ways, many of the men's movements that have sprung up in the 1980s and 1990s share a commitment to rebuilding and revaluing bonds among men, to overcoming men's fears of each other, and to pushing men to be responsible and peaceful fathers and husbands. . . . But many of these groups also share another more troubling characteristic: They clearly believe that for men to overcome their fears of other men, they must separate themselves from women. And this separation from women is spoken of in terms of men's "empowerment"—to reclaim their "natural" roles as leaders in families and communities.

The sXe ideology does not explicitly exclude women and often contains rhetoric encouraging men to *include* women and bring balance to the scene. However, men outnumber women in the scene often two or three to one, and few women occupy positions of prestige and influence. Male sXers exclude women not so much by what the men do (although certainly there are blatant examples of deliberate exclusion) but by what they do not do: that is, they may not intentionally *exclude* women, but neither do they intentionally *include* them. The result is "female exscription," a process common in youth subcultures that makes women absent or invisible (Walser 1993). Straight edge perpetuates a very masculine setting by default, and changing this can only come from intentional, persistent action. As sXe is a diffuse movement without an institutionalized bureaucracy, men cannot exclude women from defined positions of power as they could if the movement had a clear structural hierarchy. However, they can subtly and not-so-subtly discourage women from assuming positions of importance and significance (such as being in a band), thereby making women second-class citizens within the scene.

Although the scene offers many opportunities to get involved, being in a band is certainly the most prestigious role. Bands define the sXe ideology, create new meanings, and enjoy the admiration of fans. The punk/hardcore philosophy asserts that *anyone* should be able to make music, not just professional musicians and trained or talented individuals. Early punk bands such as X, the Germs, the Nuns, the Avengers, X-Ray Specs, Black Flag, and the Slits featured many female members, although men still significantly outnumbered them. During the time period of my research, however, only four *prominent* hardcore bands (Walls of Jericho, Indecision, Most Precious Blood, and Martyr AD) included women and only one all-female sXe band, the Doughnuts, had any national prominence. Clearly, the lack of female voices in the scene further ensures that it will remain male-centered and will resonate less with many women's experiences. Although most sXe men and women agree that they would welcome more women in bands, few are eager for women to be singers, a significant point since generally the singer writes the lyrics and lyrics give voice and shape to the movement. Maggie shared how she had been excluded from singing in a band:

> I've also talked to guys who are like starting bands. Can I sing, or try out? They're like, "We don't want a girl singer." I'm like, "Oh. OK." "Girl singers suck." Even though I've noticed guys like worship girls in bands. They worship the girl in Walls of Jericho. "She's so awesome!" Why can't I be awesome, too? I don't know what that's really about. Some of the bands are like, we need to support the girls in the scene, but they don't actually do it.

Brian, the singer for a local band, and other sXe men, wished more women were in bands but had difficulty explaining why so few became involved:

> It's very much male-oriented. I wish it wasn't. I want to see girl bands, I want to see girls in bands, I want to see girls at the shows. It might have to do with the way dancing goes at shows. It might be because more males play guitar out there in the world. The females that do play guitar might be into different kinds of music.

Straight edgers, both men *and women,* hold women to higher standards than they do men in the scene, often denigrating women who wear more fashionable, mainstream clothing and makeup. Women who attend hardcore shows because they have boyfriends in the scene are particularly suspect. Matthew, the young Christian sXer, acknowledged that women often face unfair treatment:

> I think sXe for girls is no different than sXe for guys. It's still a rejection of the things you don't agree with. I think unfortunately there's a slight prejudice against girls. You'll always get the people who say, "The only reason they're in the scene is because their boyfriend is in the scene or they're trying to meet guys." Which for me, I haven't really met more than three or four girls that are in the scene that have some type of boyfriend connection to it. I see no reason why they can't be just as big a part as the guys.

Sometimes men (sXe or not) who wish to dance in the pit have their girlfriends hold their coats, prompting the derogatory label "coat rack" for such women. As in other male-dominated settings, joking plays a substantial role in male bonding (Lyman 1987). Straight edge women often join in the joking, but overall it reinforces masculine relationships and thereby constructs further barriers to women's full participation.

Even the rhetoric of friendship within the scene is exclusive. "Brotherhood," not sisterhood, is a core foundation of sXe. Brotherhood implies supporting fellow sXers, whether it be during a financial crisis, helping out with shows or other projects, or "having someone's back" during a fight. "Hardcore" also has obvious masculine connotations. Straight edgers often frame abstinence in terms of "strength," "honor," and "discipline," words traditionally associated with masculine, even military, constructions of gender. Although nothing in these values is inherently restricted to maleness, and some sXe women connect strongly with them, sXe men rarely associate them with women.

The intensely physical dancing at some hardcore shows further inhibits women's opportunities to fully experience the scene. Dancing is a full contact sport. Participants stomp, swing their arms around, and collide with one another in a chaotic melee. At one particularly intense show during Salt Lake City band Clear's set, I watched as a slender teenager caught a forearm across the face, instantly knocking him unconscious. Another showgoer caught his limp form, dragged him outside, and took him to the hospital. Ian MacKaye, one of the originators of sXe, reflected on the aggressiveness at the early stages of the scene (Lahicky 1997:107–108):

> When the Minor Threat thing was happening, things were getting more and more angry, and it seemed at the time, really, like we were

under attack. Our community was under attack, fighting all the time. It got more and more aggressive, and there was this cycle of things. I am not removing myself from this—I was definitely fucking fighting. It just seemed like things were getting more and more insane, more violent. What I started to notice was this drift—women at the front of the stage drifting toward the back of the room and eventually out of the fucking room.

Straight edgers describe the aggressive dancing as a relatively harmless "release," and few serious injuries occur (although participants expect severe bruises).[6] However, the sight of (often massive) men slamming into one another and punching the air intimidates many show-goers, particularly women, and, as mentioned in the last chapter, a few men take the opportunity to intentionally strike others with relative impunity. Carrie, the nonprofit employee, shared her frustration with the intense dancing at shows:

> I've definitely been at shows where I was a little resentful of the fact that I had to stand in the back or else get hurt. I had paid just as much as everybody else. I really like this band, too. Sometimes people don't even mean it, but I've been nailed in the stomach a couple of times at shows here . . . and I think lots of people, you get hurt, you don't go back. I can understand that to an extent. That's definitely kept me from going back to a couple different shows.

The few sXe women who *do* dance with the men insist that any woman who really wants to dance could do so. However, I rarely observed more than a few women on the dance floor. The entire environment felt unwelcoming to some women, as a female contributor to the x-grrrls website suggests (www.x-grrrls.com, viewed 1/27/05):

> What males maybe can't understand is that there are countless females in this scene who are put off by certain male attitudes at shows. Because the scene always caters to them. So, just by being one of the twenty females in a room packed to the gills with shirtless males feels very awkward and uncomfortable. In every situation, females are the ones who have to adjust.

As a female colleague who accompanied me to several shows put it, "The pit is one big sausage-fest."

A show's "vibe" and the intensity of the dancing depend in large part on the band's attitude. If a singer screams to the audience, "I wanna see some blood!" or "Let's tear this place apart!" the likelihood of aggressive dancing and fights goes up. A band that called upon the audience to "Take care of each other" or "Don't be a bunch of tough guys" reduced the chance of violence significantly. Likewise, some hardcore bands earn a reputation for attracting tough guys that dance hard and fight; the Cro-Mags, Madball, and Hatebreed were a few notable examples.

Escape

I want it back again / The spirit that we once had / Showing all these new hards / They're not so fuckin' bad / You and your crew / Would have never made it through / The days we hung out in 1982 / The New York brotherhood / I can't let go / The New York Brotherhood / Where did they go? / We called it the Wolfpack / We called it United Blood / Wore chains around our waists / And construction gloves / Thompkins Sq. on a Saturday night / I see my brother, he's here to fight / They got him down, it's 3 on 1 / 10 of us show, guess who won? / We hung out on 7th and A / Friends work the door / We didn't have to pay / Boston came around one night / Push came to shove and / We were down to fight.

—"New York Crew" by Judge, 1988

The last of men's responses to the crisis of masculinity in Kimmel's (1996) analysis is escape. As industrialization brought increased compe-tition among workers and the masculine and feminine spheres increas-ingly became separate, men sought homosocial relationships in pubs, ex-clusive clubs, sporting events, and travel. Such exclusive social settings served to resist the feminization of men by women and became refuges from the fiercely competitive and alienating workplace. Men still create and recreate spaces where they can go to feel like men. There is even a sense (in sXe and other groups) that "male intimacy would be threatened by the integration of women" (ibid.:311). While single-sex settings may seem rather innocuous on the surface, "homosocial preserves—single sex colleges, fraternal orders, men's clubs — are as much about the protection of men's privilege as they are arenas to facilitate closeness among men" (ibid.:315). Promise Keepers limited women's participation to serving in secretarial and other roles and staffing stadium events. The mythopoets ex-cluded women from their gatherings entirely. The Million Man Marchers created a corresponding event in which women could participate, the Day of Absence, and had several women speak at their event, but otherwise they believed men must teach other men about manhood. Only the pro-feminist men actively include women in their organization.

The sXe men in Denver regularly socialize with women, but men still overwhelmingly populate bands, shows, and other social settings. A minority of adherents join sXe "crews," essentially cliques within the movement. A crew is generally a group of friends with common interests who may have had their own unique slogans and symbols displayed on sweatshirts or baseball caps or tattooed on their bodies. Joined by invitation only, crews represent the most exclusive aspect of sXe and are perhaps the most prominent means of reinforcing hegemonic masculinity.

Straight edge crews often center around a particular geographic locale, much like a skinhead crew, a mod "fleet," an English football supporter "firm," or a street gang. Even bands often print their city's name on their shirts, for instance Boston Straight Edge, New Jersey Hardcore, and Washington D.C. Straight Edge. Visiting sXers represent their home city with pride. New York City and Boston, boasting the largest hardcore scenes, held a special prestige among sXers,[7] and the two cities fostered an ongoing rivalry that, in the early days, occasionally resulted in violence.

Perhaps the most well known national sXe crew is Courage Crew. Formed in the early 1990s by two brothers in rural Ohio, Courage Crew has since spread across the United States, including hundreds of members at one point. The brothers were among many sXe kids from farm communities who felt constantly harassed by other young men and sometimes even the police. Although most sXe kids could recall a time they faced opposition from non-sXe peers, sXers in rural areas were especially marginal. Courage Crew emerged in response, as kids found strength and solidarity in numbers. They quickly recruited many others in the local area who shared their feelings of isolation and frustration. Each member wears military style dog tags, passed out by members of the group, and most have Courage Crew tattoos. The crew earned a reputation as being ardently sXe, physically intimidating, and, when necessary, willing to fight to defend each other and their beliefs. As one member put it, "Courage Crew put Ohio on the map for the sXe world."

Courage Crew's rapid growth spiraled out of control, and some adopted the mantle as an excuse to act tough and be violent at shows. By the late 1990s, many sXers feared and despised them, and message-board posts described intimidation and beatings by members. For many kids, the group came to symbolize everything negative about sXe, and when they spoke of tough guys they often mentioned Courage Crew in the same breath. Courage Crew's negative reputation prompted its founders to re-evaluate its membership, as Luke, a prominent Courage Crew member, explained:

Maybe it got out of hand, maybe it didn't. Whatever your opinion is. There were a few bad apples. But like sXe itself, they've all weeded themselves out pretty much. Courage Crew is definitely being cleaned up. Now there's probably . . . there's maybe, tops, sixty kids across the country. There was just a big meeting, and everything's going to be a lot more organized. There's more guidelines to a positive lifestyle. There's no messing around now. It's no doing stupid shit in the name of Courage Crew, which kids have done in the past. We're getting the blame for all this stuff. . . . It's pretty much you're a positive person or you're out. You've got goals or you've got a career in mind or you're out. You treat people with respect or you're out. It's gonna be definitely more of a standup thing.

In Denver, three members of Courage Crew were particularly prone to starting fights. Several times I saw them stand on the edge of the pit taking cheap shots at kids in the pit. It is guys like these, while vastly outnumbered in the scene, who give the scene a reputation for militancy. Shunned by most of the scene, they drifted away and were rarely at shows.

Many members of the Denver scene vehemently disliked the local Courage Crew guys and rumors regularly circulated about Courage Crew targeting various kids. Eventually, however, several members of Courage Crew came to be accepted by much of the scene, largely due to Luke's efforts. Indeed, a few of them are positive, thoughtful men who sincerely believe in bettering the sXe scene. But regardless of members' intentions, crews take on a hypermasculine mystique, based partly upon fact and partly upon fiction, which reinforces violent images of sXe as a whole and turns off many women who might otherwise participate. Crews are essentially boys' clubs, even more exclusive than sXe in general. Adele, a thirty-year-old sXer from Louisville is, as far as she knows, the only female member of Courage Crew. Shannon, the twenty-one-year-old university student, said:

I think there is [sic] a lot of guys who listen to hardcore. I think it's a masculine thing, a masculinity issue. There's just a lot of testosterone at hardcore shows. I think there's a lot of guys who have their head on their shoulders, but . . . I see it coming from guys who are really kind of into the militant part of sXe. It's like, "Do you ever listen to the lyrics of some of these songs? Do you even care?" I guess that's how life is though. . . . I guess you can't expect every sXe person to be perfect.

Straight edge women hold a variety of opinions about the masculine nature of the scene. Although most find deep fulfillment and empowerment in their sXe identities, some feel subtly snubbed. Kendra said, "You just walk into a show and you're overwhelmed with the testosterone and anger."

Conclusion

One extreme of sXe seems to further entrench a domineering hypermasculinity while the other encourages a fully profeminst ideal. In between are thousands of young men testing the boundaries of what it means to be a man, embracing certain markers of masculinity while rejecting others. Straight edge men, for the most part, have a long way to go toward truly creating an antisexist scene (as the next chapter will further investigate). However, abstaining from alcohol and possibly sexual conquest are visible, concrete ways of challenging mainstream masculinity and, for many sXe men, creating other opportunities. The movement's shortcomings emerge when sXe falls into the same traps that other men's movements have repeatedly stumbled into: exclusivity, escapism, and focusing too narrowly on controlling their own bodies and beliefs at the expense of seeing sexism as part of a larger context. Straight edgers are too quick to conclude that few women dance at shows or perform in bands simply because individual women choose not to do these things rather than acknowledging the aspects of hardcore that are very unwelcoming to women. Members of crews are quick to claim that they have no "rule" against women members, yet are blind to the behaviors that virtually ensure women will never join.

The two faces of sXe illustrate how individuals within any particular men's movement can express masculinity differently as well as the difficulties of challenging hegemonic masculinity within a masculine context. Many sXers felt caught between these two faces: negotiating a personal way of being that pushed progressive values while maintaining aspects of hegemonic masculinity. The Denver scene included many very thoughtful, progressive young men, and the young women involved generally appreciated the setting. Nevertheless, the male-dominated scene restricted women's opportunities for meaningful involvement, leaving some feeling alienated and unappreciated.

CHAPTER 6

GIRLS UNITED AND DIVIDED
WOMEN IN STRAIGHT EDGE

While I interviewed Megan in my campus office, she wept briefly as she described her struggles to feel included in the hardcore scene. Both her love of sXe and her frustrations with the scene ran deep; the interview served as a chance for her to express lingering emotions she'd kept concealed. As one of the few nonvegetarian sXers, she faced ongoing criticism from several vegan sXers whose teasing had become hurtful. "They're all so righteous. You do one thing wrong, minor, that disagrees with their philosophy and you're out. . . . Everything they do is *the* way. I don't agree with it at all. I'm accepting." For reasons not entirely clear to her, these sXers, presumably her friends, had stopped talking to her. "They'd totally gang up. I don't like them. They stop being your friends for no reason, no good reason." She felt betrayed by a scene that boasted of unity and diversity while ostracizing her for being different. Even worse, Megan felt it was harder for women to find good friends in the scene, making the loss all the more painful. Yet, demonstrating the strength of many young sXe women, she refused to give up. In one breath she could praise some sXers for refusing the "jock mentality" and criticize others for being exclusive and judgmental: "Every guy is different. I'm not going to group 'em all together." I was moved by her dedication to sXe in the face of adversity but finally asked her why she continued in a scene that had occasionally treated her so poorly. She claimed that sXe was "who she is" and she wasn't going to give it up regardless of what others thought of her.

A variety of women with different backgrounds and interests are involved in the Denver scene: Carrie, a feminist nonprofit employee; Rose, a computer technician with "sincerity" and "integrity" tattooed down her forearms; Maggie, the tattoo-covered student who loved to dance at shows (despite taking painful blows to the head on several occasions); Elizabeth, the high school counselor; Kate, the vegan animal rights activist; Jenny, a human rights activist at CU; Shannon, whose stylish appearance raised eyebrows throughout the scene, and so on. Women's numbers in the Denver scene fluctuate between very few to a fairly sizable contingent. On the whole, they feel the scene accepts them, though mostly on the men's terms. Some women feel the hardcore scene limits them to two roles, the "boy-wanna-be" or the "cute, submissive girlfriend."[1] Others see many more possibilities and vehemently oppose these images as stereotypes of hardcore girls.

As the previous chapter showed, women face significant barriers to full participation in sXe. Nevertheless, those active in the scene construct alternative meanings of femininity. Some connect sXe to feminism while pushing the boundaries of what it means to be a woman.

Studying Women in Subcultures

Most subcultural studies have focused on males (Baron 1989). When scholars *do* include women, they often focus only on their sexual attractiveness or treat them as attachments to men rather than subjects worthy of study in and of themselves. McRobbie (2000) critiques subculture theories for generally not including women's experiences: "Girls negotiate a different leisure space and different personal spaces from those inhabited by boys" (ibid.:24). Clearly young women have been present in virtually every youth subculture, making their relative absence in ethnographic studies a glaring problem.

Subcultures that ostensibly seek to challenge dominant gender relations often fall short. Faced with limited opportunities, males create subcultures that celebrate masculinity as a "solution" to a lack of upward mobility (Cohen 1955). As Brake (1985:163) notes, "subcultures are male-dominated, masculinist in the sense that they emphasize maleness as a solution to an identity otherwise undermined by structural features." In her study of female punks, Leblanc (1999:106–107) reiterates this idea:

> As they are in other numerically male-dominated youth subcultures, punk's codes and norms are heavily masculine. A number of subculture theorists have argued that males create youth subcultures in order to satisfy their need to express, affirm, and celebrate masculinity. . . . Thus, the numerical dominance of males in these subcultures is only the tip of the iceberg—these subcultures are indeed specifically constructed to be hypermasculine in order to compensate for perceived challenges to working-class boys' masculinity in mainstream culture.

Even subcultures that explicitly seek to subvert dominant gender relations rarely escape the confines of patriarchy.

Men are over-represented in many youth subcultures, including punk, skinheads, heavy metal, and hip hop. While women have a larger presence in goth, emo/indie rock, and club cultures, most music-based subcultures are seemingly dominated by men. Women played a prominent role in the early LA punk scene (Lee 1983) but their numbers dwindled as punk branched into the hardcore and sXe scenes. Hardcore, and by extension sXe, is still fairly segregated. As the previous chapter showed, in today's sXe scene, men not only outnumber women but maintain a near monopoly on the music, and therefore the ideology, of the movement. However, early descriptions of girls in subcultures only as accessories to the boys were overstated. Though sometimes less visible, women make their presence known in the sXe scene.

Women do flourish in some subcultures. McRobbie and Garber (1976) describe a "teeny-bopper," "bedroom culture" centered around girls' bedrooms where they listen to pop music, watch pop music TV shows, and read about and discuss their favorite performers. Lowe (2004) describes the "tween" scene of young female popular music fans that develop a feminist consciousness (though the girls would never call it that) by critiquing sexist representations of women in magazines and music videos. The Riot Grrrl movement emerged as a feminist offshoot of the punk and alternative music scenes, encouraging women to play music and publish 'zines (Gottlieb and Wald 1994; Schilt 2003, 2004).

Despite the presence of women in scenes such as these, young women face a variety of barriers to joining sXe. First, the scene's scarcity of women and particularly the lack of many women in bands limits opportunities for entrée. Young women had few sXe women to look up to. Certainly (male) bands inspired sXe women, but relatively few women in prestigious positions, able to give voice to female experiences and concerns, makes the movement somewhat exclusive. An article posted on the XsisterhoodX website proclaimed, "The problem is there's just not enough girls involved. Guys see their favorite bands and are inspired to start one of their own. Girls see all the guy bands and figure they should just stick behind the scenes. There's a serious lack of people to look up to."[2]

Another barrier to participation is the hypermasculine atmosphere at some shows described in previous chapters. Katherine's explanation captured the thoughts of many sXers, women and men alike: "I think maybe it's too aggressive for most girls." Maggie was one of the few women who danced in the pit with as much bravado as the men. On two occasions, I witnessed her take accidental blows to the head that would have leveled a man twice her size. This didn't stop her from continuing to have fun in the pit, but most women are not interested in such risks. Maggie explained her difficulty in forming a band and getting to the front of the crowd to watch the bands:

RH: How do you think being a woman in this scene is different from being a guy in the scene?

Maggie: It kind of sucks. Bands always say, "Yay, the girls! Blah, blah, blah." But we're really not as involved. No one wants to hear a girl singer, which sucks, 'cause I really want to sing in a band. No one will . . . it doesn't really help that I'm so little . . . but no one will let me up front. No matter how hard I push, no one lets me up front. Even my friends. No matter how much they say it. "We love you Maggie! You're such an awesome girl." They don't really notice. . . . Our voice isn't as loud. We're not as strong 'cause there's not as many of us. . . . Being a girl in the scene kind of sucks but it's good enough to stick around 'cause I have a lot of fun.

Those women who *do* join and manage to thrive in the movement often feel special or unique simply for being women in the scene. Being a man in hardcore is nothing special in and of itself. However, in many scenes women are relatively more rare, making them conspicuous; it is easy to get noticed (positively or negatively) just by being female. Further, there is an unspoken understanding that it is more difficult to be a woman in the male-dominated scene. Therefore, those who stick it out are sometimes held in special esteem. Patrick believed that more women were joining the Denver scene all the time and deserved tremendous respect:

There's so few girls that are involved with the scene, if guys can meet a girl or girls that are involved with it, it just creates such an immense amount of respect and appreciation for them, if they can be a part of such a male-dominated scene. . . . It's a pretty ballsy move for a girl that's about that age, like a teenage girl, to step up and say "I'm gonna be a part of this scene." That takes somebody with a lot of self-confidence to be able to just jump in with that. Basically all they see is just guys, and guys being tough-guys. You go to some of these shows—we all do it—if it's a band we really love you're going out there throwing the windmills in there, frickin' doin' the karate kicks and jumpin' around like frickin' madmen, lookin' like we're trying to fight each other. Fourteen- or fifteen-year-old girl is going to come to a show and see that and be like, "Yeah, this is awesome"? Most girls would be like, "Jesus Christ!" [laughs] ... There's just not a lot of girls that are just flat out into that kind of music. For one reason or another . . . you find a girl who's into hardcore, she's like a frickin' . . . that's like a rare gem. You're like, "Yeah!! [laughs] this girl likes metal! Let's go!"

Both sXe men and women believe sXe appeals less to women because the music is too "aggressive" or "angry." It may be the case that women are socialized away from enjoying such music, although clearly there are many female fans of extreme music, whether metal, hardcore, or death metal. True or not, these beliefs reinforce the dominant gender script that women are not, or should not be, angry and aggressive. Kate said, "[Women are] supposed to be more fragile and refined and maybe not into the music itself. It's loud. Maybe a lot of people think women are supposed to be into a certain thing and not so into loud stuff [laughs]." Kids viewed the girls who *do* mosh with a blend of wonder and appreciation and these girls enjoyed setting themselves apart from other girls. But if sXers see mainstream girls as passive, quiet, and ladylike there is at least some encouragement for sXe women to be the opposite (see Carr [1998] and Halberstam [1998] for a discussion of girls and women adopting masculine performances as resistance to feminine conformity).

Don't Be a Girly Girl

"Being a female in the hardcore scene means you have to be twice as dedicated to whatever you're doing because you are bound to take a lot of crap from within the same community that is supposedly set up to help you"

—[www.x-grrrls.com, viewed 10/19/05]

In the 1990s and 2000s, young girls' role models in pop music included Britney Spears, Christina Aguilera, Beyonce, and the Spice Girls. Mass media continually markets the "Midriff," a stereotypical thin, scantily clad, sexually provocative woman seemingly in charge of her sexuality, but often reduced to little more than a narrow caricature of femininity (Goodman 2001). A stroll though any suburban shopping mall reveals scores of tween-age midriff wannabees imitating the basic makeup, hair, and fashions portrayed on MTV.

Women are expected to be nurturing, passive, and pretty, following a feminine script. We *do* or *perform* femininity and masculinity (Goffman 1976; West and Zimmerman 1987), acting out our gender as we interact with others. Women are expected to act demure, sexually available but virtuous, and deferential to men. Living up to these standards requires emotional energy and failure carries sanctions (Hollender 1998). For example, a woman who gives too masculine a performance (such as being "too aggressive") risks being labeled "bitchy," "butch," "overbearing" or any number of slurs from "dyke" to "witch." Despite feeling pressure to live up to this limiting version of femininity, many women in subcultures rebel, creating their own standards. Just as sXe men contrast themselves to other men, sXe women construct an identity in opposition to their images of other women, especially stressing an independence from men.

Female sXers, particularly the younger ones, define themselves in opposition not only to youth who drink alcohol and use drugs but also to mainstream women in general. As I mentioned previously, sXe women feel they have many advantages over their non-sXe peers and this feeling gives some of them a relatively negative view of young women. Their experience is similar to that of the female punks in Leblanc's (1999:135) study: "It's almost as though being punks kept us from being girls, or at least typical girls. Instead, we were punk girls." She points out that "the possibility of rejecting or subverting her own femininity plays a large part in a girl's attraction to punk" (ibid.:141). Simply rejecting dominant standards of femininity is hardly easy. As Leblanc suggests, sXe, hardcore, and punk girls must reconcile their subcultural identities with the expectations of being women. Maggie drew a sharp distinction between hardcore girls and other girls:

> I think [other girls] are highly influenced by television. Like *Sex in the City* and *Friends*. They all think that they have to go be like that. . . . It *is* embarrassing [laughs]. Maybe that's why I don't like girls. [emphatically] But I like hardcore girls! I don't like other girls, though. Unless I've known them since like junior high.

The general sXe belief holds that "mainstream" girls are flighty, shallow, and out to impress men in whatever way possible. Jenny had many female friends both within and outside the scene. Still, as a freshman living in Denver University's dorms she felt sXe separated her from her non-sXe peers, particularly in her sexual behavior:

> RH: how do you think sXe contributes to making you different from "typical" women your age?

> Jenny: Oh, god. Typical women my age, in my dorm . . . ugh! [Straight edge] prevents me from hooking up with like ten guys in a week. Dorms are totally fucking gross. . . . [Straight edge] doesn't

separate me all that much. I have friends in sororities; I have friends who go to parties. Basically the only difference is I don't regret things. I'm not the girl crying in front of the mirror at four in the morning because she just had sex with some guy when she was drunk. It makes me very confident. It makes me feel like I'm really, really on top of my life. I also feel like I'm more academically successful than most of the people in my dorm.

Straight edge women commonly believe that other "typical" women drink, dress up, and put on feminine acts to attract guys. Rejecting alcohol also symbolizes rejecting the need for approval from men. Naomi, a twenty-year-old college dropout from an affluent family, expressed sentiments similar to many sXe women, that other women use alcohol as a crutch to impress men:

RH: why do you think there are so few women involved?

Naomi: Because girls are stupid. They're so retarded. They're always doing stupid shit just to impress people. It's almost like alcohol is their excuse to sleep with people.

Naomi repeatedly contrasted her independence from men with what she perceived as other girls' reliance on men for continual affirmation.

In the "femininity game," "the ability to sexually attract one or more men is a pretty clear indication that one is well ahead of the game" (Leblanc 1999:136). If sexually attracting men is a primary signifier that one is correctly performing femininity (that is, playing the game well), resisting social pressures to be a "good" woman means rejecting the goal of attracting men. The Denver women make *not* doing anything to impress men a virtue and especially dislike women who go to shows to attract men, as if these women had defiled a sacred space where women could feel free from those social pressures. Martyr AD, a metal-influenced band and one of the few to include a female (bassist), played a show in Denver sometime in 2004. I noticed two groups of women in the crowd. The first appeared to be typically hardcore: tattoos, spiked belts, dark band shirts. The other looked like young, giggling high school or college students: bright clothing, heavy makeup, brand name purses, completely out of place at the show. It didn't take long for the hardcore women to begin making covert fun of the other group. Undoubtedly the hardcore women believed the others were there for the "wrong" reasons—particularly to impress men.

Katherine explained how women perceived to be at shows because of their boyfriends (rather than out of their own interest) or to pick up guys were breaking an unspoken rule:

RH: Do you think quote-unquote girly women, if they got into hardcore, would be looked down upon?

Katherine: I think that they are. A lot of times they're just too girly or too wimpy to handle it. Not to say that everybody that wants to take the time to look good wouldn't thrive in the hardcore scene, but a lot of times those are the girls that are just there because their boyfriends are, or are *seen* as just being there because their boyfriends are. Or because they want to try to pick up guys. Those are the girls like, [in whiny voice] "Ow! Somebody hit me!" and start crying and making a big deal out of something that's nothing. That's not trying to stereotype them into that, but I think that's more where they fall.

Even as sXe women try to step out of the femininity game, they are caught in a trap between the expectations of their subculture and the social pressures of being feminine. Being feminine also means being "not masculine," just as being masculine by definition is "not feminine." Straight edge women have to walk the fine line between being too feminine and not being feminine enough. Spending too much time on her appearance (doing her hair, wearing makeup, dressing stylishly) might cast an sXe woman into the girly camp. However, a woman paying too little attention to her appearance risks being dismissed as well. Kendra criticized women for playing the "cutesy" role while acknowledging that they feel pressured toward such displays of femininity:

I think a lot of girls don't know about [sXe] and if girls go to shows it's usually to be an accessory. Girls are usually at shows to attract boys. I really noticed it at the show in Salt Lake. They're sitting there in their cutesy hair and all their makeup, all done up, like little dolls. Just to be on the arm of some hardcore kid. Just to be prancing around like, "Look at me, I got Joey and he's a hardass." I just really think that girls don't consciously think they have any power sometimes. You *do*. You have the choice. You can be like, "Fuck you, I don't have to be all dolled up and be all cutesy." But somehow maybe they feel like that makes them unfeminine. They don't want to be butchy, but this doesn't make you butchy. So I think a lot of girls just go to shows to catch guys. You see a lot of that and it's really depressing. You just want to pull them aside and be like, "Girlfriend, you don't have to do that."

Don't Be a Coat Rack!

This trap might be easier to negotiate if the women were united within the scene. However, even as sXe women defined themselves in contrast to "other" girls, there is often competition and mistrust among women *within* the scene. Most women I interviewed in the Denver scene expressed some difficulty in forming a supportive network of female friends. Many had very strong friendships with one another, but they also noticed an underlying competition between women. Maggie was very close with several sXe girlfriends. However, she talked extensively about how many girls disliked other girls: "Girls . . . other girls hate girls so much. I've heard so many things of how girls think about me. . . . Girls to other girls are just threats." I asked Maggie why girls saw one another as threats. Frustrated, she wasn't sure about the source of the uneasiness between girls:

> I don't know if it has to do with guys? If they're threatened by . . . like she's gonna steal my guy. I don't really know what that is. Or she's better than me. Or we need to get rid of her 'cause she has cooler hair. Girls just don't like each other. It kind of sucks cause I've noticed that if you just get to know pretty much anybody, they're pretty awesome people. Girls don't like even give each other a chance.

Maggie herself held certain standards she expected women in the scene to live up to. She had little patience for any women in the scene who, she believed, went out of the way to impress or entice guys in touring bands (sXe and non-sXe). While she thought musicians who tried to "hook up" with local women were "sleazy," she also believed that women who fell for them were "dumb."

Straight edgers in general look down upon women whom they perceived to be sXe because their boyfriends were sXe.[3] Again, they view this as another way a girl would impress a guy; some use drinking to attract men, others use sXe. Katherine said,

> I know that a lot of girls that are sXe, they're seen as being sXe only because their boyfriend is sXe. As soon as the girls aren't with [their boyfriends], they won't be [sXe]. I've seen a lot of that. The same

with vegetarianism and all of that. They're only that way because their boyfriends are. So I guess a lot of people believe that guys are better at making and more committed to making a decision like sXe than a girl is.

The most derogatory label for such women is "coat rack," meaning a woman who quietly and politely holds her boyfriend's coat while he moshes, stagedives, and sings along. The implication is that the man's participation is authentic while the woman's is not. She is, at least in part, an inanimate object there for the male's convenience.

The disdain for sXe women who became sXe to "impress" men in the scene is a double standard; men are not always held to the same standard. Many young men choose to be sXe in part to fit in with and be accepted by their sXe friends. Further, sXe men, like other young men, often do things to impress or one-up each other, whether it is dancing particularly hard or bragging about who they know in a famous band. Yet women are held to a higher standard of "proof" that they are there for the "right" reasons—because they enjoy the music and are personally committed to the lifestyle. Katherine's view reflected a theme I encountered repeatedly: many girls don't "get it" and join the scene for the "wrong" reasons.

RH: What annoys you about the scene?

Katherine: This is gonna sound really bad [laughs]. The thing . . . not so much the scene out here . . . but the scene back home, the thing that annoys me is girls. Girls generally in the scene are really snobby. They stick to themselves. It's really clique-y for them. They're friends with a few other girls in the scene and that's it. They don't accept anybody else; they don't care. It's really trendy for them to be hard-core. I sat and witnessed two girls argue over who was more hard-core. Neither one of them was [laughs]. There was a raver girl and this hippie girl. They thought because they were at this show and have a bandana and have whatever, they thought they were hard-core. They sat and argued over who was more hardcore and how guys would say, "She is so hardcore." I think a lot of girls see it as a trend. They see it as really trendy. "I'm gonna be so cool with all the guys if I go to shows and I dress this specific way." It's not about that at all. It's about your attitude, the music, the things you believe in, and having a good time with your friends. Girls . . . that's probably a big reason why girls aren't really . . . a lot of people want more girls, but at the same time a lot of girls aren't welcomed.

The most accepted girls are the ones who in some ways can be "just one of the guys." However, not only is this problematic in that women are forced to conform to a more masculine performance, but some women are never given the opportunity to be one of the guys. To make it even more difficult for women to join the scene, women are often less than welcoming to each other.

As much as sXe women scoff at the time other young women put into their appearance, many are also appearance conscious. Straight edge women mocked women they felt were too focused on their looks. Shannon was very stylish, wearing makeup, fashionable hairstyles, classy outfits, and a designer purse to shows. While she had many friends in the scene, she was never fully accepted because she looked the part of a more mainstream woman. Her seemingly unshakable self-confidence and commitment to sXe helped her follow her own path in the scene even as she recognized the absurdity of the attention her style commanded:

> It's just interesting to me that people, especially sXe kids who have this sort of "My life, my choice" attitude about sXe, think that I need to be dressing a certain way and make comments about the fact that I wear skirts. It's just like "Mind your own business." And it doesn't get to me because I'm confident enough to not care. But specifically I've had someone come up to be and go, "Do you know that people always talk about what you wear?" I'm like, "Who cares? You really sit around and talk about what Shannon wears?" [laughs] It's very conservative in a way. It's like sXe is something that's kind of liberal. It's against the norm. But there's this conflicting other side of it. People are very conservative about gender roles or whatever. [laugh]

Girls United—Resisting the Boys . . .

I can't speak about sexism / Without being misunderstood / I just wanna kill prejudice / Without sinking in the same hate / I'm just standing in front of you / And that's enough to make you lose / I won't answer to your provocations / I won't go your way to prove you're right / You're not the victim / Don't try to act that way 'cos it won't work.

—"Killing Prejudice" by French band Uneven, date uncertain

Despite the barriers sXe women encounter, the adversity they experience sometimes unites them in very strong friendships. Just as they resist mainstream femininity, they also resist the masculine overtones in the scene. Some women in the Denver scene are very close. Kate said, "I wouldn't know some of the best friends I've ever had in my life if it wasn't for being into hardcore and being sXe. I think that's made it something really special in my life." Carrie had several very close sXe girlfriends and claimed that, despite the occasional infighting, sXe helped women form more meaningful and "real" relationships with one another. She observed the competition among sXe women but still felt sXe women were closer than other women:

I think we probably get friendships that are a lot more solidly based. In lots of cases, anyway. It's just kind of a new way to approach your friendships with other women. It's not all about . . . in our junior high it was all about who'd you go make out with. I don't see [sXe] as a competition. I know, people will make jokes about the 'queen of the scene' or whatever. I don't see that so much here. I haven't seen that in general so much with sXe. Punk rock—oh yeah! . . . I think for the most part it allows you to actually be who you are and know people for who they are instead of who they are when they're [drunk] and trying to impress everyone. Or trying to be something they're not because they desperately need to fit. I think women tend to do that a lot.

Some female sXers decide that women must unite to carve out their own space in the scene and that, while the men have good intentions of overcoming sexism, equality will only emerge when women stand up for themselves. At a 1999 Floorpunch show a group of women stayed to the side of the dance area. One young woman, however, mixed it up with the biggest of the guys. Her conventional hairstyle contrasted the partial sleeve of tattoos running up her left arm and her numerous piercings. Her shirt read, "Girls coming in the pit, watch your balls." She seemed to really want to take on the tough-guy dancing crowd, punching and kicking whenever the dancing neared her. At another show Sonia, an sXer I had known since she was sixteen, used a black marker to scrawl "A girl can be just one of 'the boys' too" on a t-shirt before joining the guys in the pit.

A post on the "X-grrrls" website urged women to greater participation while recognizing that women who speak out against sexism face a difficult road:

Guys talk about sexism and how it sucks and how they're being so considerate and noble. But, when a girl does it she's just a "man-hater" or some other undesirable thing they can label us with. . . . Feminism apparently is just not cool to talk about. It's really a

11. A young woman practices her "headwalking" at a Stretch Arm Strong show. Bands such as SAS, who encourage women's participation, see more women taking an active role in their shows. Photo by Amanda Raney.

relevant issue. Girls need to start getting up there and speaking about the things that concern them; stop being so fucking content with letting other people say it for you. There defiantly [sic] are girls who are getting involved who don't think you have to wear a miniskirt to get noticed and I think it's awesome. The problem is there's still so few. It's time to make our voice strong in a scene that claims to be standing up for us. We're not made of glass; we're not going to shatter if you bump into us. We're more than just potential love interests. We're not just a decoration on the back wall. If you're a girl, go start a band. Go throw down in some pit. Tell your boyfriend to hold his own fucking jacket. It's time to show the guys that it is really "not just boys' fun" after all.[4]

In the spirit of this post, Carrie and three other sXe women formed a bowling team to compete in a "punk rock bowling tournament." They named their team "Straight Edge Pussy Crew," mostly for fun but also, said Carrie, to make a statement:

Carrie: We're taking on a word that's definitely been used to be an insult. To me that's kind of like reclaiming the word 'bitch.' Not only am I gonna be out here about being sXe, but yes I'm female and I'm not insulted by this word. It doesn't matter to me if this is supposed to be a weak thing. . . . In a way, too, it's just kind of fun. . . . What can we do to catch the eye of people and maybe freak them out a second? . . . We really got pretty positive reactions from it. I think people got it, for the most part.

RH: What exactly did they get?

Carrie: I think they got that it was kind of a joke. The whole claiming the word pussy . . . I think they appreciated the fact that we had the nerve to do that. And do it with jeans on, really tight short shirts lookin' like we're trying to go for the stripper thing or something. I think it worked. Mostly it was just fun.

The "crew" made pink bowling shirts complete with Xs. A drawing of a woman with cat ears, whiskers, and tail in a sexually suggestive pose adorned the back of the shirt. It was important to the teammates to be seen as sXe *women*, sexually empowered and engaging the scene on their terms. Megan, also on the team, wanted to say, "We are the girls. We are the not-so-PC girls." But it was equally important to them to be able to feel comfortable displaying more traditional femininity, as Megan alluded to: "We knew it was kind of a shock with the word, but I'm a big fan of the pink, so pink was natural to me, a natural choice. We knew there would be little to no other girls and we wanted to be the cutesy feminine girls." Three of the teammates wore makeup, dressed stylishly, and spent considerable time fixing their hair, things they would do less before attending a show. They seemed to enact a sort of "lipstick" feminism, enjoying dressing up and playing a role, but on their own terms. They subverted the gender expectations of young women by calling attention to their femininity in a setting that generally disdains traditional female gender displays, as if to say, "We are women, but we make our own rules!" Throwing femininity at the other, mostly male, bowlers was, in this context, an act of resistance.

Women Involved

Though rare, it is not unheard of for women to be in bands, either exclusively with other women or with men. Just a few of the sXe and hardcore bands, past and present, with female members include: Perdona (FL), Berzerk (OR), Doughnuts (Sweden), Fast Times (NJ), Walls of Jericho (MI), Indecision and Most Precious Blood (NY, same member), XLifeCycleX (Belgium), Uneven (France), the Wage of Sin (NY), Disembodied and Martyr AD (MN, same member), and Drama (Spain). Unsurprisingly, bands with female singers/lyricists frequently address issues of sexism and homophobia in both the scene and society at large. Infect, an all-female sXe band from Brazil, which reportedly has one of the largest sXe scenes in the world, scream (in Portuguese, of course) against sexism and homophobia in songs such as "Sociedade Masculina" and "Homofobia." Some sXers dislike the sound of female singers in a hardcore band, though my feeling is that few men are willing to invite women into their bands for fear of disrupting the masculine camaraderie, the "band of brothers."

In addition to occasionally being in bands, young women have often used 'zines as a space to express both their creativity and political views in male-centered subcultures (Piano 2003). The Riot Grrrl movement, especially, gave feminist 'zines a more prominent place in the subcultural landscape (Comstock 2001). Adele Collins has published the highly regarded *I Stand Alone* 'zine for many years. Several Denver sXe women created or contributed to 'zines. In the Internet age, some women create feminist-oriented sXe sites. Two of the most popular are Girls with Xs on their Hands (www.x-grrrls.com.) and xSisterhoodx (www.xsisterhoodx.com). Such sites feature all of the elements common to similar sXe sites: discussion forums, interviews, music reviews, and links to other sites. However, they also have feminist oriented articles; a few titles from Grrrls with Xs include "Proving Myself to the Boy's Club," "Are You Just a Coatrack to the Boys?" "Straight Edge Feminists Take Issue with Stereotypes," and "Holding Her Boyfriend's Sweatshirt Just Didn't Cut It for ex-sXe Woman." The site, under the slogan "Connecting and Supporting Girls in the Straight Edge Scene," sells shirts and hoodies with "x-grrrls softcore" on the front and "Coatrack Attack" on the back. They also sell thongs, boxers, lunchboxes, infant creepers, bibs, and *cooking aprons*!

In some local scenes, women play central roles aside from being in a band. Indeed, in many places without them there wouldn't *be* a scene. Kate and a few other Denver women booked shows, arranging for venues, advertising/flyering the show, and helping the touring bands find places to stay. In other scenes, women photograph bands, effectively documenting the history and culture of the times. The Louisville scene owes much to Adele Collins, who has been a central figure for a long time, doing her 'zine and setting up shows.

Straight Edge and Feminism

Man you've got a problem, who made you fuckin' king / A macho pig with
nothing in your head / No girls around you, their place is not at gigs / Don't
want 'em on the dancefloor 'cos they're weak / A woman's place, the kitchen,
on her back / It's time to change that attitude and quick / Showing us your
phobias, you're scared to see 'em think / You'd rather dress 'em up in pretty
lace, all nice and colored pink / You feel so fucking threatened, when they
stand out in front / A stupid passive piece of meat is all you really want / But
it's: Not just boys' fun / There's girls who put out fanzines, and others put on
shows / Yet they're not allowed to get out on the floor / Some make music, well
that you can accept / Hell, maybe live you'll get some tits and ass / You fucking moron, your brains have run amuck / A girl's only lot in life is not to fuck!
        —"Not Just Boys Fun" by 7 Seconds, 1984

Like many contemporary young people, both men and women, sXers are
generally cautious about, and sometimes suspicious of, feminism. While
a few, particularly a few men, dismiss feminism entirely, most wrestle
with the stereotypes spread by feminist opponents: feminist women are
obnoxious, man-hating lesbians. Though few sXers accept these stereotypes completely, the taint nevertheless remains. Still, virtually all sXers
support the goals of liberal feminism (such as equal rights, equal pay, and
questioning traditional gender roles) and some sXers (including some
men, as the last chapter revealed) self-identify as feminists, blending this
identity with sXe.

Straight edge women who have developed some sort of feminist consciousness are particularly critical of the hypermasculinity, sexism, and
machismo displayed by some men at hardcore shows. (Again, it is difficult here to separate sXe from the hardcore scene in which it finds its
home. Many women report that sXe men are more conscientious than
other men in the hardcore scene. This may generally be the case, but I certainly observed a minority of sXe men whose attitudes toward women and
displays of masculinity were virtually indistinguishable from their non-
sXe peers.) These women understand that while sXe encourages young
men to challenge many aspects of young manhood, the context of a hardcore *show* is exclusive and encourages otherwise well-meaning men toward hypermasculine behavior. Shannon saw through sXe's hypermasculine face: "I've realized that the scene in Denver is a bit chauvinistic. . . .
I think that a lot of these guys have issues with women speaking up and
voicing their opinion. They get a little more threatened by that than a

man voicing an opinion." She wasn't entirely comfortable labeling herself a feminist, but Shannon aligned herself with feminist principles.

Some women astutely make the link between homophobia and sexism, as Erica's post (titled "Building a Hardcore Scene That's Not So Fucking Sexist and Anti-Gay") on XSisterhoodX shows:

> I believe that the homophobia that exists in society at large is prevalent in some hardcore circles. Additionally, the attitudes and practices that fuel this homophobia potentially feed into the anti-female attitude that saturates hardcore. What I hope to show is the connection between gay and lesbian discrimination and oppression and straight female discrimination and disadvantage in the hardcore scene.

Though sexism and homophobia in the scene are glaringly obvious to some female sXers, a minority cannot understand what all the fuss is about. These women, while noticing the general lack of women in bands and on the dance floor, put the responsibility squarely on the shoulders of women themselves. They feel that women have every opportunity to become involved in the scene, but lack men's motivation. Most, however, recognize that all the motivation in the world can't protect a 130-pound woman from a 200-pound man swinging his fists in the pit or convince men to support women in bands.

Sexual Control

Reminiscent of radical feminism, many women make opposing rape vital to their understanding of feminism, connecting sXe, feminism, and control of their sexuality. Having power over their own bodies and sexual choices is one of their central motivations for refusing alcohol. In this case, refusing to be a man's sexual plaything means more than resisting the perceived mainstream femininity; it is a way of *embodying* feminism. Female 'zine contributors frequently demand the scene resist the "rape culture." Kendra said, "There's also that whole sXe thing about not having sex with a lot of people, or just being in a committed relationship. I definitely felt that. I don't think you should have sex with—you're at a bar, you see this guy. I'm not going to go home with him and fuck him." Though she had had sexual encounters in the past, Carrie chose to abstain from sex completely when she began identifying as sXe:

> I don't do the sex thing at all; I don't do any of that. It's not something I feel like I have to do. It's just kind of . . . I feel like it's totally

Girls United and Divided

my personal decision and I don't have to justify it to anyone. But I also don't feel like I have to advertise it either. Straight edge to me is a personal conviction but it's also something that people will recognize. Once they've been around you for a while, even if you don't tell them.

Straight edge is a more concrete way for Carrie and other women to name their personal empowerment.

Conclusion

Straight edge women simultaneously hold conflicting opinions of the sXe hardcore scene. *Every* woman I spoke with assured me that they feel empowered with greater control over their personal lives, femininity, and sexuality. Nearly every woman, however, also pointed out the gross contradictions between the movement's "positive" and antisexist ideals and the behavior of a few of its members. They overwhelmingly appreciate the profeminist and "positive" men in the scene but are disgusted by the hypermasculine tough guys. To say that sXe ultimately "empowers" or "disempowers" young women would be an oversimplification—their experiences varied greatly and each woman has good and bad things to report.

Straight edgers in general define themselves against mainstream youth, but this opposition has additional, gendered meanings. Straight edge men resist proving their masculinity through alcohol, drugs, and sexual conquest. Straight edge women refuse to prove their femininity by impressing men. Clearly, such resistance produces mixed results, for both men and women. For example, in rejecting contemporary standards of femininity, could it be that sXe women are simply adopting a more "masculine" performance, trying to be "just one of the guys?" If so, is this still a form of resistance? The Denver women show the complexity of navigating gender in a subcultural setting while still being part of the mainstream. They strike a personalized balance between dominant gender scripts and various alternatives, believing they have more *choice* in their gender performance. While the women, similar to the men, occasionally overestimate their power to resist society's pull, they do create personally fulfilling opportunities.

LIFE AFTER SUBCULTURE
HOW OLDER STRAIGHT EDGERS
REDEFINE COMMITMENT

In 2005 I briefly returned to Colorado and saw the Chicago band, the Haunted Life, play a skateboarding warehouse near downtown Denver, where skate punks flew up and down plywood ramps behind the band. At various points during the set, the singer, Matt, explained the songs' significance, warning against the casual use of the "N" word, expressing frustration with sexual offenders, and encouraging the crowd to volunteer and mentor children. Each band member is sXe and vegetarian, including three who are at least thirty: Matt, a married, thirty-six-year-old social worker; Shariq, thirty, a married anesthesiologist; and drummer Chad, thirty-three and also married. Despite their full lives, these guys found time to write and record a record as well as tour, playing shows with a five-dollar cover charge. The Haunted Life demonstrate that being part of a subculture and having an "adult" life are compatible and that the old sXe maxim "true till twenty-one" does not apply to everyone. As one member put it, "Just because you have goals in life that are more than neck tattoos and piercings, doesn't mean you have to stop being involved in hardcore and punk rock."

By the time I finished this study, I was thirty years old and the oldest *active* member of the Denver sXe scene. A few sXers older than me still lived and worked in the area, but they rarely attended shows or socialized with the younger crowd. Most left the subculture by their early- or mid-twenties. Many sXers, however, persist in their commitment to the sXe lifestyle into their late twenties and beyond. They recognize sXe's limitations, contradictions, and flaws and yet are able to personalize their commitment and reconcile ongoing participation with "adult" life. Alec's direct involvement had waned over time. After years of touring, he became discouraged with the scene in the late 1990s. Now, at age thirty, he still believes strongly in sXe ideals but he no longer identifies with the scene. Though he wore a spiked belt, denim jacket, and bright orange sneakers, little else separated him from other young instructors at the private university at which he taught—at least on the outside. Few of his students had any idea he had been a central figure in the sXe movement, playing in front of thousands of kids in several popular bands. While he had moved on from the scene he maintained a drug-free and positive lifestyle with just as much commitment as he ever had. He tried to strike a balance between giving up or contradicting the lifestyle entirely and growing old and bitter in a subculture that no longer spoke to him the way it once had:

> Let's look at the hippies. You've got your hippies that went and became yuppies. They'd maybe eat tofu, but they're crushing people's lives with their businesses. Then you have the hippies that stayed hippies but are the most disgruntled motherfuckers in the world. They're just like "Arggggg!" And they're filled with hatred. It's a good learning thing for all of us coming out of punk. I don't want to be this and I don't want to be that. I want to be happy and successful by my own right. To me, the only thing that made sense was teaching and writing. That's the only honorable thing I could do for myself. Everything else just seemed like hell. [laughs]

Though he attends few sXe shows and rarely identifies as sXe, Alec personifies sXe ideals.

Younger sXers, full of the certainty and hubris of youth, are often disgusted when older kids sell out. Newer kids believe they will persevere where their elders have failed. Despite their youthful confidence, most of these critics will nevertheless follow in the footsteps of the very sellouts they criticize. By the time I finished my seven years with the Denver sXers, about one half had stopped being sXe, including some the most vehemently self-professed "true-till-death" types. While many youth idealistically believe they will be "hardcore" forever, adults often hold the opposing view that subcultures are little more than temporary vacations from ordinary, straight society, a way to put off growing up and becoming a responsible adult. Many parents grudgingly put up with their children's eccentricities, frowning at the pink hair or black clothing but taking solace in the fact that belonging to a subculture is just a temporary phase. In many cases this may be true. Yet many former participants find creative ways to reconcile their subculture's ideals with their adult lives. The Syracuse sXe scene, for example, is full of sXers in their thirties and even beyond.

Transitioning out of a subculture is often a difficult and ongoing process (Adler and Adler 1983). Rarely do participants make a clean break. Rather, they leave and rejoin, struggling over the loss of the subculture's benefits with the pull of other commitments, often redefining commitment as their involvement wanes. Straight edge, with its clear and rigid lifestyle requirements, differs somewhat from other groups where membership is less clearly defined. When members begin using alcohol and drugs, they can no longer claim sXe, period. The transition out of the identity can be abrupt and permanent.[1] However, for those who remain drug free as they age, deciding whether to continue claiming the identity is more of a struggle. Straight edgers go through several transitions in their relationship to the movement. Many eventually find the identity is limiting rather than empowering as they critically consider inconsistencies in the scene. Those who remain sXe individualize their sXe commitment, incorporating it into a more general philosophy, and seek to set an example for other youth.

Straight Edge Becomes Limiting Rather Than Empowering

Screaming for change / But time's moved on / Look around / What the fuck have we done? Seeds of apathy / Have been sown / And we just watched them / As they've grown.

—"Sown the Seeds" by British band In the Clear, 1999

Straight edge initially challenges kids to examine and change many aspects of their lifestyles. Kids report feeling empowered to live drug free, question pressure to be sexually active, and be "different" from their peers in a variety of ways. The movement opens up new opportunities and choices and feels "liberating." Eventually, however, many sXers realize that sXe does not and cannot provide all of the answers. At some point, sXe becomes *limiting* rather than *liberating,* confining of possibilities rather than creating new ones. As Alec succinctly put it, "Life goes on outside of punk." Though he remained drug free, he came to realize that sXe no longer represented his ideals and that sXe was no longer the best expression of his profeminist, progressive values:

> [Our band] came along at a time when sXe was about vegan hardcore. It was about being tough. We were like, "Whoa! Who cares? Who cares about your sXe world?" Straight edge is a dietary choice. It's like "I don't eat cheese." It's a big thing to make that step, but after that it's like "How can I take what I've done for myself and help the community at large? Besides these suburbanites that I hang out with and listen to bands with?"

Likewise, Cedric, a member of a touring indie rock band, was still drug free, but believed the sXe label was just one stage in his personal development. He did not want to be "stuck" with a label that he felt would inhibit further growth:

I see sXe as a starting point. That's what it was for me and it gave me a lot of great ideas that I'm going to carry on in my life. I see it as people that stick with it and are totally militant about it are just kind of staying in that place and are not evolving at all. I respect someone who has the courage to say they don't want to be a part of it anymore and start drinking. I almost respect that more than someone who is going to give them a hard time about it.

Older sXers often no longer feel challenged by the movement. They worry that sXe will define them and overshadow their other accomplishments and goals. Though younger sXers are more likely to embrace the identity wholeheartedly, often defining much of their lives in relation to the scene, older sXers do not want to be defined solely in terms of sXe or hardcore. Donny, a graduate student in medical biology, was fully dedicated to the sXe lifestyle, acquiring his first sXe tattoo at age twenty-four. Yet he had little involvement with the scene and rarely associated with other sXers:

I think that being one-dimensional is really boring. I think that to have being sXe or being hardcore define me completely would be pretty sad. I don't think I could deal with having that be all there was when people would say, "Oh, do you know Donny? He's that hardcore/sXe guy." If that's all they could say about me, that would suck. I think that being sXe is really just part of your personality. Live your life. When you think about it, on a daily basis people don't drink when they do ninety percent of the stuff that they do. So why should it be a big deal that I'm not drinking at the same time? I just don't drink during the ten percent when people are getting wasted after work or something. I don't think that's that big of a difference. I guess it's a huge commitment to not give in to that social pressure, but it's not what defines me.

At age thirty-four, Joey, the former singer of a popular East Coast sXe band, still attended shows, bought records, and remained drug free. He was able to maintain his involvement in part because he had nurtured other aspects of his life:

For me personally, I think sXe isn't the be-all, end-all in life. It's not like I'm [only] sXe. It's like what are you gonna use that clear mind for? I could be sXe and sit on my couch and watch Jerry Springer all day and I'm not really helping the world at all. . . . I think I'm kind to people, I'm nice to people. I think I use my clear mind to take it a step further to start looking at the way I treat people, the way I treat animals, the way I treat others. I try to encompass sXe with all that. I think sXe is just being aware and being a nice person and being a kind person.

Some former sXers, facing the limitations of sXe, reflect upon their experiences with the movement in very pragmatic ways, claiming that being drug free served an important purpose in their lives that is no longer necessary. They report that upon approaching their mid-twenties they feel they no longer *need* the identity to help them resist peer pressure to use. Straight edge had fulfilled its purpose by helping them question the taken-for-granted assumptions of youth culture regarding drinking and alcohol use. The movement helped keep these former sXers out of trouble and empowered them to make wise choices at a crucial time in their development. Thus empowered, they no longer felt the need to maintain sXe's rigid requirements and could drink responsibly on occasion. A twenty-nine-year-old former sXer explained that while the identity had once been meaningful and useful to him, he no longer claimed the label:

Throughout high school and throughout college I remained sXe. It was cool. It was like my support system. I needed it. It was great. I'm sXe, I liked the label. But now, I'm like twenty-nine, I'm married. I don't really feel the need to call myself that. I don't see anything wrong, having a beer watching the football game. I'm so glad that I had [sXe] growing up because going through college and high school I didn't get drunk, I didn't do drugs, I didn't do stupid things. Now I'm a mature adult and I don't really feel the need to associate with that anymore. I still respect it.

Other sXers become sXe in part to resist their own addictive tendencies and put their lives in order. After maintaining a drug-free lifestyle for a period of time, they feel confident in their abilities to responsibly manage their use. Roger, a musician in a touring indie rock band, said:

One of the main reasons I started being sXe was because I wanted to stop doing drugs, I wanted to get my head back together, make sure I regained my ambition. I still definitely have that. Another thing I took from it was how much I value my friends. . . . I learned *so much* while I was sXe. I tried to get books and read about *everything*. Becoming involved in animal rights stuff. It gave me a real sense of consciousness for a world of things.

Disenchanting the Scene—Confronting Inconsistencies

You talk big when you preach / But empty promises are what you keep / You say your dedication is so deep / I know that your TALK IS CHEAP.
—"Talk Is Cheap" by Bold, 1988

As subculturists grow older they become increasingly reflexive and disenchanted about their scene. In fact, older sXers who have "been around" are often more critical of their own scene than they are of outsiders or mainstream social institutions. Older sXers critique the movement on a variety of fronts. They often have an idealized version of the scene "back in the day," grow tired of scene politics, and can't stand the intolerance of a small minority of kids. One thirty-one-year-old sXer questioned if sXe is losing its intended meaning and becoming another t-shirt slogan for sale in suburban malls: "It seems like a fad. Now it's a good way to rebel against society without . . . losing your car privileges."[2] Many become frustrated with the difficulty of making sXe and hardcore more accessible to women and are disgusted with the constant gossip and infighting. Frank, a former member of an sXe band, wrote in an email, "My whole point is, everyone is different, and we all get pleasure from different activities and social events. Being edge is all about a personal choice for me, besides, I'm twenty-eight, work full-time, going back to school to become a nurse, and certainly I don't have time for STUPID 'SCENE' POLITICS."

Some sXers eventually become "jaded scenesters," distancing themselves from the scene or dropping out entirely. Given that a scene will likely never completely live up to its ideals, a member can always find flaws. Cedric had been sXe for several years and continued to abstain from alcohol, drugs, and tobacco. However, he had mostly negative feelings about sXe as a movement, based mostly upon the intolerance and outspokenness of a minority of sXers, especially, he said, a few members of Courage Crew:

Over the years, I've just kind of stopped calling myself sXe. There's certain people who are sXe that I have no involvement with and . . . I wouldn't want to be involved with because of the way they call themselves sXe and the way they force their views on other people. As of right now, I don't call myself sXe. . . . I think once I started listening to what sXe bands were saying and noticing the people that were going to their shows and realizing that what I saw as a closed-minded point of view. . . . I decided that most sXe people that I knew were associated with it were off the level, out of touch with reality. . . . I'm definitely pointing out a lot of the negative things about sXe. I'm really into it if it's a personal decision . . . but once you start telling other people that that's the way they should be, then it's not for me.

Interestingly, nearly all of the sXers Cedric associated with fell solidly into the tolerant camp. However, I believe a few incidents, particularly Jackson's recent attack on Norman, dominated his perceptions of the movement as a whole.

Kevin, while still adamantly sXe and frustrated by sellouts, also understood how some sXers' beliefs came full circle, leading them to give up the identity:

But I think a lot of sXe guys, because they're strong or whatever, *can* [drink] in moderation. I think some of these guys were sXe to break an addiction in their lives and then they live addiction free for a long time. And then they . . . they grow up, and get a little older, lines start to grey, and they go, "You know what?" They're not drinking, not smoking, not doing drugs. They're being strong. And they realize that having that one beer is not necessarily being weak. So what's the problem? The problem with it is that it goes against a creed. . . . They have gone full circle and intellectualized and examined their life to the point where they then begin to examine sXe. They come up with the fact that moderation and each individual event taken on its own account may or may not be [weak]. So they re-intellectualize it and examine it and come to a new conclusion. . . . I hate the fuckin' sellout shit, but those people I don't necessarily consider them selling out. They never sold out the idea of living a strong life. They certainly aren't sXe any longer. It's not necessary that I be sXe to be a strong person. I've come to the same realization as those people that start drinking and stuff again. I've come to the realization that it's not that I don't drink, don't smoke, don't do drugs; it's that I am strong. However, I want my commitment to sXe to be so strong and so clear [that I won't ever give it up].

Some sXers who felt the identity is no longer relevant to their lives move on to other subcultures or leave the subcultural world entirely.

Those who stay develop a more personal commitment, expanding sXe to a more general philosophy rather than a set of rigid rules.

Personal Commitment

Reasons not rules / Six simple words / A wise man sang to me / So many years ago / Stood by me through / All of life's changes / The only advice that I have to give / Reasons not rules make us strong.

—"What Makes Us Strong" by Bane, 1999[3]

Despite recognizing the limitations and contradictions within sXe, many older members continued identifying with the movement. Straight edge kids' dedication to the identity evolves over time from a collective to a relatively individualized, personal commitment. Many kids initially claim sXe in part as a way to identify with like-minded individuals and to be part of a community, a scene. Straight edge provides a social community for kids who love fast, aggressive music and disapprove of drinking, smoking, and doing drugs. Typically, sXe youth identify strongly with their sXe peers, regularly wear sXe messages, and attend shows. The collective identity is highly salient to young sXers' lives (Stryker 1968).

As sXers grow older, however, for most, the sXe scene becomes less central to their lives. They enter careers, pursue new interests, have families, gain new friends in a variety of settings—essentially they grow up and out of the scene. Relating with fifteen- to twenty-year-olds becomes more difficult and less fulfilling. Furthermore, many or most of their sXe friends eventually move on, making older sXers somewhat of a novelty. Certainly many more mature sXers continue to attend shows, enjoy hardcore music, and maintain a sober lifestyle, but most report being less engaged in collective expressions of sXe and more committed to their own lifestyle choices. They settle into the identity, feeling they have less to prove to themselves and others, and care somewhat less that people sell out. Straight edge changes from something they are a part of to something that is a part of them. Morey, co-owner of a prominent independent record label, said,

[My commitment to sXe] has evolved over time. I'm not sure what kept me going in the first few years. Maybe my peers or the music itself. However, I'm a pretty determined person and when I set my mind on something, that's it. So that might have been all it took for the first few years. As I got older, it's become a real part of who I am. "More than the X's on my hand," if you will. I've got little or nothing to do with the sXe kids of today who are like I was when I was young—antagonistic to non-sXe people and intolerant of anything non-edge. I don't think that they represent me at this stage in my life. I may have a straight edge tattoo and wear an X watch and be an edge kid at heart, but everything is way deeper than that, so I don't sweat who drinks what and who does what and so on at my age.[4]

Many older sXers eventually claim that sXe is "more than the X on my hands," meaning more than a style, fashion, group membership, and even the choice to be drug free. This opened up opportunities to customize what sXe meant, rather than sticking solely to the group ideals of "don't drink, don't smoke, don't fuck." Joey, the thirty-four-year-old scenester, said:

> The whole thing with me is it's beyond the X on my hand, it's beyond the scene, it's beyond the music. I've always been happy my whole life without doing drugs, without drinking. When I stop going to shows, when I stop listening to the music, I'm still gonna stay sXe because I don't see any need for that stuff. I just don't see any need for that stuff. I haven't seen that really *improve* anyone's life in any way.

Ken, a twenty-five-year-old construction worker and singer in a hardcore band, explained his transition from identifying strongly with other sXers to making sXe his own way of life:

> RH: I've noticed some people, usually when they're younger and they first get into it they're really hardcore . . .

> Ken: Oh, yeah. Those are the kids that wear sXe shirts to every single show and X up at every single show and give other people shit about what they do. That's just like the same thing as skinheads. A fresh cut skinhead wears his boots and braces and freshly shaven head every single day. *Every* single day, without fail. It's the same thing. You get into it and you're all gung-ho about it. It's like a new job. You get a new job and you're like, "Hey, I like this job. I want to be part of it." Then after a while it just becomes part of you. In sXe it becomes less about being the poster boy for sXe and more about doing it for you.

Older sXers report that sXe transforms from a narrow set of rules about substance use into part of a broader life philosophy, often based upon "strength," "positivity," or "individuality." They have less connection to the sXe collective identity but have truly made sXe their own. Participation no longer primarily means going to shows, wearing X's, or buying hardcore records, but instead is a personalized expression of self. Tony, a twenty-eight-year-old from the West Coast, explained how his own understanding of sXe evolved over time:

> For me, I've evolved over time from sXe being the gospel I preached to everybody to sXe just being my own personal choice. . . . There was a time when you thought you could change the world. You thought you could change people's ideas and beliefs by shoving something down their throat. I think that was just an immature idea that a lot of us had. At a young age you can be influenced very easily. As you got older you realized "I don't want anyone shoving their opinions down my throat." You learn by just being true to yourself and being who you are, people will adapt to who you are and what you're doing—"He's living a good life, maybe *I* should try it." It's a peaceful movement, living your life on a daily basis, not trying to force someone to live your life or your ideas.

Tony had dreams of making sXe a more organized movement that would reach out beyond hardcore: "I think the basic ideology has nothing to do with the music. The music is just a part of what it is."

Going Drug Free—Losing the Label

As they age, some sXers become ever more proud of the movement and continue to claim the sXe identity. They strive to set an example for younger kids in the scene. Others, however, shed the label of sXe for various reasons and adopt a "drug-free" classification, remaining abstinent from drugs and alcohol, but distancing themselves from the baggage the identity carries.[5] The decision is not an easy one, as Megan attested:

> You know, lately I've been thinking a lot of how I don't really like many of the sXe kids out here anymore. Not because of their values or whatever, but social, like, interactions and stuff. I'm like: "Why am I still identifying myself with these people?" I'm getting to the point where I'm like: "Yes, I am drug free, I don't drink, I don't do this, that, and the other thing. But do I *really* want to be labeled with these people anymore?" I don't know. So, what's keeping me in this? Not much, right now [laughs]. . . . But I know this way of life is right

for me. I have more fun. I know that I don't need that stuff at all. I just feel like it's me. I don't have any desire to go out and get drunk *at all.*

Clarke's (2003) study of anarchist punks revealed that some contemporary punks have given up not only the spectacular punk style and music but also the very *name* "punk." Those who choose to abandon the label still feel strongly about the movement's ideals, yet refuse to be compartmentalized into a tidy stylistic or ideological box. Many older sXers find labels in general limiting. After prolonged and careful reflection, Alec, still drug-free at age thirty, decided he no longer identified with sXe:

RH: Do you still identify yourself with sXe?

Alec: Not really. Obviously there's a part of me that always will be. There's nothing I can do about that—it's my history, for years. But if somebody asks . . . it happens a lot . . . I'll go to the bars and somebody will say, "Hey, let me get you a drink." I'll be like, "Uh, root beer." And they're like, "Are you straight edge?!" My first reaction is almost to say yes, but I always go, "I'm drug free." Straight edge is such a negative thing to me. In a few years it won't be again. But for me, saying you're sXe is like saying you're part of some boys' club. I don't really need, at thirty especially, I don't really need a label like that.

Jerry, bass player for a popular band from Salt Lake City, explained how he was beginning to outgrow the sXe label as well:

Straight edge to me is not a label. Straight edge to me is not something I place on myself so I can go, "Hey buddy. I'm straight edge, you know that? I'm fuckin' bad." It's not like that at all. It's to the point I'm almost twenty-four, next month I'll be twenty-four years old, and I've been doing this for a long time. Honestly, to tell you the truth, I don't need a label. I'm not discrediting straight edge, I'm not discrediting the kids and the younger kids. I'll always respect it; I'll always think there's a place for the younger kids. But for me, I'm still drug free, I'm still alcohol free, and I'm still straight edge, but I don't like to generalize. It's nothing that I would go up to people and say, "Man, I'm straight edge! Man, I'm nailed to the X." I very rarely wear X's anymore, but I have them tattooed on my body and that's always gonna be there, you know what I mean? My convictions for straight edge, for the philosophies behind straight edge, are true. The label so much . . . I'm sort of, in a sense, and this might sound stupid to some kids, but I'm kind of, in a way, outgrowing the label itself.

Incidentally, approximately one year after I conducted this interview, Jerry began occasionally drinking.

Younger sXers, in particular, are deeply suspicious of people who claim "drug-free" rather than sXe, believing drug-free is one step away from selling out. Indeed, many of the drug-free individuals in the Denver scene eventually began using, although almost always in moderation. However, several maintain the drug-free lifestyle as strictly as they would have had they remained sXe. They are simply uncomfortable identifying with a movement containing elements (such as crews, hypermasculinity) they dislike, as George explained:

> It really is sad that I maybe don't feel comfortable identifying as sXe. I think for every great sXe kid out there, there [are] some kids that I can't trust to identify, to use the same word that they do. I'm not trying to totally be negative on sXe or anything, but it's definitely something, maybe like anything, as any underground movement grows, there are gonna be people that are alienated from that movement. While I like to think that I don't feel alienated . . . I don't *hate* sXe. If I was sXe and still don't drink or smoke and I hated sXe, I think that would be a little counterproductive. But I still live my life by example. Lead by example, lead by example, lead by example. If you can lead by example and be seen by the drinkers or the smokers or whatever, as someone who's getting things done, being positive, is totally OK with yourself, has a good time in life and everything, then that's the one-hundred-percent goal for me. I still feel I'm doing sXe's legwork. I still think I'm doing a lot of that. I just personally can't . . . I don't necessarily right away tell people, "I'm sXe." I think it's a word that sometimes, especially by people newer to the movement, it gets thrown around maybe a little too loosely among those who aren't as educated in sXe.

Like George, Kyle sometimes resisted the sXe label. However, he accepted that sXe was part of who he was and how others perceived him. Ultimately, he continued claiming sXe rather than drug free because he felt spreading the message was important:

> Kyle: To me, sXe is not drinking, not doing drugs, staying sober. To me right now, it doesn't mean a lot . . . as much as it used to. When

I first got into it, I needed it, I think. I needed it to tell people, to say: "This is how I am." Now, it's just like a label that people use on me. I don't use it as much as people use it for me. I've kind of grown out of it, saying "I'm sXe." Now everybody just kind of knows. I still put X's on my hands if I go out to a show, and I have patches and pins just cause they're fun. It's a way to talk to people without a verbal communication.

RH: Even though the label doesn't mean as much to you anymore, it's still important to you?

Kyle: It's still important to me. It's how I live my life. It's the best label that fits me. I mean, I could just say: "I don't drink," but that would just be "I don't drink." Since I stand up for that belief and tell people "You don't have to drink," I think sXe is a label that fits me. Because it is a word that means you stand up for what you believe in, you don't just *do* what you believe in.

From Fashion to Philosophy

I'm not in it for the fashion / Not in it for the fame / For you it's just a game / And in my mind it's true / But when the trend leaves this scene / Where will that take you? . . . REASON FOR THE LIFE I LIVE TRYING TO BE POSITIVE.

—"Reason" by Dutch band Vitamin X, date uncertain

At the beginning of their sXe careers, youth take great pains to "look the part" of sXers. They consistently wear shirts bearing the logos of popular bands, style their hair according to the latest hardcore fashion, acquire new tattoos, wear the latest hardcore fashion (such as baggy or tight pants, depending upon the era), and sport X's on their hands. New participants are very particular about the "rules," and the scene is central to their social life. The deviant image and opportunity to feel acceptance from like-minded peers are part of many sXers' initial attraction to the movement, as Maggie alluded to: "Yeah. I'd wear X's all the time. I'd wear X's to school [laughs]. I'd always bring it up, like, 'I'm sXe, I'm better than that' [laughs]." Luke, the twenty-eight-year-old tattoo artist who had been married for several years, explained that while sXe was first a group to feel cool about belonging to, his understanding of sXe eventually broadened into a lifestyle:

At first it was kind of like an image thing. It looks cool. It's against everything that high school is about. I got into it that way. Obviously later on I found out that it was more of a positive lifestyle, not just something I was already doing at the time.

For older sXers, the identity becomes less about following the fashion and a set of rules than about practicing a general philosophy of "positivity." Straight edge became a way of life rather than an end in itself. Andes (1998) calls this stage in subcultural life "transcendence," when the individual no longer identifies specifically with the style or community but more with the values and ideals. This philosophy encourages sXers to take up political causes (such as vegetarianism, animal rights, antisexism, and antiracism), vigorously pursue their goals, and simply re-examine many arenas of their lives. Kevin, the martial artist, revealed that sXe had encouraged him to question how he lived his life in a broad sense beyond drug and alcohol use:

It was like being sXe stopped being specific things, it stopped being "I shouldn't do X substance, I shouldn't do this practice because it is weak or against my code." Being sXe stopped being a specific dogma and started being a view of being strong. So I stopped doing the things that were weak. Because of that I had to change how I handled my personal affairs, I had to change how I handled my love interests, I had to change political beliefs, and how I deal with environmental issues. All this shit came about as a result of that idea. . . . But I think on a deeper level it became about being strong. I think that all the people who are *really* sXe, the people who are sincere, also have a lot of other things in their life. Because that expression of strength and that expression of trying to become better and stronger and do the right thing and do the strong thing and not be addicted and weak, I think it comes out in other areas. If you find somebody that's really sXe and has been for a while, you'll see a development in their growth. Almost everybody started off "We don't drink, we don't smoke, we don't do drugs" and then they go vegan, then they got militant, or then they got political, or whatever. I think it's a natural outgrowth of it because you start examining things. . . . Straight edge grew to a different level, it was more like a *lifestyle* and not so much a creed, a set of rules that you live your life by and anything out of the rules is OK. It started being like a different way to live. . . . That's what I realized I was trying to achieve.

I wasn't trying to be drug free; I was trying to be strong. To me that meant being drug free as well. But then sXe became a banner, not so much about "Look I'm drug free," or "Look what I *don't* do." It became like a banner: "Look how I *live*."

In addition to changing consciousness around substance use/abuse, participants claim that the movement motivates them to pursue their dreams and achieve their goals. For many older sXers, this message eventually supersedes sXe's antidrug message; their understanding of their involvement encompasses much more than living a clean life. Again, for some, once they feel confident in their determination to live meaningful lives on their own terms, they withdraw from sXe. Keith, twenty-eight, expressed these sentiments:

I was definitely attracted to the determination of straight edge. It fit my disposition better then the defeatist attitude of most punk bands. I hated my home town. I hated my social environment. I hated school. But I knew that getting drugged up and ruining my future would leave me trapped in that setting! The message of sXe told me to fight and transcend my environment. Songs like "Always Try" by Bold and "Flame Still Burns" by Youth of Today said more to me than any punk rock record. The straight edge message was almost secondary to me. In my mind, that was implied. I appreciated sXe's message of accomplishing everything you want to accomplish regardless of what stands in your way. The idea that you couldn't do that drunk/stoned was implicit and understood. . . . I no longer consider myself sXe. I had my first drink of alcohol in August of last year. I made the decision when I was sent to England for a week for my work. It was my first time there and I felt that I wanted to enjoy the environment as it exists. When in Rome . . . So all by myself I went to pub and ordered fish 'n' chips with a pint of Guinness. Since then, I've had occasional drinks. A glass of wine with my wife on our anniversary, etc. The main idea remains the same, though. I'm not out drinking every night. I'm not sitting in front of the TV with a six pack. That's not how I choose to spend my life.

At age twenty-three, Tony left the hardcore scene entirely for several years though he remained sXe even as a DJ in the club and rave scene:

I couldn't deal with the kids that [thought] hardcore was it, hardcore was everything they listened to. That couldn't open their minds to anything new. . . . I wanna be an sXe kid who has absolutely nothing to do with hardcore. That was my push at the time to say: "Why can't I be sXe and not listen to hardcore music?" . . . I felt that sXe needed to go to a whole new level and I was going to try to take myself to that level. . . . I said: "I'm gonna take off from hardcore and see if I could really be sXe without that music." I realized sXe isn't about those things; sXe is about what you believe on the inside.

By age twenty-eight, Tony, still sXe, had rejoined the hardcore scene while still maintaining a diversity of musical and stylistic interests.

Carrying the Flag, Setting an Example

People change everyday / Some walk their own way / But when these changes come to bring us down / We have got to stick together, stand our ground.

—"Now or Never" by Bold, 1988

Finally, for many older sXers, setting a positive example for younger kids is an important part of their ongoing commitment to sXe. They remember looking up to older members of the scene, respecting those that stayed true to sXe and feeling let down by those who left the lifestyle behind. They continue claiming sXe in part to remain true to their word. Straight edge, often framed as an "oath," "promise," or "pledge," implies that leaving the scene is a personal failure; many sXers do not want to leave this example for others to follow. For Kevin, sXe was an ideal that transcended his own experience. With his trademark focus on personal strength, he explained why he remained sXe:

It's important that I be a good example of it. That's also another reason I can't lose my commitment because it might allow a fifteen-year-old kid that I could have otherwise affected and be the one thing that saves that kid's life. But if he sees me drinkin' a beer after the fight, maybe he loses his passion. Maybe he's not as moved by my level of commitment and therefore not as inspired to achieve that level of commitment. I can't . . . this fuckin' [tattoo] on my back takes up my whole back and I feel like I'm the guy in the war carrying the flag. And the flag *can't* hit the ground. If you gotta put your gun down to pick that flag up and get shot, you're gonna fuckin' carry that flag. That's the idea to me. I could theoretically put it down and lose my integrity or my self-respect. I could live a strong life and not have the commitment to sXe that I have. Which is why

12. Seattle band Champion, one of the most popular sXe bands in 2005, plays a show at a church in Boston, rejuvenating youth crew style hardcore for a new generation. Photo by Todd Pollock.

a lot of older kids get out of it. But I just can't let the flag down. I gotta carry it so it never stops. For me or for other people.

Kevin wasn't the only one to worry about the impact leaving sXe might have on younger kids. Maggie implied that the legitimacy of the movement depended upon at least *some* members carrying on into their late twenties:

After a while, you're like an example to the young kids. If *you* can't stick with it, why would they? Why would they even start? When I see a twenty-five-year-old give it up for no reason, it's just like, "Wow . . . you're twenty-five and you can't do it anymore?" It's not hard. I don't see it as a hard thing to do. The young kids look at you and are like, "What's the point in doing it now if when I'm twenty-five I'm just going to give it up?" Or twenty-one, or eighteen, or whatever.

Luke, the tattoo artist, explained how his understanding of sXe shifted toward being a role model. Like Maggie, he had been more "militant" when he was younger, and only gradually came to focus on setting an example:

Back then, you are thinking forever because you're stubborn. "Hell yeah, I'm going to do this forever." But you're not thinking in terms of like . . . I definitely didn't think I'd be married and trying to be any-where near a role model. I think that's exactly what it turned into for me. I want to set an example, even for just younger kids at shows that I see. I definitely want to lead by example. Whereas before it was just like . . . I'd still be kind of a delinquent, I'd just be drug free. Now it's like, there's a lot more to life than running around being obnoxious and just happening to be drug free, too. Back then, I didn't give a crap, as long as I wasn't drinking or smoking.

Initially, few sXers consider setting an example for other sXe kids as a *central* meaning for their involvement. However, as they age, being a role model to younger kids becomes much more meaningful.

Conclusion

A popular misconception holds that every sXe kid eventually sells out. Indeed, prior to my research, I believed that only a very, very few kids re-main sXe into their thirties. I was wrong. Certainly, the majority of sXers eventually leave the scene and the identity behind; it's true that most people grow out of their youthful subcultures in one way or another. However, just because an older kid shows up to shows less often doesn't mean she or he is gone for good. Four members of Denver sXe band the Mutiny are in their mid- to late-twenties, including a passenger airline pi-lot, a biomedical research assistant applying to med school, a medical re-searcher, and an investigator for the U.S. government. Who can say how many sXers (or punks, riot grrrls, and so on) are out there, disguised as more-or-less everyday folks, but living their subcultural values in their own way?

As they age in the "scene," members of subcultures face more choices than simply exiting the group or maintaining their previous involvement. Many pass through a phase of deep reflection and discouragement about the scene. Yet not all members drop out entirely; indeed, most find new expressions for their subcultural values as their involvement wanes. They create new meanings and incorporate new understandings that are com-patible with life outside of the subculture. Just because they tend to be less outspoken, less visible, and less active in the scene than their younger counterparts does not mean their commitment is any less real. The irony may be that as their involvement decreases their commitment to the orig-inal ideals actually goes up.

COMMERCIALIZATION, THE INTERNET, AND THE CULTIC MILIEU

When I was growing up, I couldn't imagine punk and hardcore bands making it big. Typical shows had fifty kids, and coloring your hair actually made you *dangerous* in the eyes of school administrators. Even if the mainstream had paid us any attention, we didn't want it and we didn't want other people to like *our* music. Part of hardcore's appeal was that members had a sense of ownership of the scene. The scene was small enough that it felt like a community; we believed we were part of an incredible underground secret society that most people had no idea existed. At its best, it was like a little haven where you could be yourself and feel like you were doing something to *resist* the bland, inauthentic, impersonal, conventional world. Then in 1992, as I graduated from high school, the breakthrough success of Seattle-based grunge band Nirvana's *Nevermind* record made "alternative" music hip and fashionable to the mainstream. Around the same time, heavy metal band Metallica achieved greater popularity, opening the door for more extreme brands of metal. Suddenly kids in small-town South Dakota, many of whom never had access to much music besides Top 40, were putting down Bon Jovi and picking up Jane's Addiction. Through the nineties, punk and metal videos achieved greater rotation on MTV, and radio stations couldn't play enough Red Hot Chili Peppers and Soundgarden. By 2005, pop-punk band Green Day and metalcore bands Hatebreed and Killswitch Engage were nominated for Grammy Awards,[1] a sure sign of the music's widespread popularity. Instead of making fun of the punks, many of the cool kids are *becoming* punks, and hardcore is achieving its greatest popularity ever.

The mainstream acceptance of punk, metal, and, to a lesser extent, hardcore, calls into question these subcultures' capacities to offer some kind of meaningful, or even political, alternative to more conventional popular culture. As I complete this writing in 2005, the Denver scene continues to grow and change. Compared to punk, sXe has proven relatively resistant, though not immune, to commercialization and cooptation. Perhaps the music and lifestyle are simply too extreme to make a full-fledged leap into the mainstream world. Karl Buechner of Earth Crisis said:

I don't think sXe or veganism . . . they're lifetime commitments to sobriety or to try and be a peaceful person. That's never going to be trendy or marketable. I don't think we need to worry about that. Anything that involves a commitment contrasts a trend, so it's not something they could really sell. They could try, but it would be futile.

Hardcore music, however, continues to gain popularity, allowing an increasing number of bands to make a modest living through their music. The underground music scene thrives despite (or perhaps because of) media monopolization and corporate consolidation. Whereas in the eighties a few nationally known bands toured at any given time, now dozens of bands are constantly on the road. Both Revelation and Victory Records have long ago expanded beyond the hardcore/sXe sound into a variety of musical genres, and dozens of other independent labels promote the next underground sensations.

Beginning around 2002 and continuing as I write this, sXe is experiencing a slight lull in membership, leadership, and ideas. The resurgence of indie rock, pop punk, and emo music (such as the Strokes, Saves the Day, Modest Mouse, Thursday, AFI, Dashboard Confessional, Taking Back Sunday, Sum 41, the White Stripes) has captured the attention of many youth, sXe and non-sXe. It has become increasingly acceptable to enjoy a variety of music and it is not uncommon to see hordes of hardcore kids at popular positive rocker Andrew W. K.'s shows or concerts by legendary metal act Iron Maiden. At any given show, an sXe band might share the stage with a metal band, a punk band, or a post-core group. Though sXe kids abound, they have arguably lost a bit of their distinct identity. Indeed, many sXers are visually indistinguishable from their indie rocker peers, wearing tight black shirts, growing out and dyeing their hair black, and wearing backpacks or carrier bags covered with tiny buttons depicting their favorite bands. More importantly, no nationally recognized sXe bands command the respect that Youth of Today, Earth Crisis, and Strife did in their times. Bands such as Seattle's Champion and California's Throwdown tour extensively and attract large crowds, yet there is a shortage of distinct stylistic and substantive innovations to capture the imaginations of potential participants and set sXe apart from other youth subcultures. Straight edge will no doubt survive its current lull as it has in the past (for instance, in 1991–1992) and eventually experience a resurgence of interest. The movement's longevity is at least partial proof that it occupies a meaningful place in youth culture. In the near future an individual or band will likely bring forth a new innovation to reinvigorate the scene, and reunion shows (Youth of Today, Bold, 108, Good Clean Fun, Trial) have spurred interest.

Straight edge, like virtually every other youth subculture, has had to grapple with commercialization and "competition" with other subcultures. Subculturists often condemn corporate involvement in their scenes, but the pull of a secure livelihood is difficult to resist. Likewise, they acknowledge the benefits and drawbacks of the Internet as well as blending with other scenes. Straight edgers' reactions to commercialization and their use of the Internet inform my later reflections on how sXe fits into alternative culture, or the "cultic milieu."

Commericalization

I've seen kids hungry for their idols / Standing in front of club / They all wear just the same clothes / To follow their music revolution . . . / You don't need myself / To tell you how to live / Don't be a follower / Of every latest trend / All those fucking rock stars / Just want to sell their crap / So take your skate and fuck them all / Be punk the leader of your own / Just imitating your heroes / Just following your flock of sheeps / Just buying your revolution / In nearest skate shop changing your mind / By pierce on your head / If this is hardcore now / Just kill your hero . . . today.

—"Kill Your Hero" by Czech band Underfire, 1999

From the late 1990s to the early 2000s, hardcore music, particularly *metal*-influenced hardcore, became increasingly commercial: Hatebreed toured with eminent metal band Slayer, played Ozzfest, and singer Jamey Jasta hosted MTV2's *Headbanger's Ball* program; California sXe band Eighteen Visions signed with Epic Records; Poison the Well signed with Atlantic; Killswitch Engage, including their sXe singer Howard Jones, toured with popular nu-metal band Slipknot; and Snapcase, an sXe band formed in the early 1990s, packed large venues and toured the world before finally calling it quits in 2004. Many bands now produce music videos, once considered the domain only of corporate sellouts.[2] As bands moved away from the DIY ethic to become somewhat more commercially successful, many downplayed their ties to sXe (Earth Crisis was a notable exception). Whereas in the past finding the latest hardcore music meant frequenting a local independent record store, buying from a distro at a show, or ordering from a fanzine, by the 2000s national chain stores such as Best Buy and Target carried a substantial selection, and with Amazon.com, owning the latest hardcore CD was just a mouse

TABLE 1. MAINSTREAM REALITY VERSUS DIY HARDCORE IDEALS

Mainstream	*Hardcore*
Impersonal (such as barriers at shows)	Personal relationships
Musicians = professional performers	Musicians = fans
Commercial business	Art
Commodity	Community
Professionalization (such as promoters)	DIY

click away. These developments potentially signaled the death of DIY sXe hardcore.

Straight edge has always had a commercial side. Many sXers collect records and bands often press variations to meet the collectors' demands, releasing a limited number on colored vinyl. If the music is popular enough to require later repressings, the first pressings increase in value. Collectors buy, sell, and trade records through 'zines and, more often, the Internet. Yet this sort of commercialization still reflects the DIY roots of the scene. When more mainstream media and the culture industry become involved, professionals (many of whom have some roots in the scene) often replace local DIY entrepreneurs.

Straight edgers are ambivalent about the growing popularity of hardcore. Most don't mind that more bands are able to make some kind of living off of their music. (To my knowledge, very, very few bands are getting rich off of hardcore.) At the same time, they question the convictions and authenticity of highly commercial bands that claim hardcore or sXe roots. They feel participating in hardcore has become too "easy;" kids no longer have to work at it. Aaron Bedard, singer of popular Massachusetts band Bane (a band many sXe kids felt epitomized the hardcore ethic) expressed his uneasiness with the commercialization of hardcore in an interview with a Denver 'zine:

> It just always scares me a little bit to see that stuff start to get commercialized, ya know? To see it start to get tainted and . . . because it's such like our thing, ya know? It's just like this thing that we have that the whole rest of the world doesn't understand. . . . And this is our heart, this is our blood, this is our whole lives and it gets kind of scary to think that its gonna be like this easy . . . marketable thing that any kid can sorta like pick up on and make his own. Like to be a hardcore kid, you still have to like work at it. . . . When I see these

dudes on fuckin' MTV jumping around with straight edge shirts on, it scares me a little bit.

Many sXers also have mixed feelings about bands signing to major labels. Some believe the exposure is good while others see signing with big labels as a betrayal of the DIY ethic. Still others find a middle ground where going major is OK so long as the band then helps other bands, doesn't forget its roots, and doesn't change its style to accommodate record executives. Darren, being in a touring band, was supportive of bands signing to a major but was wary of being exploited: "I think selling out would be completely altering your sound for someone else. But if you're signing to a major label, the main concern should be that you're not getting screwed over. Everyone knows how major labels can be." A post on a hardcore site in reaction to the Sounds of the Underground (a hardcore/metal bill similar to Ozzfest) tour showed the mixed feelings many kids have when bands become successful.

> I've seen half of those bands at VFW halls 2–4 years ago, and I want those days back. If I saw a kid with a Poison the Well shirt on, and god forbid a fucking Unearth shirt on in 2000, that was the rarest of the rare. Now you can get an entire wardrobe of these bands at Hot Topic. I'm glad that these bands are getting popular and can make some sort of living doing what they love, but I dunno, it always kinda sucks when bands and moreover an entire genre of music that's a personal part of your life move into the mainstream. It's like something is taken away from you. (http://www.milehighhardcore .com, viewed 6/8/2005)

Cassell judged the distinction between hardcore and other bands by the bands' relationship with fans and the DIY ethic. If a band no longer takes time to interact with fans, they are no longer hardcore: "As soon as a band gets escorted in from their bus and doesn't help load their own equipment they are not hardcore." Through no particular intent, however, a band may gain widespread popularity and suddenly be playing in front of thousands of kids, making personal interaction unlikely. Bands then face the uneasy balance of continually proving their authenticity to their initial (underground) fan base and enjoying their newfound success.

13. The Memphis hardcore "family," goofing off and flashing "gang" signs. Photo by Amanda Raney.

Media

The impact of mainstream popularity and media attention on subcultures and their potential to be subversive has long interested scholars. The popular media tend to first demonize subcultures as alienated, delinquent youth, before eventually incorporating and absorbing them into the mainstream (Cohen 1972). Clarke (1986) claimed that subcultural style goes through two processes: diffusion and defusion. As the popularity of a style grows, it is diffused throughout the public, spreading to other regions via television, magazines, and now the Internet. As a style is diffused it is also *defused,* that is stripped of its power to meaningfully challenge mainstream culture. In this case, it seems media attention and commercialization destroys the authenticity of the subculture by making it a meaningless commodity. Writing about punk, Clark (2003:223–224) suggests that as the mainstream gradually becomes "acclimatized" to a spectacular subculture's shocking style the group loses its ability to "shock and dismay":

> In this climate, constrained by the discourse of subculture, deviation from the norm ain't what it used to be. Deviation from the norm

seems, well, normal. It is allegedly common for a young person to choose a prefab subculture off the rack, wear it for a few years, then rejoin with the 'mainstream' culture that they never really left at all. Perhaps the result of our autopsy will show that subculture (of the young, dissident, costumed kind) has become a useful part of the status quo, and less useful for harbouring discontent. For these reasons we can melodramatically pronounce that subculture is dead.

Despite (or perhaps because of) the hyper-commercialization of subculture, Clark insists that truly authentic punks have traded spectacular resistance to the mainstream for resistance in daily life, much like the older sXers I described in the previous chapter. Clark claims, "Having been forced, as it were, out of a costume and music-based clique, punk is evolving into one of the most powerful political forces in North America and Europe, making its presence felt in the Battle of Seattle (1999), Quebec City (2001), EarthFirst!, Reclaim the Streets, and in variety of anti-corporate movements" (ibid.:234). Subcultures may have "died," but declaring that subcultures have become completely depoliticized and absorbed into the mainstream ignores the fact that youth recognize and react to the "normalization" of subcultures. Recognizing the power of commercial culture to co-opt subcultural style, some youth circumvent the problem by focusing on the core values rather than style. Gosling (2004:168) points out, "to a large extent the development of the underground punk scene was a reaction of disappointment with 'mainstream' punk." As the Clash and the Sex Pistols gained mainstream attention, later bands Dead Kennedys, Crass, Minor Threat, and others reinvigorated the underground.

It took nearly fifteen years for the mainstream media to take more than a passing notice of sXe and even then the attention was mixed. Some applauded the movement for its stand on drugs and sex, but the national news especially picked up stories about Salt Lake City's scene and the "gang" label spread. The introduction to this article is fairly typical (AP April 29, 1997):

LOGAN, Utah—Cache Valley law enforcement officials are wary of a group of teenagers—part of a nationwide movement called "straight edge"—who pressure other young people not to take drugs. . . . [Head of Cache County sheriff's gang unit Wayne] Lewis said the movement is dangerously close to becoming a street gang because straight-edgers have been linked to quasi-terrorist groups like the Animal Liberation Front, and have been known to beat up people who don't agree with them.

Many stories explain that only a small minority of sXers is violent and then go on to focus exclusively on that small minority. The media does not necessarily defuse or destroy subcultures. Building on the work of Thornton (1995) and Osgerby (1998), Muggleton (2000) claims that the media and commercialization *create* rather than *destroy* subcultures by bringing together and labeling unconnected individuals to form a coherent group.[3] In particular, local niche media, such as 'zines and independent music catalogs, can help solidify a scene; rather than defusing the subversive potential of subcultures, media can bring cohesion to a formerly scattered group. A subculture may not even *be* a subculture until the media label it so. This seems evident for sXe in the late 1990s. As mass media took notice of the movement, Earth Crisis, in particular, gained a platform for their drug free, vegan message. As I have previously mentioned, many Denver sXers joined the movement at this time, some literally after seeing sXe covered on MTV or *ABC News*. However, sXe has been a subculture for twenty-five years despite relatively little *mainstream* media coverage; the DIY media of 'zines, records, and websites have done more to bring coherence to sXe. By and large it seems that the increasing attention paid to metalcore, emo, and indie rock bands has not led to a similar growth in sXe.

Straight edgers struggle with the problem of the scene's popularity as a result of media exposure. Some look forward to a time when sXe will gain greater visibility and numbers, wanting as many kids as possible to be exposed to the movement's ideals. Others jealously guard the scene's underground tradition, fearing that numbers alone will dilute, distort, and weaken the meaning behind sXe.

Fashion/Style

Straight edge has gone through more than its share of fashions. Longtime scenesters remember the Champion hoodies, Krishna beads, camouflage pants, sports jerseys, and bandanas popular in times gone by. A few of today's kids dress in *ironic chic,* purposely wearing silly shirts of bands they do not really like (or at best are guilty pleasures)—shirts bearing the names and logos of hair metal or heavy metal bands such as Pantera, Whitesnake, and Guns N' Roses are popular. Youth music subcultures have always been characterized by their style (Hebdige 1979) and commodification of subversive style is nothing new. Ken Gelder (1997:374) writes, "Style is the most self-absorbing feature of a subculture. . . . It is also highly vulnerable to commodification, easily sliding into the more diffused realm of 'fashion'." Indeed, some scholars have characterized youth subcultures primarily in terms of their consumerism (Clarke 1975). However, while the early teddy boy, punk, mod, and goth styles were formerly marketed to kids through small boutiques and independent shops, now subcultural style is mass marketed via the Internet and suburban shopping malls in stores such as Hot Topic.

Hot Topic is the nation's largest chain of subculture shops, with over five-hundred stores in malls across the country. The store sells merchandise to meet the demands of a variety of subcultures. Shoppers enter a store where goth leather hangs next to Hello Kitty figures, and heavy metal t-shirts sit by hipster kitsch such as Cabbage Patch Kids lunchboxes. The chain's website asks, "What's your scene?" and then provides the categories—club, gothic, lounge, punk, street, rockabilly, indie—as if with the click of the mouse aspiring subculturists could purchase a starter kit for the scene of their choice (www.hottopic.com, viewed 11/11/03). Hot Topic has at various times carried sXe t-shirts; buttons; and small, canvas patches and they sponsored a stage at the 2004 Hellfest event. While, for the most part, sXe has remained below the radar of most mainstream youth, Hot Topic has the potential to expose even more kids to the movement, though it appears that this potential hasn't been realized.

On the one hand, Hot Topic *may* broaden the subcultural possibilities of youth in suburban and rural areas by exposing them to a variety of styles and music. On the other hand, the chain routinizes and standardizes subcultures into neatly purchasable packages. Anyone may be able to look the part of a punk, but without experiencing an underground punk show, any understanding of punk, according to insiders, is incomplete; there is much more to being punk, rockabilly, goth, sXe, or whatever than the look and even the music. Subculturists frequently used Hot Topic as yet another signifier of authenticity. Most "true" subculturists would never shop for their merch at a suburban mall—frequenting and supporting the local independent record store and buying band shirts at shows separated the "real" sXers from the pretenders. Never interested in wearing the latest band shirt, Kate disliked Hot Topic and the fashionable side of hardcore. She was wary of hardcore fashion trumping hardcore politics, but did not believe that fashion had replaced what she saw as the more crucial aspects of the movement:

> I see kids that were super-pumped about all these different movements and now all they care about is their clothes and looking a certain way. That's too bad when you see that happen to people. But there's so many people that it hasn't happened to; that's part of the reason I still love it.

TABLE 2. MOST TO LEAST AUTHENTIC WAYS OF ACQUIRING A RARE SXE SHIRT

MOST	You were at the show.
	A friend gave it or traded it to you.
	You purchased it at your local independent music shop.
	You bought it off eBay for an exorbitant amount of money.
Least	You bought a reproduced shirt of a band that broke up ten years ago (seminal goth-punk band Misfits shirts are among the most popular).

Having the right shirt is not enough to demonstrate authenticity; how one acquires the shirt holds just as much significance. One may be able to purchase one's way into a subculture; purchasing true authenticity, however, proves more difficult.

Subcultures have often taken mainstream commercial icons and transformed them into subcultural statements. One Denver sXer had a shirt that read "Straight Edge—Can't Beat the Real Thing" written in the Coca-Cola logo. Another shirt features straight edge written in Star Wars logo lettering and still another parodies the Adidas brand. In an ironic turn, the shoe company Nike created an advertisement based upon the Minor Threat LP jacket, showing a young punk sitting on a stoop (wearing Nikes), shaved head down and skateboard by his side.[4] The ad, using the same font, replaces "Minor Threat" with "Major Threat" and features the XXX logo complete with bars underneath. Nike has a history of co-opting subcultures and protest movements critical of its use of sweatshop labor, using 'zines and fake countercultures to advertise their products. Statements of disgust from Dischord Records and Minor Threat fans apparently convinced Nike to drop the ad, but counterculture chic continues to sell.

The Internet

U spend your days and nights online, your website makes U proud. But if U had a single friend at all they would LOL. Well it seems I may have crossed the line, I've gone and made U pissed. Now UR going to take me off your buddy list. If you can't get a date because you live with your mom, then you'll feel right at home at Loserdotcom. If you don't have a life but you have plenty of ROM, then you'll feel right at home at Loserdotcom. U tell me that your sex life, it has not been bland, since U learned how to click and type with just 1 hand. UR a keyboard Casanova, UR a Digital Don Juan, UR a chat room Romeo and U want to get it on. URL IRC MSN HTTP AOL ISP LOS ERUB. I guess U can't see what is wrong, you've got your modem and your mouse and U think you've got it going on. U once had a life but it is gone. www.loser.com.

—"Loserdotcom" by Good Clean Fun, 1999

Just as the commercialization of subcultures has a variety of effects and meanings for members, so does the Internet. The World Wide Web provides unprecedented access to the music and history of subcultures as well as a much more efficient way to network with sXers across the United States and even around the world (Wilson and Atkinson 2005). Booking shows, signing and promoting bands, and finding venues are all easier with the advent of email. For these reasons, many sXers believe the Internet has greatly benefited the underground music scene.

The Internet plays a significant role in subcultures including goth, alternative country, and Phish fans, not to mention Star Trek and Star Wars fans, online gamers, and hackers (Hodkinson 2002; Lee and Peterson 2004; Ross 2000; Shields 2003; Smith and Kollack 1999; Thomas 2002). Participants create online communities, and some interact on a daily basis. If some sense of community is central to subcultures, how does *virtual* community compare to communities centered around a physical location? Internet chat rooms can be "subcultural spaces" (Bassett 1991) in which members socialize much as they might at a club, record store, or pub. Most of the Denver sXers have access to the Internet and many spend considerable time perusing websites, frequenting sXe-themed chat rooms, trading and buying records, and communicating with sXe and hardcore friends. Milehighhardcore.com, created and maintained by a young woman in the scene, keeps locals informed of shows, new music, and other scene events as well as providing space to gossip, share ideas, and build community. Message boards provide a forum to discuss the movement's values, such as the benefits of a vegetarian/vegan diet, the merits of hardcore/metal festivals, and various political issues. Polls are exceptionally popular, including questions ranging from "Are you vegetarian?" and "Who will you vote for in the next election?" to "What are the top five sXe hardcore records?" and "What is your favorite brand of shoe?" For many sXers, being part of an online community is a pleasant pastime. A significant number, however, feel at least some ambivalence about the changes brought on by the Internet. Straight edgers such as Andy appreciate how the Internet makes the scene more accessible and streamlines the process of booking tours but also believe something is lost in translation:

It's just made every band a lot easier to have their message spread. Everybody who has a computer or who has access to a computer can hear it no matter where they are in the world. Which is awesome for the scene. But it also adds for the kids who are actually in the cities with a lot of shows and good bands, it makes them not care as much, not have to go to a show to buy a CD or see what else is coming out. Nobody has a decent distro anymore. It's horrible. I miss the days where you could go back into the room and there was the one guy with forty-million fucking crates full of any record that you wanted. Nobody does that anymore. It's kind of sad. Kind of the end of an era.

It is worth noting that some of the distros have simply moved online, but somehow this feels less DIY, less authentic to some older sXers. Other sXers who participate primarily online claim *they* are more authentic than direct participants in the hardcore scene, precisely because they focus more on sXe values rather than music and fashions (Williams and Copes 2005).

The Internet has also magnified the hardcore rumor mill and provided a new forum to criticize and attack others ("flaming," in Internet jargon). Scene gossip, what I call "hardcore hearsay," is no longer limited to one's local scene. Each day, dozens of sXe and hardcore-related chat rooms and message boards fill with gossip about scenesters and band members. Who has sold out, who slept with whom, and which band is breaking up or re-forming provide continual material for speculation. Straight edgers nearly universally complain about Internet rumors, yet many still participate. In an interview with a hardcore 'zine,[5] Ed McKirdy of Face the Enemy said:

> I am honestly sick of the Internet, and the rumors and the gossip and the bullshit that the Internet has. The ability to hide behind a computer and say anything you want about anybody regardless of having to stand behind anything you say or face them face to face is shit. It's really taken a lot of fun out of hardcore.

Ed's band mate Tim McMahon weighed the Internet's consequences:

> It's kind of a two-way street with the Internet. In one way, it's incredible because all kinds of new kids will get on the Internet and find out about all these bands and communicate with people all around the world. There's a lot of positive things that can come out of the Internet. But Ed's right that a lot of people take advantage of the fact that you're just a faceless . . .

Darren used the Internet to announce his band's shows and to sell records, but the anonymity of "shit-talkers" frustrated him:

Even in the short time I've been around, honestly two or three years, the Internet has *completely changed* the way kids go about hardcore. The shit-talking on message boards is completely ridiculous. People have like their personas and feel like they can say whatever they want and not have consequences for their actions. Before that, if you said something to offend someone, they'd let you know, whether it was a punch in the face or a look. On the Internet it seems like kids can go back and forth and—this sounds corny—hurt each others' feelings. People take stabs at things, personal, personal things. Personally I see no reason for it. It wasn't like that even two to three years ago.

One site, www.howsyouredge.com, even offers a sellout list where people can post the names of former sXers and the circumstances under which they sold out. This online shaming may serve as another method of informal social control.

Sites and services such as Friendster, Makeoutclub.com, and Myspace foster online communities of people (not just sXers) from all over the United States. Members of such sites create profiles describing their interests, from music to books to hobbies, and create lists of friends with whom they regularly interact. Several Denver sXers, both men and women, initially contacted their romantic partners via the Internet. They began chatting online, then moved to the phone, and finally arranged face-to-face visits. Most sXers believe that chat rooms are relatively harmless, so long as chat room participants didn't take it "too far" by spending virtually all of their free time plugged in. Andy had a roommate who fit the bill: "I think it's OK, to some extent—as long as people don't go overboard with it. But some of these people, that's all they do. People who are online all the time are obnoxious." With their characteristic humor, Good Clean Fun mocked the "losers" who do not have a life outside of the Internet in their song "Loserdotcom."

A minority of sXers actually participate in the movement *primarily* via the web, and for some sXers the virtual community is their *only* connection to sXe (Williams 2005). Most use the Internet as an additional form of communication and interaction. Many in the new generation of sXers (born from about 1985–1990) have grown up using the Internet, and some encounter sXe not through music recordings or shows but online. Particularly for individuals isolated in rural areas or otherwise unable to participate in the non-virtual scene, the Internet provides an opportunity to feel connected to others with similar interests. Despite some sXers' exclusively online participation, discussions often arise from lived experience. For example, many topic threads on sXe sites find sXers reviewing the latest music recordings, describing the last show they attended, finding out the location of the next show, or gossiping about who recently sold out. Other topics abound as well, including exchanging vegetarian/vegan recipes and intense discussions regarding who can be considered an authentic member. While exclusively virtual subcultures are likely growing in number and membership, many subculturists use the Internet in conjunction with their participation, on some level, in an offline scene (Wilson and Atkinson 2005). As Bennett (2004:165) writes, "Rather than viewing the Internet as a 'cultural', or 'subcultural' context, it is perhaps better conceptualized as a cultural resource appropriated within a pre-existing cultural context, and used as a means of engaging symbolically with and/or negotiating that context." Perhaps one of the clearest examples of sXers using the Internet is record selling, buying, and trading. Online auction sites such as eBay make purchasing a piece of subcultural history easier than ever before. Rare first pressings of classic sXe records sometimes sell for one hundred dollars or more and a Judge "Chung King Can Suck It" record sold for over $1000.

Younger sXers are part of the music downloading and CD burning generation, which raises its own set of questions within the scene. Does downloading or burning music fit into the hardcore philosophy? Downloading may thwart the commercial aspects of making music but it also potentially undermines independent records labels' abilities to make enough money to produce the next record. Darren's band recorded a record with a smaller label:

> A lot of bands and a lot of labels that put money into records are losing a lot of money because of [downloading]. A lot of people say hardcore's not about money. But I've put so much money into this band. It's dumb, how much. A lot of people are like, "Why are you doing that? You're not huge." It's 'cause I love to do it, but it would be nice if everyone else could pull their share.

Downloading was acceptable to Darren only under certain circumstances: 1) to see if you like the band enough to later purchase the record, 2) to acquire old, out of print, and otherwise unavailable music, and 3) to obtain music from major-label mega-stars such as Madonna. While some sXe and hardcore kids *do* avoid downloading or burning struggling bands' music, the temptation is great.

In addition to the relatively benign discussions in sXe chat rooms and Internet commerce, a number of alternative culture-themed dating and erotica sites emerged around 2000. Though associated more with the independent music scene[6] and body modification subcultures, rather than sXe specifically, many sXers have visited these sites and a few post pictures and messages of their own. Some sXers view these sites as a corruption of the indie/punk ethos, exploiting the independent music scene and young people's sexual curiosity for profit. Others view such sites as simply silly, relatively harmless fun.

Suicidegirls.com is a very popular site featuring nude women with tattoos and piercings. Each woman creates a profile to accompany her photo set. In addition to asking about "turn-ons," the SuicideGirls profiles list which piercings a woman has. The site's managers profess to challenge norms of beauty by showing women with tattoos, dyed hair, and multiple piercings rather than displaying women who fit more standard norms of female attractiveness.[7] The site frames posting pictures of oneself as an act of confidence that may lead to further opportunities.[8] SuicideGirls also features celebrity interviews, news briefs, message boards, and an online "community" of alterna-kids. Burningangel.com, another so-called punk rock porn site, offers music, game, and movie reviews, almost like a 'zine with pictures of nude women.

A message board forum on the feminist oriented Grrrls With Xs on Their Hands site reveals mixed opinions about SuicideGirls, though most find the site "trashy:" "[SuicideGirls is] Just another way of exploiting women in the scene! We don't need that shit in punk and hardcore."[9] Trashy in this context seemed to imply that the girls were not authentic members of a punk/hardcore scene but were "groupies" who used their bodies to attract male attention. A few posters had different opinions:

> I have no problem with sexual photos. The girls get off on doing them, probably make some money, and those that go looking for them must want to see them too. I don't love all the photos of these girls, but some of them are beautiful, with beautiful bodies. They're proud of that and wanna show it off . . . it's a choice and I think that's cool.

At least one member claimed to have submitted nude photos to the site. Another member wrote, "I know that Suicide Girls is making a fetish out of females in the hardcore scene as well as the indie scenes etc. I don't necessarily think that is a good thing, but I don't see it as being a threat— at least not presently."[10]

Straight edgers struggle with what to make of these sites. On the one hand, the sites seem to fly in the face of sXe's focus on women's empowerment and freedom from exploitation as sexual objects. Andy said, "How does a movement turn into *that?* 'I'm depressed, I like Elliot Smith, take a picture of me with my shirt off'!"[11] On the other hand, some sXers do not see what is wrong with nude pictures, so long as they are not misogynist or coerced. Women covered with tattoos likely have a different understanding of their bodies than many women and women have substantial involvement in maintaining SuicideGirls. Still, for many sXers such sites undermine the authenticity of the underground music movement as well as potentially degrading women. If "mainstream" men are surfing porn, it can't be very punk rock.

Metalcore and More—The Cultic Milieu

I entered the hardcore scene in 1996 mainly because I felt an affinity to the Straight Edge community. It was great to meet so many people who shared my distaste for drug culture. Although I don't really know any of those kids anymore, the main thing that struck me about the hardcore scene was their die hard independence. It showed me that there is no shame in presenting my ideas and manufacturing my music in any possible manner, just as long as I was doing something and involving myself.

—straight edge hip hop artist/emcee/slam poet Sage Francis[12]

From the beginning, sXe was influenced by a variety of subcultures. Early hardcore occasionally crossed with skinhead culture with bands like TSOL, Agnostic Front, and Cro-Mags, and kids were influenced by punk, classic rock, heavy metal, and skate-thrash bands (Blush 2001). By 2005, the sXe/hardcore crossover into other scenes sometimes made it difficult to pick sXers out of a crowd. For instance, when I saw metalcore band Martyr AD play in a small Denver club, the usual array of hardcore kids was there, but it was becoming increasingly difficult to tell the difference between punks, indie rockers, goths, and sXers. Nearly everyone dressed in black and looked like some conglomeration of punk/indie/hardcore/ metal. The body modification subculture's impact on sXe (and other groups) is evident in the ubiquitous tattoos, stretched ears, and piercings. I also saw metalcore band Killswitch Engage play with European metal bands Dark Tranquility and Cradle of Filth. As Killswitch took the stage the numerous hardcore and sXe kids literally cleared the floor of metalheads, making room for their exhibition-style dancing. A few minor scuffles aside, the kids from opposing scenes moshed alongside one another, some with shaved heads, others with hair down the middle of their backs. These experiences raise one of the central questions of contemporary subculture scholars: do distinct subcultures even really exist (Redhead 1997)?

Are subcultures blending beyond recognition or are they fragmenting into ever more specific subcategories? The answer, it seems, is both.

Subcultures tend to blend and overlap with time. Colin Campbell (1972) proposed that alternative lifestyles, religions, and activist groups of the 1960s counterculture together formed a "cultic milieu," a collective underground of seekers and radicals who share a common consciousness of deviance. He claimed that the cultic milieu tends toward syncretism, meaning that groups gradually, through magazines, books, meetings and other forms of communication, come to share similar ideas and ideals. Later authors (see Kaplan and Lööw 2002) demonstrated that even groups with seemingly radically different beliefs and goals, such as environmentalists and neo-Nazi groups, have similar ideologies.[13] "Post subculture" scholars claim that distinct divisions between subcultures have dissolved, leaving a marketplace from which youth pick, choose, and reconstruct pieces of style into their own bricolage of personal taste (Redhead 1990; Muggleton 1997). Youth are involved in fluid, overlapping "tribes" rather than distinct subcultures (Maffesoli 1996). Indeed, sXe has much in common with other underground youth scenes. As subcultures overlap and blend, sharing and borrowing styles, music, lingo, and ideas, perhaps Hot Topic's question "What's your scene?" becomes a bit obsolete.

Commercialization and the Internet have accelerated the process of syncretism so that today it can be increasingly difficult (though not impossible) to distinguish sXers from their subcultural peers without the telltale X's. Andy and Darren rarely X'd up:

Andy: people aren't as open about it as they used to be. You'll be at a show with like 600 kids and there might be 200 sXe kids there but there's only two kids with X's. People aren't televising the fact that they're sXe anymore.

Darren: which isn't necessarily a problem.

Andy: It's more of a personal [thing].Nobody's trying to preach at anybody. I haven't X'd up in quite some time.

Darren: I don't have to wear my pride on my sleeve. . . . People aren't dressing to impress anymore.

While some sXers still listen exclusively to hardcore, many are exploring other types of music. Straight edge and hardcore share musical styles with more than just metal.[14] In California, hardcore meshed with hip hop as bands such as Downset incorporated a rap-like cadence to their lyrics. Zach De La Rocha, singer for early Revelation Records hardcore band Inside Out, went on to front popular '90s band Rage Against the Machine's fusion of rap, metal, and hardcore. In New York, bands such as Scarhead also incorporated hip hop fashion and sensibility. Hip hop artist and slam poet Sage Francis claimed sXe though he had relatively little connection to the hardcore scene. Punk bands AFI, H2O, and Good Riddance have or have had sXe members, as do indie rock bands such as Vaux, Saves the Day, and New Found Glory. Ska-punk band the Mighty Mighty Bosstones and metal group Slayer both covered Minor Threat songs. Youth may still adamantly align themselves with a particular scene and *against* other scenes ("I'm *hardcore*, not *punk!*"), but they generally recognize the influence other groups have upon their own.

Branches of sXe have also overlapped with Christianity and Krishna Consciousness. The clean-living ideology meshes nicely with the more puritanical aspects of Christianity and the monastic Hare Krishna lifestyle. Though the Krishna influence is rare in the Denver scene, several sXers connect sXe to their Christian beliefs. Matthew, seventeen, attended Christian youth gatherings as well as sXe shows. While he believed these parts of his life were essentially separate, he also saw the connections:

I *do* believe—this is really cheesy, but I still believe it—I should never put the X above the cross. That's just the way I feel. I have my God and that's me. That's like inside of me. And sXe is my outside, it's who I am outside. . . . But my beliefs also have to do with sXe. You see in the Bible "Do not allow yourself to become drunken." You see through stories, fables, whatever you want to call them of men who have become drunk and it showed what it led to. It's just more evidence not to do those things. Myself, I believe in the "temple of God" statement. As a Christian, God lives in me, so I want to show respect to that. If I'm gonna be someone who believes this and has so-called God inside of me, I want to keep my body clean for those reasons, too.

Face Down Records produced Christian hardcore bands such as No Innocent Victim, Bloody Sunday, and ALove for Enemies [sic]. From Equal Vision Records came Krishna bands Shelter, 108, Prema, Baby Gopal, and Refuse to Fall.

Just as subcultures tend toward syncretism, they also fragment into a variety of subgroups.[15] With such a web of micro-cultures some overlap is inevitable; boundaries become more porous as particularistic sub-groups borrow from one another. It becomes more difficult to speak of "punk" except as an umbrella identity encompassing the variety of punk-influenced genres that fragmented from the original incarnation: gutter punk, emo, hardcore, straight edge, screamo, anarchist punk, pop punk, goth punk, post punk. The process continues as fragments break up even further—sXe emerged from hardcore, itself a fragment of punk. Each sub-group becomes more particularistic, more specialized and often believes it is more *true* to the original spirit of the movement.

Such fragmenting produces ever greater options in the subcultural marketplace. Kids customize their identity, and some periodically switch from one to another (and sometimes back again!). Straight edgers were sometimes also skinheads, punks, ravers, and hip hoppers at the same time. I observed Louis, a young Denver man, morph from an old-school punk to a skinhead to an sXe skinhead and, finally, to a club kid who regularly used drugs. Youths not only jump back and forth between a subculture and the mainstream, they often wend their way through a variety of different subcultures, trying on costumes and beliefs until they find the best fit. The difference with sXe is that the ideology is specifically framed as a lifetime choice and a one-chance opportunity. The basic borders are strict, the essential behaviors clear-cut.

It is easy to overstate the amount of culture-hopping. While many of the Denver sXers experimented with a variety of styles, cases such as Louis's were rare. Most kids eventually settled on sXe while occasionally moonlighting to a hip hop or death metal show.

Conclusion

Commercialization has not killed sXe. It may defuse some of the movement's original intent, but it also simultaneously creates resistance to homogenization. The Internet creates new opportunities for community and exchange of ideas, promoting ever-greater overlap between subcultures but also prompting new, specialized combinations of styles and beliefs. While sXers complain that "negative" media coverage hurts the movement, Muggleton (2000:135) suggests it "can help to render subcultures subversive and increase their longevity." Indeed, the mass media gave more militant sXe a platform, but it did not *create* vegan sXe and in focusing on the very small minority of truly militant sXers, the negative coverage brought law enforcement in addition to increased exposure. Negative press may actually make subcultures more attractive to some kids while overexposure and commercialization undermine a movement's resistance potential (Moore 2005).

Given that no openly and vocal sXe band has truly gained national notoriety on a large scale, it is difficult to say what the outcome of such a development might be. Perhaps with such a platform sXe would finally reach the masses, making abstinence a viable option for hundreds of thousands of kids. Maybe an sXe band with Green Day's popularity could significantly shift youth culture. More likely the message of sXe would get lost in the glitz, leaving a hollow shell of the movement after the fad declined. However, this would also give the underground a shot in the arm. Studying goths, Hodkinson (2004) shows that the decline in commercial interest during the early 1990s led to smaller, intimate networks spread over vast geographical areas. Mainstream attention is bound to fade as new, fresh (and more profitable) styles emerge. As mass media coverage moves on, so too do many of the poseurs and profiteers associated with the scene, leaving the truly committed to reinvigorate the underground. The rise and fall of a commercialized scene does not foretell its impending death.

CONCLUSIONS

I don't think any of the original DC sXe kids could have imagined what sXe would eventually become, or even that it would still be around twenty-five years after its modest beginnings. Tens of thousands of kids from countries around the world have passed through the sXe ranks, assuring the movement's place in the history of youth subcultures. Straight edge stretched the boundaries between subcultures and social movements, sharing characteristics of both. As Martin (2002) points out, neither subculture nor new social movement theories adequately explain the complexity of some forms of collective action. This study allows me to draw some conclusions to a variety of questions posed in the previous chapters: Do subcultures really *resist* anything? How does collective identity form the basis of new social movements? How do moderate and radical factions coexist in the same movement? How do young men and women wrestle with the meanings of masculinity and femininity? What happens to kids as they grow up and out of the scene? And finally, what are the impacts of commercialization and media on the future of sXe and subcultures more broadly?

Subcultural Resistance

While scholars have established that resistance, even when ineffective, is a key feature of youth subcultures, the nature and impact of youth resistance is still under dispute (Leblanc 1999). The Centre for Contemporary Cultural Studies (CCCS) has drawn substantial criticism for ignoring participants' subjectivity, failing to empirically study the groups they sought to explain, focusing too much on Marxist/class-based explanations and grand theories, and reifying the concept of subculture (Muggleton 2000; Blackman 1995; Widdicombe and Wooffitt 1995). Based on solid ethnographic work, contemporary theorists have acknowledged the fluidity of subcultures and retooled the notion of resistance to include the subjective understandings of participants. Leblanc (1999), studying female punks, found that resistance included both subjective and objective components. Leblanc redefined resistance broadly as political behavior, including discursive and symbolic acts. Postmodern theorists have further questioned CCCS ideas of resistance, suggesting that, depending on one's perspective, many narratives can be "true" simultaneously. They encourage us to examine subcultural quests for authenticity from the participants' point of view, paying particular attention to the individualistic, fragmented, and heterogeneous natures of subcultures (Muggleton 2000; Grossberg 1992; Rose 1994).

Straight edge demonstrates that subcultural resistance has many different meanings, targets, and methods. Theorists working in the CCCS tradition hint at multiple levels of analysis. Cohen (1984) claims that subcultures must be examined at the historical, structural/semiotic, and phenomenological levels and Clarke (1986) analyzes subcultures in terms of structure, culture, and biography. Yet these writers shortchanged the phenomenological and biographical levels, respectively, missing the subjective, lived experiences of participants. This work provides an analytical framework for understanding the complex meanings, multiple targets, and various methods of resistance of any subculture.

Meanings of Resistance

Members of youth subcultures construct both individualized and collective meanings for their participation. Various members of the group may hold individualized meanings that are not central to the group's ideology while simultaneously maintaining collective understandings of the subculture's significance. Widdicombe and Wooffitt (1995:204), for example, found that "punk may be constituted both through shared goals, values and so on, and through individual members."

Straight edge resistance has many diverse, but intensely personal, meanings for individual members: maintaining good health, overcoming personal addiction, creating feelings of personal control and freedom, bringing satisfaction at being different from mainstream youth, and partially empowering other identities (such as queer, feminist, Christian, and activist). Straight edge women often mentioned safety as a meaningful reason they were sXe; they would never be taken advantage of while under the influence. For some, sXe is the foundation of an entire progressive worldview that includes environmentalism, restructuring gender, and antiracism, among other things. Subcultures help people define who they are during the uncertainty of coming of age (Widdicombe and Wooffitt 1995:25). They offer a space for experimentation and a place to wrestle with questions about the world, creating a "home" for identity in a modern era when personal identity suffers a homelessness brought about by the impersonal, bureaucratic forces of modernity (Melucci 1989; Giddens 1991).

Subcultures offer more than individualized meanings of resistance. Individualized resistance is symbolic of a larger, collective, oppositional consciousness. For sXers, the collective meanings central to the group's identity include defying the stereotypical "jock" image (through clean living and abstinence), setting a collective example for other youth, supporting a drug-free social setting, and avoiding society's "poisons" that dull the mind. For some, sXe becomes a "family," a "brotherhood," a supportive space in which they can be different together. Youth adopt the sXe identity rather than simply remaining "drug-free" in part because they believe their individual choices will add up to a collective challenge.

Everyday resistance has political consequences (Scott 1985) and (collective) resistance and (individual) authenticity are not mutually exclusive (Muggleton 2000). "In the case of life politics, the politicized self and the self-actualizing self become one and the same. The microphysics of power also points to identity as the battleground in contemporary forms of resistance" (Buechler 1999:151; Giddens 1991). Melucci (1996:115) writes, "To an increasing degree, problems of individual identity and collective action become meshed together: the solidarity of the group is inseparable from the personal quest." All this is to say that people pursue personal empowerment/enlightenment while also working for social change. As sXe shows, subcultures advocate core meanings of resistance, but then offer space for individuals to customize their resistance and subcultural identity.

Sites of Resistance

Youth subcultures engage macro-, meso-, and micro-level sites of resistance. Leblanc's (1999) work with punk girls illustrates multiple sites of resistance to dominant gender constructions. At the macro level, these young women resist society's dominant constructions of femininity; at the meso level, they resist gender roles in punk; and at the micro level, they challenge gender constructions in their families and focus on personal empowerment and self-esteem. Past theorizing on resistance has privileged mainstream, hegemonic, adult culture; the class structure; or the state as the macro-level target of subcultural resistance: each youth subculture has emerged in relation to the larger social structure, reacting against some prior conditions and reflecting other current conditions (Hall 1986). For example, skinheads glorified their working-class roots and led "exemplary" working-class lives in reaction to an ongoing decline of working-class culture as they knew it, a shrinking job market, and resurgence in immigration in the late

1960s (P. Cohen 1972). Straight edgers challenge a larger culture they believe promotes alcohol and tobacco products to kids, makes alcohol use normal and even expected, and glorifies casual sexual encounters.

In addition to challenging mainstream, adult culture at the macro level, youth movements offer resistance at the meso level. While sXe challenges dominant values, sXers focus much, if not most, of their message of resistance towards their fellow youth, reacting against mainstream youth and perceived contradictions in other subcultures.[1] They resist what they see as youth culture's fixation on substance use and sex; punks' "no future" and nihilistic tendencies; skinheads' patriotism, sexism, working class ideology, and some members' racism; and hippies' drug use, passivity, and escapism—believing that these undermine the resistance potential each of these groups shares. They respond with clean living, abstinence, self-actualization, antiracism and antisexism, and ideally, positivity. It is clear that previous subcultures profoundly impacted the nature of sXe. Lahickey (1997: xviii) writes, "straight edge provided an untraditional form of rebellion—rebelling against the traditional forms of rebellion." Resistance may also be the "hyper-acceptance of dominant norms rather than the deliberate violation of cultural standards" (Atkinson 2003:201). In many ways sXers strictly live out certain middle-class values to counter perceived contradictions in mainstream society; parents may preach abstinence but themselves indulge. Self-control, individuality, and delayed gratification—middle-class values—become subcultural virtues when youth use them to challenge mainstream hypocrisies.

Despite its insistence on countering counterculture, sXe co-opts many values from previous youth movements, clearly owing its "question everything" mentality to punk, its intimation of self-actualization to hippies, and its relatively clean-cut image and sense of pride to skinheads. It also borrows punk's aggressive music, hippies' goal of cultural challenge through lifestyle, and skinheads' insistence on personal accountability. Analyzing youth movements at the meso level in terms of their relationship to other youth cultures is vital to an accurate understanding of these groups, as is recognizing the identity battles within the group. Youth reflexively examine their own groups and often attempt to resolve intragroup contradictions. LeBlanc (1999:160) notes, for example, that female punks "subvert the punks' subversion" just as some sXers resist militant "tough guys" within their scene. All youth movements share disdain for the mainstream; how they express their contempt and challenge existing structures depends in large part on current and previous youth subcultures, which often become meso-level targets for change.

Finally, sXers offer micro-level resistance as they reject the substance abuse within their families and make changes in their individual lives. Many sXers report that they abstain from drugs and alcohol at least in part in reaction to family members' substance abuse. Others claim that sXe is a powerful commitment against their own addictive tendencies, enabling them to maintain control over their lives and, as Brake (1985) suggests, providing them with a space to work out their identities. Straight edge women, in particular, felt they resisted the threat of sexual assault and had greater control over their physical safety and well-being than their non-sXe counterparts. Self-actualization and control are themes in other youth subcultures as well. Clearly, subcultures' targets extend beyond contradictions in adult culture and the class structure.

Methods of Resistance

Straight edge demonstrates that subcultures employ many methods of resistance, both personal and political. Rather than confine resistance to political challenges, organized social activism, or overturning the class structure, subcultures often embody a less overt opposition. Many sXers do seek to change youth culture, but their primary methods are very personal: leading by example; personally living the changes they seek; expressing a personal style; and creating an enclave, a space to be "free" from the perceived constraints of peer pressure and the demand to conform to mainstream culture. They turn a mirror back on society, their peers, their families, and themselves, encouraging each to live up to their ideals. The style-focused resistance of past theories misses the variety of methods subcultures employ. Theorists must, as Gary Clarke suggests, "transcend an exclusive focus on style" (1997 [1981]:178). Clearly sXe has a visible style like any other youth subculture, but adherents also combine personal and social transformation, exemplifying resistance in daily life and creating and living a new way of being rather than simply resisting and/or trying to change the old. As Widdicombe and Wooffitt (1995:204) note in their study of punk identity, "We observed in particular that these oppositional narratives do not invoke radical activities or public displays of resistance; rather, they are fashioned around the routine, the personal and the everyday." Lifestyle changes, leading by example, and creating safe spaces for expression of alternative ways of being challenge systems of meaning and values: the hippie movement transformed materialism through idealism, skinheads glorified working-class values over middle-class values, and punks rejected order and stability in favor of chaos and anarchy. An overemphasis on "style" undermines the significance of youth ideology apart from the manner they present and live it.

Though focused on personal methods of resistance, sXe has political ramifications as well. Straight edgers' abstinence from drugs, alcohol, and casual sex are essential components of a broader resistance to dominant society and mainstream youth culture. The movement engages in what Giddens (1991:214–215) calls "life politics"—a "politics of choice," a "politics of lifestyle," a "politics of self-actualization," and a "politics of life decisions." Through their individual actions, sXers seek a "remoralizing of social life" (Buechler 1999:150). Wearing a shirt with an sXe message may be a personal stylistic decision, but when an entire group of people wears such shirts, that so clearly defy the norm, style has the potential to become collective challenge. Likewise, becoming a vegetarian or vegan may be an individualistic dietary choice, but when a subculture does so and advertises their choice, it opens up possibilities for other youth. As Leblanc (1999:18) notes, the intent to influence others is an important component of resistance: "accounts of resistance must detail not only resistant acts, but the subjective intent motivating these as well. . . . such resistance includes not only behaviors, but discursive and symbolic acts."

Finally, personal methods of resistance often encourage involvement in more political struggles. As Buechler (1999:150) points out, "Although this form of politics originates on the micro level of personal identity, its effects are not likely to remain confined to this level." Straight edgers advocate for animal rights and environmental causes, punks are involved in programs such as Food Not Bombs, antiracist skinheads champion groups like Anti-Racist Action, and hippies participate in antiwar rallies and other forms of activism. Subcultures are themselves politically meaningful and they often serve as a bridge to further political involvement.

Cultural Reproduction and Resistance

Looking at resistance through the lens of meanings, sites, and methods forces us to reexamine the "success" of subcultural resistance. Is youth resistance "magical," more style than substance, as CCCS theorists might suggest? Straight edge, like the other subcultures, also has illusory tendencies and reproduces prevailing ideology in several ways. In fact, the group embraces values that would resonate with many Americans and part of adherents' message is for people to live out the values they likely already hold. Oppositional subcultures do not emerge in a vacuum (Kaplan and Lööw 2002); both the conservative and progressive elements of the sXe ideology have links to the dominant cultural milieu from which the group emerged, links that sometimes contradict the group's goals. The movement's contradictions included its antisexist yet male-centered ideology. The almost complete lack of female musicians in bands, the hypermasculine dancing at shows, and the male cliques reinforce the movement's own unspoken gender norms that make women seem less important to the scene and ensure that many women will never feel completely at home. Straight edge's critique of corporate power comes from a class-privileged position. In addition, sXe promotes individuality and clear, free thought, but for some adherents the rigid lifestyle requirements create conformity, closed-mindedness, and intolerance, a far cry from the "positivity" the movement promulgates. Finally, sXe's image and fashion surpass the ideals for some sXers and, despite their clean ways of living, the movement becomes little more than a style. No doubt the contradictions in sXe will provoke new innovations both within sXe and from other subcultures seeking to transcend sXe's limitations.

Despite these contradictions, sXe resists dominant ideology in several ways, transcending the level of "signs" such as style, demeanor, and dress (Hebdige 1979:17). Straight edge creates a space for youth to reject the drug and alcohol culture, stretch the boundaries of gender expectations, experience a deeply supportive community, and pursue personal and social change. Resistance goes beyond the subjective/postmodern sensibilities of a subculture's adherents; it has real consequences for the lives of its members, other peer groups, and possibly mainstream society. Resistance implies grandiose, even revolutionary, notions of a large group of people overturning dominant ideals and social structure. Under this limited conceptualization, resistance only becomes meaningful when youth movements surpass some imaginary threshold of societal change. Resistance is contextual and many-layered rather than static and uniform. It often centers on individual opposition to domination, "the politicization of the self and daily life" (Taylor and Whittier 1992:117), and subjective redefining of societal norms. Social actors practice the future they envision (Scott 1985; Melucci 1989, 1996). Therefore, personal actualization and social transformation are not mutually exclusive (Calhoun 1994). Straight edge has not created a revolution in either youth or mainstream culture. It has, however, for twenty-five years, provided a haven for youth to contest these cultures and create alternatives.

The "Newest" Face of Social Movements

In addition to redefining subcultural resistance, sXe provides new ways to think about the roles of collective identity in diffuse social movements.

Straight edge is among the "newest" of social movement forms (that is, least structured, most reliant on collective identity), illustrating how, in the absence of formal structure, collective identity becomes the foundation of social movement activity. Johnston, Larana, and Gusfield (1994:8) write "in contrast to cadre-led and centralized bureaucracies of traditional mass parties, new social movement organizations tend to be segmented, diffuse, and decentralized." Though social movement scholars have developed a rich theoretical tradition explaining how movement organizations challenge institutionalized politics, they have been less sure of how to account for diffuse, extra-institutional challenges that target civil society, as Snow (2001:2) suggests:

> While theoretical elegance and conceptual tidiness may be gained by limiting the conceptualization of movements institutionally and in terms of the institutional locus of changes sought, it is important to ask about the costs of doing so. If movements are conceptualized under the rubric of contentious politics, for example, what is to be done conceptually and analytically with collective challenges or adaptations outside of traditional political arenas, such as retreatist and communal movements, movements of self-help and -renewal, lifestyle movements, not to mention the array of religious movements?

Collective identity not only provides potential constituents for social movement organizations, a receptive audience to a variety of more formal movements, and an arena for cultural change: it can form the foundation of a movement in and of itself.

Melucci (1988) recognized that collective identity is created in "submerged networks," or small groups of people concerned with the "ongoing routines of everyday life" (Mueller 1994). A variety of less structured movements rest on submerged networks and symbolic challenges. Examples of diffuse social movements include simple living (Schor 1998; Elgin 1993), What Would Jesus Do (www.wwjd.com/), groups responding to postpartum depression (Taylor 1996; 2000) and other self-help movements, and some men's movements (Kimmel 1995; Jesser 1996). The example of sXe suggests that, for diffuse movements, collective identity gains greater importance and must resonate with participants even more. Lacking a powerful collective identity, a diffuse movement has no formal structure to ensure continuity, consistency, action, and commitment. Collective identity provides a sense of belonging and immediate connection between movement adherents. It is a "shorthand way of announcing status" that creates obligations for individual and social action. Collective identity may be important to participation in all movements (Buechler 1993), but in diffuse movements it is critical.

Collective Identity and Commitment

In focusing on participants' commitment to conventional social movement organizations and movement tasks, researchers have overlooked the fact that many individuals have instead committed to collective identities that reflect personal value identities (Gecas 2000). Strong convictions support identity politics and collective identities (Robnett 1997; Taylor and Raeburn 1995; Taylor 2000; White 1989; Whittier 1995), but not everyone with strong convictions joins a movement organization. For example, the 1999 World Trade Organization protests in Seattle featured thousands of individuals acting out their convictions and their commitment to an "anticorporate" or "fair trade" collective identity. While many participants belonged to social movement organizations, many others were committed to the "fair trade," "global justice," or "antiglobalization" collective identities rather than a specific group or groups. Commitment to the larger movement's collective identity may outweigh commitment to a movement organization (see Hunt and Benford 1992). The "anticorporate" identity governs behavior in adherents' everyday lives and creates a pool of willing participants when massive protest actions arise.[2] Commitment to a collective identity *may* lead to involvement in a social movement organization, which in turn reinforces commitment to the identity. However, commitment does not rest on membership to a formal organization.

Most of the adherents of a collective identity will never become active in a movement organization. For example, many Americans now claim the "environmentalist" collective identity, yet only a small minority are active in environmental organizations. Rather, based on their commitment to the identity, they recycle, buy some environmentally friendly products, send a check to a social movement organization on occasion, compost, buy organic food, and take other eco-friendly actions in their daily lives. Straight edge demonstrates how collective identity supports a commitment to putting personal values into action. Collective identity is a *support structure;* people call on collective identity (that is, look to the identity for guidance) in a variety of situations where they might otherwise rely on the guidance of an organization and/or a leader.

Collective Identity and Individualized Participation

In an individualistic culture, many people live out their values as individuals connected by a collective identity. Individuals bonded by a collective identity experience a *community of meaning* that makes the personal political and gives new, politicized meaning to everyday actions. It creates an oppositional consciousness and a framework for understanding social problems which leads to a politicization of everyday life (Whittier 1997). Adherents committed to the collective identity live out a set of core values and/or behaviors, but they are then able to fit the identity to their individual preferences, for example simple living. They connect to the core of a collective identity and then tailor the identity to match their interests, biographical availability, and values. They define what participation and commitment mean, blending their own preferences and interpretations with those of the collective identity, to forge a personally empowering identity.

New Social Movement scholars contend that collective identity is especially important in modern societies characterized by complex power relationships (Giddens 1991; Habermas 1984; Mulucci 1989). In an increasingly individualized world, the New Social Movement assertion that the politicization of everyday life becomes central to movement activity makes sense. "The insistence that the construction and expression of a collective vision is politics, or the politicization of the self and daily life, is . . . the core of what is 'new' about the new social movements" (Taylor and Whittier 1992:117). Less-structured movements may have different goals and targets. "Activism" has become embedded in daily life (Scott 1985), supported by a loose community of meaning, and is therefore more sustainable for many people; "many contemporary movements are 'acted out' in individual actions rather than through or among organized groups" (Johnston, Larana, and Gusfield 1994:7). Diffuse movements are not *replacing* formal social movement organizations; the growth and number of social movement organizations suggests otherwise. However, focusing nearly exclusively on social movement organizations excludes a variety of significant social actions.

Collective identity creates personal, as well as collective, behavioral expectations. As individual and collective values overlap, failure to act according to the collective identity amounts to a personal failure as well: "To falter or fail in the pursuit of these values, therefore, is to falter morally" (Gecas 2000:97). Likewise, individuals experience satisfaction when they live in accordance with their values (Shamir 1990). Again, collective identity creates a support system for individual participation via everyday life. The values and meanings inherent in a collective identity encourage individuals to live an integrated life, a life in line with their values. People experience unease or even cognitive dissonance when they realize their actions contradict their values (for instance, "Can I call myself an environmentalist if I don't recycle?" "Can I call myself a feminist if I don't attend the local 'Take Back the Night' march?"). Likewise, they experience efficacy and fulfillment when they consciously act according to their values and are more likely to participate in something that strengthens their sense of efficacy:

> It could be argued that the value identities provided by social movements have a clarity and forcefulness that is lacking in most other aspects of modern society. . . . Some of the appeal of social movements in modern times might be the clarity of the values and value identities they provide. (Gecas 2000:105)

The sXe collective identity provides sXers with a clear value identity that empowers them, shapes their personal actions, and combines movement participation with everyday life.

Collective Identity and Cultural Challenge

Collective identity gives meaning to individual participants' actions, adding an additional layer of meaning to what could be isolated, individual acts (Taylor and Whittier 1992). Calhoun (1994:28) writes, "the politics of personal identity and the politics of collective identity are . . . inextricably linked." Personal actualization and social transformation are not mutually exclusive. For example, coming out of the closet for lesbians or gay men became more than a personally fulfilling and beneficial choice. It became a political act. At the height of the gay and lesbian movement, coming out was a social statement, an action that ultimately made the world a better place for *all* lesbians and gays. While most sXers refuse alcohol, drugs, and tobacco for personal reasons, their collective choices add up to meaningful resistance to youth and mainstream culture. Abstinence is an individualized means to a collective end; sXers' intention is not only to live fulfilling lives as individuals, but also to create new options for youth culture. Having a "clear mind" and bonding with the sXe collective identity encourages young people to question and subvert *many* aspects of society. Not drinking becomes an act of resistance and defiance that creates new possibilities for other youth (Haenfler 2001).

Melucci's (1988) concept of submerged networks sheds light on how diffuse movements such as sXe issue cultural challenge as members live lifestyles of opposition (Melucci 1985). Mueller (1994:238–239) explains:

> The basic thrust of Melucci's conception of submerged networks is the proposition that the initial challenge to the prevailing order takes place principally on symbolic grounds. That is, the status quo must be challenged at the cultural level in terms of its claims to legitimacy before mass collective action is feasible. Thus Melucci argues that submerged networks "challenge and overturn the dominant codes upon which social relationships are founded. These symbolic challenges are a method of unmasking the dominant codes, a different way of perceiving and naming the world." (Melucci 1989:75)

A vast movement constituency focuses very little on conventional institutional politics, if at all. Rather, its members are busy creating and living alternatives that reflect the world they want to live in, seeking "social change through the transformation of values, personal identities, and symbols" (Scott 1990:18). They contest entrenched values. While the goal of such social movements is to create communities of meaning that support individual efforts at living according to value commitments, the results amount to more than "safe spaces" and subcultures. Such movements pose a meaningful cultural challenge. I do not mean to suggest that cultural challenge and lifestyle-based movements are replacing more "political" forms of social protest, nor do I claim that cultural/lifestyle change is more important or significant than challenging institutionalized politics. I simply suggest that expanding our focus outward from "political" and even "organized" new social movements to cultural, lifestyle-based, diffuse movements will reveal interesting and significant forms of social change.

The Impact of Diffuse, Culture-Based Movements

The field of social movement studies must account for such diffuse, extra-institutional challenges that target civil society.[3] Scholars have known for years that the vast majority of people will likely never become actively involved in causes that they support (Lichbach 1996). Yet we continue to focus our attention on the minority of social movement actors actively participating in social movement organizations, who, while certainly important, do not account for the full range of participation in social change. Ultimately, participation in diffuse social movements depends on creating a sustainable *community of meaning*. The more individual and collective identities link, the greater participants' commitment to the cause (Gamson 1990, 1991). Actors in movements are creating personally customizable identities and action repertoires based upon guidelines and structure provided by a community of meaning/collective identity. Changing everyday actions and living out value identities is more sustainable for the vast majority of people—"Linking personal change with external action, collective action functions as a new medium which illuminates the silent and arbitrary elements of the dominant codes as well as publicizes new alternatives" (Melucci 1989:63). More people participate in this level of social change and such movements often serve as a bridge to further political involvement.

Straight edge and other diffuse movements seeking cultural change deserve consideration as *social movements,* albeit as "newer" forms than even most challenges branded new social movements. Such movements may not only involve a greater number of participants than formal social movement organizations, they may also ultimately have greater impacts on social life. I do not mean to suggest that every trend, subculture, or interest group is potentially a social movement. However, the current scope of study leaves much room for expansion.

Indeed, the cultural outcomes of movement activity may generate longer-lasting and more far-reaching consequences than political or legislative victories. The black civil rights movement's legal victories overturning segregation and other injustices were important, but "de facto" segregation is still prevalent over forty years later, affirmative action is under assault, and blacks still face structural discrimination. Perhaps of greater significance are the ways the movement changed cultural norms regarding interaction between whites and blacks. The same could be said for the women's movement. Certainly, suffrage, legalized abortion, Title IX, and other legal rights have proven pivotal in advancing the power and status of women. But the movement's greatest impact lies in how it changed relations between men and women, made the personal political, and destabilized taken-for-granted gender expectations on a cultural level. Gay and lesbian liberation movements have fared rather poorly in the political realm; gay marriage is still illegal, some states still have antisodomy laws, and lawmakers pass various "antigay" initiatives. Yet the movement has had an undeniable cultural impact, shifting attitudes, uncovering homophobia and heterosexism, and becoming a legitimate area of study in many universities. I do not mean to declare culture the victor in the debate around the relative influence of culture and politics; it is not an either/or question, as each has its importance, and one is in continuous dialectic with the other. However, in focusing primarily on political challenges and outcomes we miss cultural challenges and changes that ultimately impact social relations on a deeper level than laws. We need to study movements that seek, exclusively or primarily, to change culture, including behaviors, norms, and values, rather than politics, instead of implying that cultural change is a byproduct of political collective action.

Managing Boundaries—Balancing Inclusion and Meaning

Straight edge's internal struggles between tolerance and militancy reflect a ubiquitous movement dynamic: movements are rarely completely unified, and internal contention produces change.[4] Movement identities are interactional accomplishments rather than manifestations of macro social change (Hunt, Benford, and Snow 1994).[5] Friedman and McAdam (1992) make a useful distinction between inclusive and exclusive collective identities. An inclusive identity is accepting of many different attitudes and/or beliefs. Perhaps counterintuitively, an inclusive collective identity likely appeals to fewer potential participants than an exclusive identity. This is due to two reasons. First, if a collective identity espouses many different attitudes, most people will likely find at least one that they disagree with, turning them away from the group. Second, a group will have more difficulty controlling the selective benefit aspect of an inclusive identity. Collective identity can be a selective incentive motivating participation, that is, a "good" available only to those who participate (ibid.). If everyone is welcome to be a member, the benefits of being a member seem less special/selective. This point leads to another observation: collective identity often becomes a public good over time. Everyone has access, therefore limiting the selective incentive potential. People can assume the identity without significantly contributing to the movement.

Closed collective identities are more likely to have a formal hierarchy, narrow and intense membership requirements (both beliefs and actions), rigid ideology/narrow frames, high time commitment (for instance, an entire lifetime for sXe), less reflexivity, and a high degree of exclusivity. Open identities have less hierarchy, fluid boundaries, flexible belief systems, relatively few behavior requirements, a high degree of reflexivity, and require little commitment. Therefore a wide range of individuals can relate to and claim the identity, participating in their own way. Compared to exclusive identities, inclusive ones often establish a weaker connection between the individual and the collective. Again, we must be careful to avoid painting a particular collective identity with a broad brush; each movement has open and closed elements. However, we can recognize the consequences of the relative widening or constricting of identity boundaries in the ongoing life of a movement.

Progressive movements in particular often go to great lengths to construct open, accepting identities. These efforts are beneficial in that they account for the needs of diverse groups and allow movements to bridge their causes to a variety of supporters (Snow et. al. 1986). Straight edge demonstrates, however, that open, inclusive identities may have unintended consequences, primarily in a loss of meaning that can precipitate decreased commitment. If sXe gravitates towards a more open, "anything goes" identity, it might lose its sense of special connection and meaning for many adherents. For example, environmentalists worked very hard to create an open identity that encouraged a variety of people to identify with the ideology. They succeeded—a wide variety of people consider themselves environmentalists, everyone from people who enjoy hiking and send checks to The Nature Conservancy once a year to individuals who recycle paper and to Earth First!ers who wreck logging equipment. The identity has become *relatively* meaningless (in terms of what the identity requires) for most people who identify—what must one *do* to earn the right to claim the identity? Is there a minimum set of requirements one must fulfill to maintain one's claim?

The feminist movement is perhaps one of the most informative cases for examining the balance between inclusion and meaning.[6] In her book *Feminism is for Everybody* (2000:5–6), hooks describes how feminism lost some of its meaning and significance when it became a "lifestyle" (essentially an open identity) that individual women could express in innumerable ways:

> Lifestyle feminism ushered in the notion that there could be as many versions of feminism as there were women. Suddenly the politics was slowly removed from feminism. And the assumption prevailed that no matter what a woman's politics, be she conservative or liberal, she too could fit feminism into her existing lifestyle. Obviously this way of thinking has made feminism more acceptable because its underlying assumption is that women can be feminists without fundamentally challenging and changing themselves or the culture. . . . Feminist politics is losing momentum because the feminist movement has lost clear definitions.

The widening of the feminist identity may have swelled the ranks of self-identified feminists, but hooks (2000:11) suggests the *meaning* inherent in feminist identity was watered down or lost:

By the early '80s the evocation of a politicized sisterhood, so crucial at the onset of the feminist movement, lost meaning as the terrain of radical feminist politics was overshadowed by a lifestyle-based feminism which suggested any woman could be a feminist no matter her political beliefs. Needless to say such thinking has undermined feminist theory and practice, feminist politics.

As the feminist identity's new inclusiveness not only undercut feminism's political significance, it pitted women against one another along race and class lines (hooks 2000:16).

Like feminism, sXe faces the possibility of having many members who claim the identity but dilute the meaning and significance of the group's resistance. A diluted, less-exclusive identity may lose some of its "selective incentive" value—if everyone has access to the desirable identity (that is, the benefits) regardless of their efforts, the identity becomes less attractive, as Friedman and McAdam (1992) suggest. Given this point, the importance of sXe's stringent lifestyle requirements and careful (though informal) policing of sXe boundaries becomes apparent.

Exclusivity thus has several strategic benefits. Certainly, the feminist movement has received a great deal of criticism for being *too* exclusive, too centered on white, straight, middle-class women at the expense of women of color, lesbian women, and working-class and poor women (Rich 1980; Collins 1986; Zinn, Cannon, Higginbotham, and Dill 1986; Hirsch and Keller 1990). But it seems that complete openness of identity is not the solution either. Taylor and Rupp (1993:44), writing about lesbian feminist communities, found that "separatist events and caucuses remain important for women who are disenchanted with the politics of the mainstream; separatism is a means of both drawing sustenance and maintaining feminist identity." The more "radical" or "militant" factions of a movement often bring passionate new recruits ("young blood"), innovative strategy, invigorating enthusiasm, and inspiration for future cohorts (see Taylor and Rupp 1993). ACT-UP, Queer Nation, and the Lesbian Avengers, sometimes disavowed by the larger feminist and queer movements, challenged the hegemony of older movement cohorts. Short of invoking the wrath (and repression) of authorities, the radicals or "ultramilitants" of any movement serve a vital function, forcing the more moderate constituencies to re-evaluate their commitments and tactics.

For sXe, exclusivity has helped the movement preserve much of its original meaning and resist, to a large extent, commercialization and cooptation. Punk, on the other hand, has a more open identity, has exceedingly high turnover, and has such a varied membership few can say exactly what it now stands for. One can buy all essential punk accessories at the Hot Topic store in any suburban mall. In some cases, exclusivity may, in fact, attract a greater number of people because the identity provides some certainty and stability in an uncertain and unstable world. Millions of people have flocked to the conservative Christian identity in part because it provides sure answers, tells people what they want to hear, and creates strict boundaries between "us" and "them" (that is, saved or not saved, Christian or non-Christian) (Rozell, Wilcox, and Green 1998). Particularly in a postmodern world rife with uneasiness, disconnection, and confusion, a solid, black-and-white identity might be appealing: hence the allure of hardline sXe. But, like the exclusive New Christian Right (Bruce 1994), hardline sXe faced an uphill struggle and could not ultimately sway the scene in its more closed direction. Ironically, most of the more militant sXers eventually sell out. Radical views attract some people who will be more committed to the movement, at least in the short term. But by making sXe so central to their lives, hardline sXers are unable to adapt as they grow older; for many, their beliefs are too rigid to be sustainable in the "adult" world.

It is tempting for outsiders and even many sXers to dismiss the more militant branch of sXe as nothing more than narrow-minded hooligans enforcing an exclusive boys'-club mentality. Movements regularly disassociate themselves from the more "extreme" factions within their ranks (for instance, the Sierra Club vs. Earth Liberation Front) (Benford 1993).[7] Militancy *does* push some older, disenchanted sXers out of the movement. Also, for good or ill, militant sXe garners a great deal of negative mainstream attention, provoking minor moral panics among the mainstream public and efforts to de-legitimize the entire movement based on the actions of a minority of individuals. The closed identity appeals to a hypermasculine demographic and, had it not provoked an impassioned response from the more positive sXe elements, the exclusive branch of sXe likely would have quickly stagnated and declined, taking much of the movement's constituency with it. A balance between inclusion and meaning thwarted stagnation (from too open an identity) and dogma (from too closed).

Despite these drawbacks, bands such as Path of Resistance, the attention focused on Salt Lake City kids, crews, and the urgency and passion of sXe "militancy" attract more than simply jersey-wearing thugs: they attract thousands of positive, *dedicated* kids looking for a place to belong. Militant sXe offers youth previously unexposed to the movement a new possibility and inspires many to new levels of sXe "activism" or outreach. The massive shift towards veganism, environmental awareness, animal rights, and other issues would have been neither as widespread nor as quick were it not for the intensity of sXers labeled "militant." The "positivity" master frame that so guided the Youth Crew era has brought the movement back to a relative balance between inclusion and meaning, tolerance and militancy.

Multiple Expressions of Masculinity

The contentions in the sXe movement go beyond militancy versus tolerance. Blending conservative and progressive ideals, the movement attempts to redefine gender. Straight edge's masculine subtexts, issues around control, and its exclusionary and escapist tendencies paint a contradictory portrait of a group which, on the surface, desires a more progressive masculinity. Indeed, sXe is rife with contradictions. However, to characterize sXe in narrow terms, either progressive or hypermasculine, fails to capture the complexity of gender constructions within the movement.

While it is legitimate to point out the general characteristics of any particular movement, such generalizations may obfuscate more diverse interpretations of gender at the micro level by both men and women associated with the movement. Gender relations are contextual (Cornwall and Lindisfarne 1994), and therefore "sweeping generalizations about gender make little sense of our own realities" (Cornwall 1997). Straight edge illustrates that there can be multiple expressions of masculinity within any particular movement. There is a constant tug-of-war between hegemonic masculinity and more progressive expressions of manhood. Though I have dichotomized the constructions of sXe masculinity into two faces, in fact there is a continuum of gender behavior and consciousness that ranges from reinforcing hegemonic masculinity to being completely profeminist. Straight edge men fall across the range of this continuum. Straight edge masculinity emerges differently in various contexts: an sXer might be hypermasculine at a show, but progressive in other arenas. This observation almost certainly applies to many contemporary men's movements as well. Though the Promise Keeper ideology clearly reinforces a patriarchal ideal, different Promise Keeper men may redefine masculinity in multiple ways, and their wives may be grateful their husbands are involved.[8] As Williams (2000:1) writes, after reviewing a number of empirical studies, "It is a disparate movement, made up of many men and with a vast array of motives, ideologies, and outcomes."[9] Furthermore, while the nonfeminist men's movements lean towards hegemonic masculinity, they each had progressive rhetorical elements: the Promise Keepers emphasize racial harmony, the Million Man March/Day Of Absence was antiviolence and called for participants to honor and respect women, and the mythopoets tried to break through emotional barriers that confine many men. Such themes do not eliminate the patriarchal rhetoric and practices of nonfeminist men's movements, but rather add complexity to our understandings of such groups' multiple masculinities.

Reconstructing Masculinity in a Masculine Context

Despite the range of expressions of masculinity, sXe shows that reinventing masculinity in a masculine context is problematic. In giving up defining aspects of masculinity such as alcohol, sexual conquest, and eating meat, it seems that some sXe men compensate by glorifying other aspects (such as hard dancing, an athletic look, physical fitness, and crews). Straight edgers call for more egalitarian constructions of gender, but undermine their own efforts by constantly reinforcing and recreating a masculine context. This is unsurprising given the pervasive influence of hegemonic masculinity. There may be many ways to "be a man," but dominant culture values some over others (Carrigan, Connell, and Lee 1985). Men who do not adhere to hegemonic expressions of masculinity trade some of their male privilege for potential disadvantages, a difficult bargain for any man but perhaps most especially for *young* men. Even young men who genuinely desire a more profeminist masculinity will find themselves caught between the profeminist movement and a society that substantially rewards hegemonic masculinity. As Messner (1997:xiv) points out, "It's actually getting harder and harder for a young male to figure out how to *be* a man."

Several characteristics of sXe inhibit its potential as a movement towards a more progressive masculinity. The lack of female voices in positions of influence, an inadequate context for women to voice their concerns and needs, an unbroken cycle of male-only camaraderie, an insufficient understanding of *structural* discrimination and disadvantage, and little work towards systematic institutional change all limit sXe's efforts to create a new masculinity. As Christian (1994:194) suggests, "Men do not need a new exclusively male organization, rather we need a mixed-sex anti-sexist movement." If they truly want to change gender relations and create more fulfilling relationships, men must make an active, intentional effort to include women, because the default is to maintain homosocial boundaries. This is indeed possible, as the profeminist men have demonstrated. Men *can* create a progressive support system for one another, but not in isolation from women.

Despite sXe's shortcomings, the fact that such *young* men are questioning and taking steps towards a more progressive masculinity is remarkable. Abstinence from alcohol and drugs is significant in and of itself. Beyond that, sXe empowers many men to express a wide range of emotions, share their regard for one another, and undermine many aspects of hegemonic expressions of masculinity. It is possible that because sXers are engaging in "men's work" at a relatively early age the effects of the movement will be more significant and longer lasting than the those of men's movements, whose members are typically older and more invested in the dominant social order. In a study of profeminist men, Christian (1994:20) found that nearly all of the men had "early life experiences with some unconventional features which departed from traditional gender expectations. . . . It is unlikely that adult men will develop an anti-sexist outlook or be converted from a conventional sexist one without having some aspect of their early life experience which has prepared them for this." Most of the older sXe or formerly sXe men I interviewed hold onto many of the core values of the movement.

The Future of Profeminist Men

Feminist women and profeminist men call upon men to renounce patriarchy and male privilege, offering a vision of a more egalitarian, safe, and fulfilling society for both women *and* men. However, redefining masculinity, or giving up the hegemonic male identity entirely, is a daunting undertaking for most men. As Cornwall (1997:11) writes,

> asking men to abandon these identities altogether without having anything of value to hold on to is clearly unreasonable. But if men become aware that in their own everyday lives they are already behaving differently in different settings without losing a sense of their own identities, then it may be easier to recognise some of the implications of 'hegemonic masculinity' without feeling attacked or threatened.

Straight edgers, for the most part, have little interest in being part of an organized profeminist movement, following a religious doctrine, or engaging in pseudo-spiritual rituals. They focus on interpersonal relationships rather than systemic oppression. Individual men enact masculinity within the movement in different ways, some of which reflect patriarchy. However, "if empowerment means enabling people to expand their 'power within' in order to have power to make their own choices" (Cornwall 1997:12), then sXe provides a context for young men to subvert narrow definitions of masculinity and "take pride in kinds of manliness which do not oppress women" (Christian 1994:18). The affirmation of some sort of traditional manhood is clearly a need for most men and helps explain why the Promise Keepers can attract one million men to their events in a year while the profeminists' annual conference draws about two hundred. Connell (1997:65) writes

> Men who try to develop a politics in support of feminism, whether gay or straight, are not in for an easy ride. They are likely to be met with derision from many other men, and from some women—it is almost a journalistic cliché that women despise Sensitive New Age Guys. . . . Since change in gender requires reconstructing personal relations as well as public life, there are many opportunities for personal hurt, mistaken judgments, and anger.

It seems men's movements will be more successful in redefining masculinity in profeminist ways when they both challenge oppressive aspects of manhood *and* value certain traditional expressions of masculinity. A profeminist politics must do more to "meet men where they are" rather than asking them to abandon hegemonic masculinity and immediately challenge sexism at a systemic level. Straight edge is not burdened by the Million Man March, mythopoets, or Promise Keepers' strict exclusion of women, rigid gender roles, and patriarchal rhetoric. But the movement also lacks the profeminists' understanding of structural inequality, more intentional involvement of women, and thorough comprehension of the gendered nature of society. Straight edge is an example of an imperfect movement struggling with a middle ground, creating contexts where young men can express various masculinities while simultaneously undermining dominant notions of what it means to be a man.

Straight Edge Women

Straight edge also offers women an opportunity to bend gender rules, engaging them in a *double resistance* as they simultaneously challenge dominant gender scripts and a male-oriented subculture. Negotiating the continual push and pull between their subcultural values and society's demands results in a battle between radical and lipstick feminism, reflecting the ongoing project of redefining feminism(s) in the broader culture.

Straight edge women want to challenge oppression and mainstream expectations of women, sometimes combining their sXe identity with a feminist identity. Yet just as it is costly for men to completely turn their backs on conventional masculinity (an impossible goal anyway), women face sanctions if they abandon the "femininity game" entirely. Rather than overturn every aspect of femininity, sXe women reinterpret some traditionally feminine characteristics, giving them new symbolic meanings. Fussing over appearance to impress a man might be taboo, but crafting one's own style, conventionally feminine or not, can be a fun form of personal expression. They feel more free to play with gender, blending subversive and traditional femininities, making sXe work for them, regardless of what men (or less-sympathetic women) think. Feminism is useful in reconciling the disconnection between style and politics by politicizing subcultural production (see Piano 2003). In the case of sXe, women's personal avoidance of alcohol becomes political when understood as resisting pressures to impress men or as a safety issue.

Straight edge women believe dependence upon men (for emotional reassurance, self-validation, personal fulfillment) is a weakness. In fact, weakness, connoting dependency and attributed to "girly girls," is generally looked down upon. Straight edge women in some ways adopt a masculinized femininity. Halberstam (1998:9) notes that female masculinity "has been vilified by heterosexist and feminist/womanist programs alike." Though still restricted, sXe women can express a more masculine presentation of self and rather than being stigmatized, female masculinity is celebrated, up to a point. The celebration might be less enthusiastic if lesbianism were to enter the picture, and sXe girls generally do not feel free to replace all feminine cues with masculine. Nevertheless, there is room for women to experiment with masculinity.

Both women and men engage in *embodied resistance,* or resistance directly related to and enacted through their physical bodies. Instead of just spouting ideals, sXers physically live out their beliefs through their drug-free bodies. The "clear mind" and "pure body" values have physical connotations. Some sXers literally feel they are defending their bodies from a power structure that uses drugs and alcohol to pacify or control. The sXe core value of *control* takes on additional meanings for sXe women beyond the general sXe ideal of control of mind, health, and actions. It is different from men's masculine, sometimes obsessive, self-control. Control means being a woman on one's own terms: in control of one's own sexuality, appearance, behavior towards men, expressions of femininity, and—most importantly—*body.* Tattooing is clearly another example of embodied resistance, as Atkinson (2003:197) writes of Canadian sXers: "tattooing is not constructed as a flamboyant form of social protest by them, but rather a highly controlled method of cultural dissent." Tattoos signify control of one's body, permanence of commitment, communicating (whether ultimately true or not) a lasting bond to the community (see Vail 1999) while fulfilling the sXe value of spreading the message. Tattooing is increasingly popular amongst many types of people (DeMello 1995), including women, from sorority girls and female athletes to lesbians and New Agers. However, despite increased mainstream acceptance, tattoos still carry a social stigma (Sanders 1989), particularly for women. A woman with tattoos may be perceived as less feminine. Many women defuse some of the gendered stigma associated with tattoos by getting a "feminine" image (such as a butterfly), choosing a small tattoo, or placing the tattoo in an inconspicuous location (Irwin 2001); the topic, size, and placement of tattoos have gendered meanings and can therefore be political statements. College-aged women might get small tattoos on their lower backs (especially prevalent now, given the popularity of bare midriffs and low-rise jeans) or flowers on their ankles, but sXe women tattoo their biceps, forearms, calves, and sometimes entire upper chests. For some people, tattoos symbolize "liberation, independence, and freedom" (Irwin 2001), and for sXe women they are, in particular, a way to resist conventional standards of feminine beauty. Particularly for middle class youth, the body becomes a site of resistance. Spiked belts, black clothing, and unconventional body modifications (such as stretched ears) are other examples of how female sXers embody resistance, injecting ambiguity into gendered bodies (see Halberstam 1998). "Throwing down" (dancing hard) in the mosh pit empowers some girls, who see it as symbolic of being able to do anything a man can do and more.

Why aren't more women involved? Perhaps the stakes are simply too high. Girls face enough pressure to perform femininity; why take on the added trouble of walking the razor's edge between subcultural identity and fitting into the mainstream world? Of course, many sXe girls report feeling more free once they became involved, but taking that initial plunge is intimidating, as is the ongoing burden of dealing with some sympathetic yet immature young men who are not exactly sure what to make of girls. As feminist-sXe websites, 'zines, and bands continue to push for a more egalitarian scene, some men remain significant obstacles. To truly resist restrictive gender scripts, women must continue to carve out their own space in the scene, and men must encourage them and get out of the way. The potential is there. Clearly sXers, male and female, recognize the power *both* genders have to create less-oppressive masculinities and more-empowering femininities *under one movement*. Until sXe men, especially, renew their stance against sexism and put their words into action, that potential will remain unfulfilled.

Growing Up
The boundaries between adult and alternative youth culture are porous, and not every sXer grows up and out of the scene. Even those who leave often carry their subcultural values with them. Youth subcultures, in encouraging participants to question everything, sow the seeds of their own demise. After critiquing their perception of conformist mainstream youth and adult cultures, participants inevitably turn their critical lenses upon themselves, uncovering the inconsistencies within their own movement. The resulting disenchantment contributes to participants leaving the subculture for other pursuits.

Some adherents, however, persist, despite the contradictions between their movement's ideals and lived experience. This research suggests that those who are able to make the beliefs their own, transcend involvement in sXe just for acceptance or style, and individualize their commitment last the longest, as opposed to sXers who stick stringently to the beliefs they held when they were seventeen. Flexibility is central to ongoing participation, even in a movement such as sXe with fairly rigid, black-and-white prerequisites for membership. Commitment evolves from being outward-focused to inward-focused, collectively to individually oriented. Older sXers may be less committed to the collective, yet just as (or more) committed to subcultural ideals than their younger counterparts. Those adherents who are able to creatively balance their dedication to these ideals with their adult work lives, families, and friendships are most likely to maintain involvement into their late-twenties and beyond (see Downton and Wehr 1997 for notes on long-term commitment).

Ironically, older members who have less direct involvement in the scene may uphold the scene's values more completely than their younger counterparts. While they seem to be less involved, less "true," they have thoroughly considered and critiqued the values, reconciled the inconsistencies, cut out the superfluous trappings, and recommitted to the core ideals. Older sXers are generally neither enmeshed in scene politics nor obsessed with the latest fashions and styles. With nothing to prove, they live relatively more "free" from social (and subcultural) constraint than the younger sXers who, though they may deny it, often seek status and lose the potential of sXe in scene drama and internet message boards. For older sXers, resistance comes full circle; in exiting the scene, but upholding their commitment to the sXe collective identity, they achieve the individuality the scene claimed to offer all along. Rather than "growing out" of the movement they "grow up" within it. As Clark (2003:234) claims of punk, "The threatening pose has been replaced with the actual threat."

However, as disenchantment with the collective aspect of sXe pushes older participants to live their commitment as individuals, it robs the scene of their experience and perspective. Relating less to the younger scene, many withdraw to other settings, taking their critical, and potentially inspiring, understandings of sXe with them. Musicians are the exception; members of touring bands are often somewhat older than their fans and shape the ideology through their music, lyrics, and performances. Nevertheless, the lack of a significant older presence directly in local scenes limits sXe's growth in positive directions.

Commercialization, the Cultic Milieu, and Postmodern Identity

By 1979, and many times hence, music critics, fans, musicians, and others had declared "punk is dead," believing the movement's political potential and stylistic innovations to be exhausted. Punk's moment is gone and any attempts to revitalize it are futile, even sad. Blush (2001:10) writes of hardcore, "Face it, hardcore ain't the same anymore. It can still make for powerful music, but it's an over-with art form. It's relatively easy to be into now, but back [in the early eighties] it was an entirely different story." The same could be said of sXe. But over twenty-five years since its inception, there are still kids who identify themselves as sXe; there are still sXe bands; and there are now hundreds, if not thousands, of sXe-related websites. Cynics would claim that contemporary punks and sXers wear the trappings of the movement without *really* understanding the essence of the original scenes, especially their potential as a foundation of personal and social change. To some degree they are right, but the story is more complex.

Subcultures tend to go through continual cycles of commodification and resistance to that commodifcation. As a band or genre gains popularity it attracts new, generally younger, members into the scene. Numbers quickly swell as kids jump on the popularity bandwagon, more bands emerge, and the fashion becomes homogenized. While this may dilute the group's original meanings and frustrate the core members, it also invigorates an underground response as the self-styled "true" kids return to the roots of the movement. For every hardcore band that has gained significant popularity, filling concert halls and selling hundreds of thousands of records, there are a dozen underground bands playing in front of fifty kids in basements, peddling their low-budget CDs. As much of hardcore has gradually fused with the metal scene, kids form "old school" and "youth crew" style bands in resistance to the prevalent trends. So while many veteran hardcore kids express dismay at their scene's growing popularity, they sometimes overlook that this popularity also energizes a new cohort of youth to "keep it real." Commodification provides another way for "authentic" members to differentiate themselves from poseurs. With hardcore's entrance into the mainstream, the underground members have yet another way to claim their authenticity. By displaying knowledge of the underground they set themselves apart from their mainstream counterparts. Also, once a band makes it big, "authentic" sXers can claim to have seen them when they were playing $5 shows in front of one-hundred kids, inspiring a bit of respect and appreciation. For example, Hatebreed may host MTV's Headbangers' Ball, but those who saw them play in a Denver warehouse with forty kids and who own an original pressing of their first 7″ score scene points that add to their prestige.

The Internet has created new opportunities and pitfalls for sXe and other youth subcultures. Bennett (2004) suggests that the Internet makes the idea of subcultures with distinct styles and boundaries highly problematic. Instead, "youth cultures may be seen increasingly as cultures of 'shared ideas,' whose interactions take place not in physical spaces such as the street, club or festival but in the virtual spaces facilitated by the Internet" (ibid.:163). Given that sXe existed long before the Internet, it is more likely that the Internet is "a cultural resource appropriated within a pre-existing cultural context, and used as a means of engaging symbolically with and/or negotiating that context" (ibid.:165). The Internet is not re-placing more conventional subcultural spaces. However, it has become a vibrant new arena in which to exchange ideas, debate values, organize events, and purchase subcultural fashions. The Internet accelerates commercialization, syncretism, and fragmentation. It also provides a forum for youth to experiment with a variety of identities, mixing, matching, and exchanging to create their own bricolage of styles. In addition, the online sXe community, contrary to the opinions of some sXers, may actually facilitate resistance by providing easier access to the movement's ideals and community. The line between the virtual and the real is blurry; sXers "do not differentiate between on- and offline performance; to them, both are included as part of walking the Straight-edge" (Wilson and Atkinson 2005:303).

Straight edge's future is bound up in the larger theoretical question regarding the future of subcultures in general. Contemporary subcultural studies challenge the very idea of stable, coherent subcultures with recognizable boundaries. Subcultures have been redefined as "club cultures" (Redhead 1993; Thornton 1995), "post-subcultures" (Muggleton 1997; Muggleton and Weinzierl 2003), and "neo-tribes" (Bennett 2000). Each label questions the usefulness of conceptualizing subcultures as distinct entities, focusing instead on the fluidity, heterogeneity, tastes, and overlap of youth cultures. Polhemus (1997) describes a "supermarket of style" in which diverse subcultures are linked (and linked to the mainstream) in a fragmented community through their fashions. It is increasingly difficult to determine where dominant culture ends and subcultures begin, calling into question the very notion of hegemonic and resistant cultures. All of this implies that youth movements' potential political impact, already marginal at best, is perhaps even less than it once might have been.

Still, Carrington and Wilson (2004) argue that post-subculture theorists downplay the political significance of subcultures by focusing on hyper-individuality and taste. Rave and dance cultures, while seemingly apolitical and hyper-individualistic, actually challenge racism, sexism, and homophobia: "Those who dismiss the politics of popular music too readily miss out on the nuanced ways in which racialized and gendered identities have been reformed in these increasingly globalized urban cultural spaces in performing important 'identity work' concerning the collective identities we inhabit" (ibid.:74). It is undeniable that subcultural boundaries are fluid, perhaps increasingly so—adherents switch between scenes or combine multiple tastes and identities. Some are weekend participants, taking off their subcultural costume once Monday morning and work roll around. It is my feeling, however, that the post-subculture theorists focus too much on style and overemphasize the breakdown of subcultural divisions. The differences between rockabilly, goth, and club kids are still readily apparent. As much as scenes overlap, members still define themselves largely in opposition to other scenes. Furthermore, subculturists' experiences and understandings of resistance are not fixed. As they age they often re-emphasize the roots of their beliefs and leave the latest fashions to the younger set. Postmodern subcultural identities are transient, fluid, and often a pastiche of styles and ideologies. Yet they are still distinguishable and still have political importance.

Epilogue: Living Somewhere between Hopeful Idealist and Jaded Scenester

Straight edge meant a lot to me as I was growing up and it continues to mean a lot to me now. As I began this project, I was acutely aware of two potential pitfalls that might influence the scholarly potential of my work *and* my personal views of sXe. First, there of course existed the possibility that my affinity for the group could produce a biased account, despite my four-year absence from the scene. To combat this possibility, I adopted an extracritical eye throughout my study, and particularly during the final stages of data gathering and analysis. Through cross-checking reports, consulting colleagues, and continually questioning my assumptions, I tried to navigate this danger and produce a sociological account of the group. The second trap may have proven more difficult to overcome.

While "starting where you are" is sound advice for the novice ethnographer, the downside to studying one's "own group" is that one enters the shadows, meets the unsavory characters, notices the hypocrisies, and begins to see the group for what it really is rather than what one wishes it might be. The process is disillusioning, in both positive (literally, a freeing from illusion) and negative (discouraging) ways. Far from being an idealistic, biased observer, the temptation for me was to follow in the footsteps of the many aging subculturists before me and adopt the mantle of the jaded old scenester.

Every scene has its jaded scenesters, those older kids who still hang around occasionally at shows but firmly believe that everything was better, more pure, "back in the day," and that the current scene is going to shit. As my thirty-second birthday approaches, I am almost always one of the oldest "kids" at any given show. Many of my initial Denver contacts, who had fervently sworn they would be "True Till Death," have, of course, sold out. The process of encouraging more young women to be involved was slow, at best; there were still no women in local hardcore bands. The scene seemed to be gradually losing its political edge, despite the efforts of numbers of kids in the Denver scene. Finally, and somewhat obviously, I suppose, living among and studying youth ten to fifteen years younger than I was began to feel somewhat alienating. Towards the end, hanging out with sXe youths was still often invigorating, but rarely challenging on a personal level. While I adored the kids, I fit in less and less. I had to find my heroes, new inspiration, elsewhere. And yet all I have to do is play Minor Threat, Insted, Outspoken, Trial, Good Clean Fun, or Champion to remind me of the powerful role sXe has played in my life and the lives of so many young people. It is for these reasons and a true belief in the potential of the movement that I remain committed to sXe.

After reading this account, some sXers may feel discouraged; I've pointed out some troubling aspects of the scene, things we all acknowledge at some level, but would often rather not talk about. I hope you will take this work as a challenge to shape and create the scene many of you

14. The author, flanked by sXe friends Collin Ahrens and Matt Ramirez, joking around dressed as "mosh pit referees." Photo by Jen Brown.

really want, a scene that truly welcomes women and seeks to have a meaning beyond the music. Straight edge has helped so many of us resist the potentially destructive patterns of our peers, creating better lives for ourselves and, hopefully, for those around us. This is a great legacy for you to build upon.

Outsiders may be tempted to dismiss sXe as violent, sexist, or narrow-minded, despite my repeated observations that most sXers participate in the movement precisely to counter these tendencies. Like the news media, we are often drawn to the spectacular stories of violence or antisocial be-havior; kids who don't drink *and* like to fight make a better story than kids who simply don't drink. The fact is, sXe kids are neither the saints nor the devils outsiders make them out to be. Most of them are your typical young adults searching for meaning and taking a stand for what they believe in the best way they know how. I hope that sXe will continue to be a vibrant part of the larger subcultural world. For all of its flaws, the movement has provided a home for thousands of kids, a haven from which to escape peers who make fun of their abstinence; parents who don't understand and may use to excess themselves; and a culture that encourages them to drink, smoke, use drugs, or have sex at every turn. Straight edge often faces accusations of being "preachy," but certainly sXe is a drop in the bucket compared to the "preaching" alcohol and tobacco companies undertake on a daily basis.

I hope that current and future sXers might learn from my work as well. Any subculture must constantly be on its guard against both commercialization at the expense of ideals and consistency that breeds rigidity or stagnation. Innovation keeps a movement vibrant. If sXe is to truly thrive as a source of change, it must find ways to include women as full participants. It must also continue to find creative ways to hold onto its core meaning while welcoming the next generation of kids. Militancy may occasionally have its place, but dogma allows no room for growth and ultimately blows up in your face. The best, most lasting way to influence people is through patient, positive, personal example. As the early Victory band Billingsgate said at the beginning of their song "Reach Out":

Try to change a person's style or beliefs with your fists? That's bullshit, man. Scars heal, the truth sticks. Do you really want to make a change or do you just want to get a cool reputation? Knowledge leaves an imprint greater than any punch. Reach out and pass it on.

This is a rough outline of bands that have influenced the straight edge movement beyond their local scene. It would be impossible to include here every straight edge band that ever existed, so I have only listed those that left some kind of lasting mark—for example, through extensive touring or recording. Note that not all of these bands have or had all straight edge members, and some members

TIMELINE OF STRAIGHT EDGE BANDS

	OLD SCHOOL (1979–1985)	YOUTH CREW (1985–1991)		EMO-INFLUENCED /POLITICALLY CORRECT (1989–1995)
BOSTON AREA	SSD DYS Negative FX	Slapshot		Bane (still playing)
NEW YORK AREA	The Abused	Youth of Today Bold Gorilla Biscuits Judge Straight Ahead Project X Side by Side	Crucial Youth Wide Awake Turning Point (NJ) Upfront Life's Blood Beyond Rise Above	Mouthpiece (NJ) Shelter (Krishnacore) 108 (Krishnacore) Battery
WASHINGTON, D.C.	Teen Idles Minor Threat Faith			
CALIFORNIA	Justice League Uniform Choice Stalag 13	Uniform Choice Insted Hardstance/Inside Out Unit Pride Chain of Strength No for an Answer/411 Against the Wall Chorus of Disapproval		Forced Down Outspoken
OTHERS	7 Seconds (NV)	Brotherhood (WA)		Endpoint (KY) By the Grace of God (KY) Trial (WA) Stretch Armstrong (SC) (still playing)

stopped identifying as straight edge at some point during their careers. My goal here is not to judge what constitutes a straight edge band but rather give some idea which bands have been most influential. All dates are approximate, as bands often break up and reform. Some bands are listed twice if they bridge two or more eras.

VICTORY STYLE (1991–2001)	YOUTH CREW REVIVAL (1997–2006)	METALCORE (1998–2006)
	Ten Yard Fight	
	In My Eyes	
	Fastbreak	
	Have Heart (still playing)	
Snapcase (Buffalo)	Floorpunch (NJ)	
Earth Crisis (Syracuse)	Ensign (NJ) (still playing)	
Path of Resistance (Syracuse)	Shutdown	
	Hands Tied	
World's Collide	Good Clean Fun	
	Count Me Out	
	Down to Nothing (still playing)	
Strife	Carry On	Throwdown (still playing)
	Allegiance (still playing)	Eighteen Visions
Integrity (OH)	Champion (WA) (still playing)	Torn Apart (MD)
Confront (OH)	Time Flies (VA)	Prayer for Cleansing (NC)
One Life Crew (OH)		

Chapter 1. Straight Edge 101

1. Throughout the book, I will abbreviate "straight edge" as "sXe" and "straight edgers" as "sXers." Straight edge kids use the sXe abbreviation. The *s* and the *e* stand for *straight edge;* the *X* is the straight edge symbol. Other abbreviations include SxE and XsXeX.

2. Straight edge individuals only occasionally refer to themselves as "straight edgers," and many find the term quite funny. Rather, they call themselves straight edge "kids," regardless of age. The term "straight edger" likely comes from media portrayals of the group. I use straight edger in this work simply for ease of communication.

3. Windmilling involves spinning around with arms fully extended. Speed skating is rocking side to side as if on ice skates. Picking up change and floor punching entail bending at the waist and rapidly touching the floor with first one hand and then the other. Kung-fu kicks should be self-explanatory. Circle pits are as old as punk rock. Kids stomp around in a massive circle, bobbing their heads, bouncing off one another, and pumping their fists in the air.

4. Wood (1999), Helton and Staudenmeier, Jr. (2002), Atkinson (2003), Haenfler (2004a, 2004b, 2004c), Williams (2005), and Wilson and Atkinson (2005) are recent exceptions.

5. Punks and straight edgers draw a sharp distinction between "shows" and "concerts." Shows attract a much smaller crowd, are less expensive, feature underground bands, often showcase local bands, and are set up by local kids in the scene at little or no profit. Concerts are large, commercialized, for-profit ventures typically featuring more mainstream bands.

6. For a history of the early D.C. punk/hardcore scene, see Anderson and Jenkins (2001).

7. Some claim that "hardcore" is the American equivalent of British "punk." Hardcore, then, is simply Americanized punk. American hardcore long ago became a distinct genre of its own with many different forms and styles, generally faster and more aggressive than punk.

8. Other hardcore bands such as Cro-Mags and Cause for Alarm had dabbled in Krishna Consciousness before Youth of Today did (Davis 1995).

9. Veganism had been part of the punk and hardcore scenes previous to Earth Crisis. However, their efforts helped veganism grow exponentially.

10. Strife later reformed, first under the moniker Anger Means, then once again as Strife, though several members were no longer sXe or even drug free. This latter development caused a fair bit of controversy in the sXe scene as some adherents took offense to a band that made its name advocating sXe playing under the same name with non-sXe members.

11. Including metal-influenced hardcore bands on the Ozzfest bill has since become a tradition.

221

12. All names are pseudonyms with the exception of a few musicians who gave permission to be identified.

13. Punks typically disdain both slamming and hardcore dancing. Just as hardcore kids think metal fans are crazy for intentionally running into one another, so do punks think hardcore dancing is too violent. Punks also prefer the more communal circle pit to what they view as more egoist, exhibitionist dancing in the hardcore scene.

14. Alec, a thirty-year-old musician, told an amusing story about a large show he put on. He'd hired off-duty police as security and spent the evening pointing out which "confrontations" were dancing and which were fights.

15. As bands became more popular, they could play larger clubs that inevitably had a barrier (usually a steel railing) between the stage and the crowd. In the gap between the stage and railing, burly security guards, sometimes off-duty police officers, made sure no kids jumped onto the stage. True hardcore aficionados despised barriers as symbols of "corporate rock," and many singers would leap over the guards and rail to be with the crowd.

16. Some of the most prominent annual fests include Hellfest in Syracuse, NY; Krazyfest in Louisville, KY; and the More Than Music Fest in Columbus, OH. In 2005, a new touring festival called Sounds of the Underground brought metal and hardcore bands to cities across the United States.

17. The order in which bands played sometimes caused friction in the scene. Generally, the "biggest," or most successful, band, with the greatest longevity and/or the most recordings, played last, while the newer bands opened the show. Bands were not supposed to care when they went on—quibbling about this was a sign of ego or of being a "rock star." Nevertheless, when someone set up a show and put a band without any recordings on after a band with a record, resentments flared.

18. The most prominent record labels that distributed sXe recordings included Revelation Records, Victory Records, Equal Vision, New Age, and Conversion.

19. Katherine, the twenty-two-year-old working class woman, told me: "I don't think I've ever heard anyone say anything bad about you. A lot of people *do* look up to you. Like, wow, look at Ross, he's a college teacher and he's in the scene, or Ross just wrote a book. Everything you do. Everybody in the scene that I know of, they do look up to you. I've never heard anybody say anything bad about you. I don't think there's anything bad to be said."

Chapter 2. Straight Edge Core Values

1. Later researchers have recognized that subcultures are not exclusive to working-class youth (Baron 1989).

2. Willis's (1977) classic study of English working-class school boys serves as another example. The working-class "lads" eschewed middle-class, intellectual pursuits and glorified manual labor as real work, goofing off in school and mocking the quiet middle-class kids who listened attentively to teachers, diligently did their homework, and conformed to the school's rules. However, by delegitimizing education and white-collar work, the lads rein-

forced the existing class structure and ensured their place in its lower rungs. Although they felt they were resisting their subordination, the lads merely reinforced their subordinate class position, effectively ensuring they would never achieve upward mobility.

3. Movements often appropriate and modify their opponents' or oppressors' symbols. The gay and lesbian liberation movement changed the pink triangle from a Nazi death camp label for homosexuals into a symbol for unity and pride. The American Indian Movement turned the American flag upside down to demonstrate its disgust with the U.S. government.

4. The Institute for Social Research at the University of Michigan reported, in their "Monitoring the Future" study, that in 1996–2000 between 40.2% and 42.4% of twelfth graders reported using an illicit drug in the last year, while between 24.6% and 26.2% used in the last thirty days. The same study reported that between 72.5% and 74.8% used alcohol in the last year and between 50.0% and 52.7% had used in the last thirty days. Approximately 33% reported being drunk in the last thirty days. (Monitoring the Future study 2000, www.monitoringthefuture.com).

5. Stretching ears involves gradually enlarging the piercing with a series of hoops of increasing diameters. Plugs are thin "earrings" without a ring; they simply fill ("plug") the piercing. Some plugs (and therefore piercings) are as much as one inch in diameter.

6. The popular bands Earth Crisis, Outspoken, and Good Clean Fun encouraged listeners to challenge homophobia. At one time there was even a website dedicated to "Queer Edge."

7. Earth Crisis sings, "An effective revolutionary, with the clarity of mind that I've attained."

Chapter 3. Straight Edge as a Social Movement

1. For example, the Student Nonviolent Coordinating Committee emerged during several political shifts. The civil rights movement had won important Supreme Court rulings, President John F. Kennedy and Attorney General Robert Kennedy pledged their support, and liberation struggles around the globe created at least a sense of the possibility of revolution. Increasing urbanization made networking and organizing easier. Finally, the political disorder in Birmingham, Alabama, surrounding the electoral contest between "Bull" Connor and Albert Boutwell created a focal point for change that the SNCC and other civil rights groups capitalized on.

2. Many aspects of the gay and lesbian liberation movement transcend typical organizational structures (Gamson 1997). Certainly, there are formalized gay and lesbian groups, but the movement is more than the sum of its organizations. Lesbians and gays have created a politicized subculture intent on destabilizing cultural norms. This political collective identity is not necessarily tied to social movement organizations. The gay and lesbian liberation movement may be the quintessential new social movement. It centers on a specific identity, is not revolutionary (in the traditional sense), and focuses

on creating safe cultural spaces in addition to challenging the state. Certainly, various factions of the movement focus their energies on the state (for instance, on changing marriage and sodomy laws), but for many members culture, lifestyle, and identity expression are the focal points of resistance.

3. See Calhoun (1993) for a discussion of nineteenth-century movements with "new" social movement characteristics.

4. "Contrary to culturalist interpretations, no categorical distinction can be drawn between social movements, pressure groups and parties. Social movements are best understood in terms of a continuum stretching from informal network-like associations to formal party-like organizations" (Scott 1990:132).

5. New social movement theory acknowledges the active process of identity construction by problematizing "the often fragile process of constructing collective identities and identifying group interests, instead of assuming that conflict groups and their interests are structurally determined" (Buechler 1995:442).

6. By 2000, distros had been increasingly replaced by online selling. Also, as hardcore grows in popularity, it is now easier to find in conventional stores.

7. Another Floorpunch song, "Persevere," illustrated a common theme that, while others may sell out, the remaining sXers' commitments will stay strong: "Then that day finally came / You lost the edge, but I'll never change / . . . You're long gone, but I'll never quit / Through thick and thin, I'll stick with it."

8. The relatively small Clearweather scene included eight sXers, aged twenty-nine to thirty-two. Though most were much less active in the scene than they had once been, their commitment inspired younger kids.

9. Calhoun (1993:408) discusses this mix-and-match process of commitment construction: "One may thus combine feminism with pacifism and not be much moved by environmental concerns, and no organization will divert one's feminist and pacifist dollars or envelope licking to environmentalist uses. This is described sometimes as a consumerist orientation to political involvement, with a variety of movement products to choose from. The various movements are knit together into a field but not a superordinate umbrella organization."

Chapter 4. Positivity versus Militancy

1. In 2004, it was a measure of hardcore's growing popularity that Hellfest continued to grow. Promoters expected 8,500 kids at the 2005 event.

2. It is worth noting that this shirt is generally meant as a joke and a parody of another sXe shirt slogan: "Straight edge—if you're not now, you never were." However, such messages often reflected an underlying seriousness and outsiders or newcomers would not understand the humor of such an inside joke.

3. Lesbian feminists and the broader women's movement have never completely come to terms with their differences (Eder, Staggenborg, and Sudderth 1995). Likewise, the gay and lesbian liberation movement has struggled over the inclusion of transgendered individuals (Gamson 1997).

4. Gamson (1997:178) shows that movement conflicts over who is in and who is out are actually messages to the public rather than hard-and-fast rules within the social movements: "internal movement debates are best understood as public communications, depending heavily on the communicative environment." Thus, participants may create *symbolic* boundaries to convey an image to the public. In the case of lesbian and gay liberation, some groups will exclude drag queens for the public's benefit but informally accept them when out of public view.

5. See Gamson (1997) for more discussion on how movements' internal debates send a message to and create an image for outside observers.

6. It should be noted that the few sXers who wore such shirts often did so more for their humor or shock value than because the message reflected their true sentiments.

7. These events occurred just weeks prior to my own confrontation with Jackson and another Courage Crew member, Clint, described in chapter 2.

8. During several Good Clean Fun shows I witnessed, Issa reminded the crowd, "Remember, no one should be dancing so hard that the smallest person is afraid to come up here and sing along." Indeed, more women appeared to participate in the dancing and singing at GCF shows than at other shows I attended.

9. Both of these songs are from the Good Clean Fun record *On the Streets Saving the Scene from the Forces of Evil*. Phyte Records #20. Washington, D.C.

10. The situation is similar to that of the environmental movement, detractors of which cite Earth first! or Earth Liberation Front to discredit the entire movement (including peaceful groups such as the Nature Conservancy and the Sierra Club).

11. In the 2000s, both the University of Colorado's athletic department and the U.S. Air Force Academy (located in Colorado Springs) faced scandals involving athletes and airmen raping female students and cadets.

Chapter 5. Masculinity in Contradiction

1. Straight edgers did not use the label "jock" to mean "athlete" per se; many sXers are or were athletes. Rather, the connotation of "jock" was an arrogant, selfish, hypermasculine jerk.

2. On October 16, 1995, the Million Man March/Day of Absence attracted approximately one million black men to Washington, D.C., for a day of "prayer, fasting, confession, forgiveness of sin, atonement, repentance, reconciliation, and responsibility" (Walker 1998:9). Nation of Islam leader Louis Farrakhan and others centered the day's events around three of these themes, "atonement, reconciliation, and responsibility" (Madhubuti and Karenga 1996:5).

3. Formed in 1991 by former college football coach Bill McCartney, the Promise Keepers are an evangelical movement that traces society's problems to a variety of broken promises, especially those between men and God, men and their wives, and men and other men (Stepnick 2000; Abraham 1997).

Men had failed to fulfill their "natural" roles as spiritual leaders, faithful husbands, and devoted fathers, pushing their familial duties onto women who, the men felt, were less suited to the task. A Promise Keeper vowed to "take back" his leadership role and fulfill his obligations as a man.

4. In the mythopoetic movement's seminal book, *Iron John: A Book about Men,* Robert Bly claimed that men have become passive, losing their adventurous and victorious spirit, resulting in a sense of ineffectiveness and unhappiness (Bly 1990). Bly believed the primary cause of this crisis of masculinity was fathers' absence during boys' upbringing.

5. The profeminists' three main tenets were "profeminist, gay-affirmative, enhancing men's lives." They renounced sexist, homophobic, and racist behavior and thought. Perhaps the most political and least spiritual of the contemporary men's movements, the profeminists worked to stop sexual harassment in the workplace, end date rape, and fought against AIDS (see Kimmel 1997; Harding 1992).

6. Only once during the seven years of my research (and since) did I witness an injury significant enough to require a trip to the emergency room—the incident I just mentioned. The vast majority of shows produced no significant injuries.

7. The Denver/Boulder area was home to many kids originally from Boston. While they appreciated being able to see a greater variety of bands back home more frequently, most of them disliked the Boston scene, saying it was "too big" or "too trendy."

Chapter 6. Girls United and Divided

1. See Gottlieb and Wald's (1994:26) discussion on how women performers are often restricted to two roles, either "the to-be-looked-at sex object, or the woman with balls."

2. From "Calling All Girls" by Laura Greco at www.xsisterhoodx.com [viewed 11/22/03].

3. It is worth noting that *men* whom sXers perceived went to shows to "hook up" or pick up girls were also ridiculed and viewed as there "for the wrong reasons." The difference, of course, is that hardcore kids attributed this motivation to women much more frequently than to men. There was less pressure for men to *prove* their motivations were "true" or pure.

4. "Calling All Girls" by Laura Greco at www.x-grrrls.com [viewed 11/22/03].

Chapter 7. Life after Subculture

1. Some sXers did attempt to "reclaim" their "edge" after experimenting with alcohol and/or drugs. The majority of sXers believed this was ridiculous and refused to acknowledge such individuals as sXe.

2. Martha Irvine, *Star Tribune,* Minneapolis, MN, May 4, 2003.

3. Bane's song is inspired by an old D.C. band.

4. www.TrueTillDeath.com, viewed 11/13/03.

5. Owing to their roots in the punk scene, many sXers were suspicious of labels even as they adopted the sXe lifestyle. Adopting a label might imply unquestioningly, wholeheartedly accepting a dogma, a sentiment contrary to punk ideals. I recall struggling with my own decision to actually take on the sXe identity, and others reported thoughtfully considering whether or not to actually claim sXe.

Chapter 8. Commercialization, the Internet, and the Cultic Milieu

1. Green Day was nominated for several awards. Both Hatebreed and Killswitch Engage were nominated for the "Best Metal Performance" Grammy.
2. A few of the many hardcore bands that produced videos in the 2000s included H2O, Most Precious Blood, Throwdown, Bleeding Through, Hatebreed, Killswitch Engage, and Sick of it All. Youth of Today famously (or infamously) made a video for their song, "No More," but the trend failed to catch on until much later.
3. Muggleton (2000:133–134) writes: "Rather than self-contained and clearly defined subcultures being diffused and dissipated by media attention and commercial exploitation, authentic inception is characterized here by a lack of cohesion and demarcation, with the media playing a homogenizing and clarifying role."
4. www.nike.com/nikeskateboarding/v2/assets/botttomBar/threat/major_threat-bg-v2.gif, viewed 6/24/05.
5. From *Impact: A Hardcore Fanzine* issue 2, 2002.
6. Such sites catered to members of a variety of music-based subcultures, including indie rock, emo, rockabilly, goth, punk, hardcore, and metal.
7. I heard rumors they had begun a section of Suicideboys, though I could not find pictorials of men.
8. Viewed 1/27/05.
9. Viewed 1/27/05.
10. Viewed 4/12/05.
11. Elliot Smith was perhaps the archetype of emo-themed music. His somber, acoustic songs made him a favorite of the emo crowd. Sadly, he killed himself in 2003.
12. www.music-news.com/ShowReview.asp?nReviewID
13. White-power racists and radical environmentalists, for example, both construct ideals of *purity*: the former purity of race, the latter of the natural world.
14. There is even a festival called the New England Metal Hardcore Festival.
15. Heavy metal, for instance, fragmented into glam/hair metal (such as Poison and Ratt), thrash/speed (Exodus, Megadeth), death (Death, Cannibal Corpse), Christian (Stryper), and black metal (Venom, Dimmu Borgir).

Chapter 9. Conclusions

1. Brake (1985:115) claims, "We can see that middle-class subcultures, whether political, bohemian, or militant, are also the result of contradictions in the

social structure." For example, the generation that produced the hippies and New Left grew up in a time of affluence contrasted with poverty and materialism versus idealism (Gitlin 1993 [1987]); structural contradiction produced a sense of powerlessness and/or strain which youth attempted to resolve via subcultural participation.

2. Some examples of the post-Seattle protests included massive demonstrations and civil disobedience at the IMF/World Bank meetings in Washington, D.C. (2000), the Democratic National Convention in Los Angeles (2000), the Republican National Convention in Philadelphia (2000), and the Free Trade Area of the Americas meetings in Quebec City (2001). Though central social movement organizations played a large role in organizing the events, it appears that many unaffiliated participants joined the protests based upon their connection to an antiglobalization/fair trade/global justice collective identity.

3. As the American Sociological Society's section on Collective Behavior suggests: "While theoretical elegance and conceptual tidiness may be gained by limiting the conceptualization of movements institutionally and in terms of the institutional locus of changes sought, it is important to ask about the costs of doing so. If movements are conceptualized under the rubric of contentious politics, for example, what is to be done conceptually and analytically with collective challenges or adaptations outside of traditional political arenas, such as retreatist and communal movements, movements of self-help and -renewal, lifestyle movements, not to mention the array of religious movements?" (Snow 2001:2).

4. For more on the various sXe factions see Wood (1999).

5. New social movement theories problematize "the often fragile process of constructing collective identities and identifying group interests, instead of assuming that conflict groups and their interests are structurally determined" (Buechler 1995:442).

6. Some radical feminists are adamantly against widening the feminist identity to include men (see Roszak and Roszak 1969). Other feminists encourage men to claim a feminist identity, believing that an inclusive movement will ultimately prove more effective (Schacht and Ewing 1997). Connell (1987:xii) writes, "There are currents in feminist thought which do not welcome men's involvement, and there is a fine line to tread between intruding on women's business and sharing the work on common problems." A growing constituency favors men's involvement as *profeminists* rather than *feminists,* thus preserving the feminist identity for women while still encouraging men's participation.

7. The second wave feminist movement, for example, ostracized lesbian feminists who critiqued heterosexism within the movement (Cruikshank 1992).

8. For a discussion of evangelical feminist women and their appreciation for their evangelical husbands, see Stacey and Gerard (1990).

9. Lockhart (2000:73) found that the Promise Keepers movement "includes at least four different ideologies of gender."

Abraham, Ken. 1997. *Who Are the Promise Keepers?: Understanding the Christian Men's Movement*. New York: Doubleday.

Adler, Patricia, and Peter Adler. 1983. "Shifts and Oscillations in Deviant Careers: The Case of Upper-Level Drug Dealers." *Social Problems* 31, 2:195–207.

———. 1987. *Membership Roles in Field Research*. Newbury Park, Calif.: Sage Publications.

Agar, Michael H. 1996. *The Professional Stranger: An Informal Introduction to Ethnography*. 2nd ed. San Diego: Academic Press.

Anderson, Mark, and Mark Jenkins. 2001. *Dance of Days: Two Decades of Punk in the Nation's Capital*. New York: Soft Skull Press.

Andes, Linda. 1998. "Growing Up Punk: Meaning and Commitment Careers in a Contemporary Youth Culture." In *Youth Culture: Identity in a Postmodern World*, ed. Jonathon S. Epstein. Malden, Mass.: Blackwell.

Atkinson, Michael. 2003. "The Civilizing of Resistance: Straightedge Tattooing." *Deviant Behavior* 24:197–220.

Azzerad, Michael. 2001. *Our Band Could Be Your Life: Scenes from the American Indie Underground, 1981–1991*. Boston: Little, Brown.

Baron, Stephen W. 1989. "Resistance and Its Consequences: The Street Culture of Punks." *Youth and Society* 21, 2:207–237.

Bassett, Caroline. 1997. "Virtually Gendered: Life in an On-line World." In *The Subcultures Reader*, ed. Ken Gelder and Sarah Thornton. London: Routledge.

Bearman, Peter S., and Hannah Brückner. 2001. "Promising the Future: Virginity Pledges and First Intercourse." *American Journal of Sociology* 106, 4:859–912.

Becker, Howard S. 1960. "Notes on the Concept of Commitment." *American Journal of Sociology* 66:32–40.

———. 1963. *Outsiders: Studies in the Sociology of Deviance*. New York: Free Press.

Becker, Howard S., and Blanche Geer. 1960. "Participant Observation: The Analysis of Qualitative Field Data." In *Human Organization Research: Field Relations and Techniques*, ed. Richard N. Adams and Jack J. Preiss. Homewood, Ill.: Dorsey Press.

Benford, Robert D. 1993. "Frame Disputes within the Nuclear Disarmament Movement." *Social Forces* 71:677–701.

Benford, Robert D., and Scott A. Hunt. 1992. "Dramaturgy and Social Movements: The Social Construction and Communication of Power." *Sociological Inquiry* 62:36–55.

Bennett, Andy. 1999. "Subcultures or Neo-Tribes? Rethinking the Relationship Between Youth, Style, and Musical Taste." *Sociology* 33, 3:599–617.

———. 2000. *Popular Music and Youth Culture: Music, Identity and Place*. London: Macmillan.

———. 2001. *Cultures of Popular Music*. Buckingham, UK, and Philadelphia: Open University Press.

229

Bennett, Andy. 2004. "Virtual Subculture? Youth, Identity and the Internet." In *After Subculture: Critical Studies in Contemporary Youth Culture*, ed. Andy Bennett and Keith Kahn-Harris. New York: Palgrave Macmillan.

Berger, Bennett M. 1967. "Hippie Morality-More Old Than New." *Trans-Action* 5, 2:19–26.

Biernacki, Patrick, and Dan Waldorf. 1981. "Snowball Sampling." *Sociological Research and Methods* 10:141–163.

Bjorgo, T., and R. Wilte, eds. 1993. *Racist Violence in Europe*. New York: St. Martin's Press.

Blackman, Shane J. 1995. *Youth: Positions and Oppositions-Style, Sexuality, and Schooling*. Aldershot, UK: Avebury.

Blush, Steven. 2001. *American Hardcore: A Tribal History*. Los Angeles: Feral House.

Bly, Robert. 1990. *Iron John: A Book about Men*. Reading, Mass.: Addison-Wesley.

Bottomore, Tom. 1984. *The Frankfurt School*. Chichester, UK: Ellis Horwood.

Boyd, Herb. 1995. "The March." *The Black Scholar* 25:12–16.

Brake, Mike. 1985. *Comparative Youth Culture: The Sociology of Youth Culture and Youth Subcultures in America, Britain, and Canada*. London: Routledge and Kegan Paul.

Brod, Harry, ed. 1987. *The Making of Masculinities: The New Men's Studies*. Boston: Allen and Unwin.

Bruce, Steve. 1994. "The Inevitable Failure of the New Christian Right." *Sociology of Religion* 55:229–242

Buechler, Steven M. 1993. "Beyond Resource Mobilization? Emerging Trends in Social Movement Theory." *Sociological Quarterly* 34:217–235.

——. 1995. "New Social Movement Theories." *Sociological Quarterly* 36: 441–464.

——. 1999. *Social Movements in Advanced Capitalism: The Political Economy and Cultural Construction of Social Activism*. New York: Oxford University Press.

Butler, Judith. 1990. *Gender Trouble: Feminism and the Subversion of Identity*. New York and London: Routledge.

Calhoun, Craig. 1994. *Social Theory and the Politics of Identity*. Oxford and Cambridge, Mass.: Blackwell.

Campbell, Colin. 1972. "The Cult, the Cultic Milieu and Secularization." A *Sociological Yearbook of Religion in Britain* 5:119–36.

Campbell, D. T. 1975. "Degrees of Freedom and the Case Study." *Comparative Political Studies* 8: 178–193.

Cappo, Ray. 1993. *In Defense of Reality: Conversations between Ray Cappo and Satyaraj Das*. New York: Equal Vision Records.

Carr, Lynn C. "Tomboy Resistance and Conformity: Agency in Social Psychological Gender Theory." *Gender and Society* 12, 5:528–553.

Carrigan, Tim, Bob Connell, and John Lee. 1985. "Toward a New Sociology of Masculinity." *Theory and Society* 14, 5:551–604.

Carrington, Ben, and Brian Wilson. 2004. "Dance Nations: Rethinking Youth Subcultural Theory." In *After Subculture: Critical Studies in Contemporary Youth Culture*, ed. Andy Bennett and Keith Kahn-Harris, 65–78. New York: Palgrave Macmillan.

Cashmore, Ernest Ellis. 1984. *No Future: Youth and Society*. London: Heinemann.

Charmaz, Kathy. 1983. "The Grounded Theory Method: An Explication and Interpretation." In *Contemporary Field Research: A Collection of Readings*, ed. R. M. Emerson. Boston: Little, Brown.

Christian, Harry. 1994. *The Making of Anti-Sexist Men*. New York: Routledge.

Clark, Dylan. 2003. "The Death and Life of Punk, the Last Subculture." In *The Post-Subcultures Reader*, ed. David Muggleton and Rupert Weinzierl. Oxford: Berg.

Clarke, John. 1986. "Style," In *Resistance Through Rituals: Youth Subcultures in Post-war Britain*, ed. Stuart Hall and Tony Jefferson. London: Hutchinson.

Clarke, John, Stuart Hall, Tony Jefferson, and Brian Roberts. 1975. "Subcultures, Cultures, and Class: A Theoretical Overview." In *Resistance Through Rituals: Youth Subcultures in Post-war Britain*, ed. Stuart Hall and Tony Jefferson. London: Hutchinson.

Clarke, Gary. 1997 [1981]. "Defending Ski-Jumpers: A Critique of Theories of Youth Subcultures." In *The Subcultures Reader*, ed. Ken Gelder and Sarah Thornton. New York: Routledge.

Coffey, Amanda. 1999. *The Ethnographic Self: Fieldwork and the Representation of Identity*. London and Thousand Oaks, Calif.: Sage Publications.

Cohen, Albert. 1955. *Delinquent Boys: The Culture of the Gang*. London: Collier-Macmillan.

Cohen, Jean L. 1985. "Strategy or Identity: New Theoretical Paradigms and Contemporary Social Movements." *Social Research* 52:4.

Cohen, Phil. 1972. "Subcultural Conflict and Working Class Community." *Working Papers in Cultural Studies* 2. University of Birmingham: Centre for Contemporary Cultural Studies.

——. 1984. "Subcultural Conflict and Working-Class Community." In *Culture, Media, Language*, ed. Stuart Hall, Dennis Hobson, and Paul Willis. London: Hutchinson.

Cohen, Stanley. 1972. *Folk Devils and Moral Panics: The Creation of the Mods and the Rockers*. Oxford: Martin Robertson.

Collins, Patricia Hill. 1986. "Learning from the Outsider Within: The Sociological Significance of Black Feminist Thought." *Social Problems* 33:S14–S32.

——. 1989. "The Social Construction of Black Feminist Thought." *Signs* 14, 4:745–773.

Comstock, Michelle. 2001. "Grrrl Zine Networks: Re-composing Spaces of Authority, Gender, and Culture." *Journal of Advanced Composition* 21, 2:383–409.

Connell, Robert W. 1987. *Gender and Power: Society, the Person and Sexual Politics*. Sydney: Allen and Unwin.

——. 1995. *Masculinities*. Berkeley and Los Angeles: University of California Press.

——. 1997. "Gender Politics for Men." *International Journal of Sociology and Social Policy* 17, 1–2:62–77.

Cornwall, Andrea. 1997. "Men, Masculinity and 'Gender in Development'." *Gender and Development* 5, 2:8–13.

Cornwall, Andrea, and Nancy Lindisfarne, eds. 1994. *Dislocating Masculinity: Comparative Ethnographies.* New York: Routledge.

Cruikshank, Margaret. 1992. *The Gay and Lesbian Liberation Movement.* New York: Routledge, Chapman and Hall.

Davis, Erik. 1995. "Hare Krishna and Hardcore." *Spin Magazine* (summer 1995).

Davis, Fred. 1967. "Focus on the Flower Children, Why All of Us May Be Hippies Someday." *Trans-Action* 5, 2:10–18.

——. 1968. "Heads and Freaks: Patterns and Meanings of Drug Use among Hippies." *Journal of Health and Social Behavior* 9, 2:156–164.

DeMello, Margo. 1995. "Not Just for Bikers Anymore: Popular Representations of American Tattooing." *Journal of Popular Culture* 29:37–52.

Douglas, Jack D. 1976. *Investigative Social Research.* Beverly Hills, Calif.: Sage Publications.

Downton, James, Jr., and Paul Wehr. 1997. *The Persistent Activist: How Peace Commitment Develops and Survives.* Boulder, CO: Westview Press.

Durkheim, Emile. 1951 [1897]. *Suicide.* New York: The Free Press.

Earisman, Delbert L. 1968. *Hippies in Our Midst.* Philadelphia: Fortress Press.

Earth Crisis. 1995. The Discipline. On *Destroy the Machines* [CD]. Chicago: Victory Records.

Eder, Donna, and William Corsaro. 1999. "Ethnographic Studies of Children and Youth: Theoretical and Ethical Issues." *Journal of Contemporary Ethnography* 28, 5:520–531.

Eder, Donna, Suzanne Staggenborg, and Lori Sudderth. 1995. "The National Women's Music Festival: Collective Identity and Diversity in a Lesbian-Feminist Community." *Journal of Contemporary Ethnography* 23:485–515.

Eder, Klaus. 1985. "The 'New Social Movements': Moral Crusades, Political Protest Groups, or Social Movements?" *Social Research* 52:869–901.

Elgin, Duane. 1993. *Voluntary Simplicity : Toward a Way of Life That Is Outwardly Simple, Inwardly Rich.* Rev. ed. New York: William Morrow.

Farrell, Warren. 1974. *The Liberated Man: Beyond Masculinity; Freeing Men and Their Relationships with Women.* New York: Random House.

——. 1993. *The Myth of Male Power: Why Men Are the Disposable Sex.* New York: Simon and Schuster.

Ferree, Myra Marx. 1992. "The Political Context of Rationality: Rational Choice Theory and Resource Mobilization." In *Frontiers in Social Movement Theory,* ed. Aldon D. Morris and Carol McClurg Mueller. New Haven: Yale University Press.

Floorpunch. 1996. Stick Together. On *Division One Champs* [LP]. Hudson, N.Y.: Equal Vision Records.

Fox, Kathryn Joan. 1987. "Real Punks and Pretenders: The Social Organization of a Counterculture." *Journal of Contemporary Ethnography* 16, 3:344–370.

Freeman, Jo, ed. 1983. *Social Movements of the Sixties and Seventies.* New York: Longman Group.

Friedman, Debra, and Doug McAdam. 1992. "Collective Identity and Activism: Networks, Choices, and the Life of a Social Movement." In *Frontiers in So-*

cial Movement Theory, ed. Aldon D. Morris and Carol McClurg Mueller. New Haven: Yale University Press.

Frith, Simon. 1985. "The Sociology of Youth." In *Sociology: New Directions*, ed. Michael Haralabos. Ormskirk, UK: Causeway.

Gamson, Josh. 1989. "Silence, Death, and the Invisible Enemy: AIDS Activism and Social Movement 'Newness'." *Social Problems* 36:351–366.

———. 1996. "The Organizational Shaping of Collective Identity: The Case of Lesbian and Gay Film Festivals in New York." *Sociological Forum* 11, 2:231–261.

———. 1997. "Messages of Exclusion: Gender, Movements, and Symbolic Boundaries." *Gender and Society* 11:178–199.

Gamson, William A. 1990. *The Strategy of Social Protest*. 2nd ed. Belmont, Calif.: Wadsworth Publishers.

———. 1991. "Commitment and Agency in Social Movements." *Sociological Forum* 6, 1:27–50

Gans, Herbert J. 1999. "Participant Observation in the Era of 'Ethnography'." *Journal of Contemporary Ethnography* 28, 5:520–531.

Gecas, Viktor. 2000. "Value Identities, Self-Motives, and Social Movements." In *Self, Identity, and Social Movements*, ed. Sheldon Stryker, Timothy Owens, and Robert W. White. Minneapolis: University of Minnesota Press.

Geertz, Clifford. 1974. *The Interpretation of Cultures*. New York: Basic Books.

Gelder, Ken. 1997. "Introduction to Part Seven." In *The Subcultures Reader*, ed. Ken Gelder and Sarah Thornton. London and New York: Routledge.

Gelder, Ken, and Sarah Thornton, eds. 1997. *The Subcultures Reader*. London and New York: Routledge.

Giddens, Anthony. 1991. *Modernity and Self-Identity: Self and Society in the Late Modern Age*. Stanford: Stanford University Press.

Gitlin, Todd. 1993 [1987]. *The Sixties: Years of Hope, Days of Rage*. New York: Bantam Books.

Glaser, Barney G., and Anselm L. Strauss. 1967. *The Discovery of Grounded Theory: Strategies for Qualitative Research*. Chicago, Aldine.

Goffman, Erving. 1959. *The Presentation of Self in Everyday Life*. Garden City, N.Y.: Doubleday.

———. 1974 [1963]. *Stigma: Notes on the Management of Spoiled Identity*. New York: Jason Aronson.

———. 1976. "Gender Display." *Studies in the Anthropology of Visual Communication* 3:69–77.

Good Clean Fun. 2001. Today the Scene, Tomorrow the World. On *Straight Outta Hardcore* [CD]. Washington, D.C.: Phyte Records.

Goode, Erich. 1993. Drugs in American Society. 4th ed. New York: McGraw-Hill.

Goodman, Barak, director. 2001. "Merchants of Cool." *Frontline* [television program]." Boston: WGBH Educational Foundation.

Gordon, Milton M. 1947. "The Concept of Subculture and Its Application." In *The Subcultures Reader*, ed. Ken Gelder and Sarah Thornton. London and New York: Routledge.

Gosling, Tim. 2004. "'Not for Sale': The Underground Network of Anarcho-Punk." In *Music Scenes: Local, Translocal, and Virtual,* ed. Andy Bennett and Richard A Peterson. Nashville: Vanderbilt University Press.

Gottlieb, Joanne, and Gayle Wald. 1994. "Smells Like Teen Spirit: Riot Grrrls, Revolution, and Women in Independent Rock." In *Microphone Fiends: Youth Music and Youth Culture,* ed. Andrew Ross and Tricia Rose. New York: Routledge.

Greenwald, Andy. 2003. *Nothing Feels Good: Punk Rock, Teenagers, and Emo.* New York: St. Martin's Griffin.

Grossberg, Lawrence. 1992. *We Gotta Get Out of This Place: Popular Conservatism and Postmodern Culture.* New York: Routledge.

Habermas, Jürgen. 1981. *Selections.* Frankfurt am Main: Suhrkamp.

———. 1984–1987. *The Theory of Communicative Action,* trans. Thomas McCarthy. 3 vols. Boston: Beacon Press.

Haenfler, Ross. 2001. "Rethinking Subcultural Resistance: Core Values of the Straight Edge Movement." A paper presented to the annual meeting of the American Sociological Association, Anaheim, Calif.

Halberstam, Judith. 1998. *Female Masculinity.* Durham, NC: Duke University Press.

Hall, Stuart. 1986. "Popular Culture and the State." In *Popular Culture and Social Relations,* ed. Tony Bennett, Colin Mercer, and Janet Woolacott. Milton Keynes, UK: Open University Press.

Hall, Stuart, and Tony Jefferson, eds. 1976. *Resistance Through Rituals: Youth Subcultures in Post-War Britain.* London: Hutchinson.

Hammersley, Martyn, and Paul Atkinson. 1995. *Ethnography: Principles in Practice.* 2nd ed. London: Routledge.

Harding, Christopher, ed. 1992. *Wingspan: Inside the Men's Movement.* New York: St. Martin's Press.

Harrison, James, James Chin, and Thomas Ficarratto. 1995. "Warning: Masculinity May Be Dangerous to Your Health." In *Men's Lives,* ed. Michael S. Kimmel and Michael A. Messner. 3rd ed. Boston: Allyn and Bacon.

Hayano, D. M. 1979. "Auto-ethnography: Paradigms, Problems, and Prospects." *Human Organization* 38:99–104.

Hebdige, Dick. 1979. *Subculture: The Meaning of Style.* London: Methuen.

Helton, Jesse J., and William J. Staudenmeier, Jr. 2002. "Re-imagining Being 'Straight' in Straight Edge." *Contemporary Drug Problems* 29:445–473.

Henry, Tricia. 1989. *Break All Rules!: Punk Rock and the Making of a Style.* Ann Arbor, Mich.: UMI Research Press.

Heylin, Clinton. 1998. *Never Mind the Bollocks, Here's the Sex Pistols: The Sex Pistols.* New York: Schirmer Books; London: Prentice Hall International.

Hirsch, Eric L. 1990. "Sacrifice for the Cause: The Impact of Group Processes on Recruitment and Commitment in Protest Movements." *American Sociological Review* 55:243–254.

Hirsch, Marianne, and Evelyn Fox Keller, eds. 1990. *Conflicts in Feminism.* New York: Routledge.

Hodkinson, Paul. 2002. *Goth: Identity, Style, and Subculture.* Oxford: Berg.

Hodkinson, Paul. 2004. "The Goth Scene and (Sub)Cultural Substance." In *After Subculture: Critical Studies in Contemporary Youth Culture*, ed. Andy Bennett and Keith Kahn-Harris. New York: Palgrave Macmillan.

Hoffer, Eric. 1951. *The True Believer; Thoughts on the Nature of Mass Movements*. New York: Harper and Row.

Hollander, Jocelyn A. 1998. "Doing Studs: The Performance of Gender and Sexuality on Late-Night Television." In *Everyday Inequalities: Critical Inquiries*, ed. Jodi O'Brien and Judith A. Howard. Malden, Mass.: Blackwell.

hooks, bell. 1992. *Feminist Theory: From Margin to Center*. Boston: South End Press.

———. 1995. *Killing Rage: Ending Racism*. New York: Henry Holt and Company.

———. 2000. *Feminism Is for Everybody*. Boston: South End Press.

Hunt, Scott, and Robert Benford. 1992. "Constructing Personal and Collective Identities: Identity Work in the Peace and Justice Movement, 1982–1991." A paper presented to the August 1992 annual meeting of the Society for the Study of Symbolic Interaction, Pittsburgh.

Hunt, Scott, Robert Benford, and David Snow. 1994. "Identity Fields: Framing Processes and the Social Construction of Movement Identities." In *New Social Movements: From Ideology to Identity*, ed. Hank Johnston, Enrique Laraña, and Joseph R. Gusfield. Philadelphia: Temple University Press.

Hunter, James Davidson.1987. *Evangelism: The Coming Generation*. Chicago: University of Chicago Press.

Irwin, Darrell. 1999. "The Straight Edge Subculture: Examining the Youths' Drug-Free Way." *Journal of Drug Issues* 29, 2:365–380.

Irwin, John. 1977. *Scenes*. Beverly Hills, Calif.: Sage Publications.

Irwin, Katherine. 2001. "Legitimating the First Tattoo: Moral Passage through Informal Interaction." *Symbolic Interaction* 24, 1:365–384.

Jesser, Clinton J. 1996. *Fierce and Tender Men: Sociological Aspects of the Men's Movement*. Westport, Conn.: Praeger.

Johnston, Hank, Enrique Laraña, and Joseph R. Gusfield, eds. 1994. *New Social Movements: From Ideology to Identity*. Philadelphia: Temple University Press.

Kanter, Rosabeth Moss. 1968. "Commitment and Social Organization: A Study of Commitment Mechanisms in Utopian Communities." *American Sociological Review* 33:499–517.

———. 1972. *Commitment and Community: Communes and Utopias in Sociological Perspective*. Cambridge, Mass.: Harvard University Press.

Kaplan, Jeffrey, and Helene Lööw, eds. 2002. *The Cultic Milieu: Oppositional Subcultures in an Age of Globalization*. Walnut Creek, Calif.: AltaMira Press.

Kimmel, Michael S., ed. 1995. *The Politics of Manhood: Profeminist Men Respond to the Mythopoetic Men's Movement (and the Mythopoetic Leaders Answer)* Philadelphia: Temple University Press.

———. 1996. *Manhood in America: A Cultural History*. New York: Free Press.

———. 1997. "From Conscience and Common Sense to "Feminism for Men": Pro-Feminist Men's Rhetoric of Support for Women's Equality." *International Journal of Sociology and Social Policy* 17, 1/2:9–33.

Kimmel, Michael S., and Thomas E. Mosmiller, eds. 1992. *Against the Tide: Pro-Feminist Men in the United States, 1776–1990, A Documentary History*. Boston: Beacon Press.

Klandermans, Bert. 1994. "Transient Identities? Membership Patterns in the Dutch Peace Movement." In *New Social Movements: From Ideology to Identity*, ed. Hank Johnston, Enrique Larana, and Joseph R. Gusfield. Philadelphia: Temple University Press.

Kornhauser, William. 1959. *The Politics of Mass Society*. New York: Free Press.

Kupers, Terry A. 1993. *Revisioning Men's Lives*. New York: Guilford Press.

Lahicky, Beth. 1997. *All Ages: Reflections on Straight Edge*. Huntington Beach, Calif.: Revelation Books.

Leblanc, Lauraine. 1999. *Pretty in Punk: Girl's Gender Resistance in a Boy's Subculture*. New Brunswick, N.J.: Rutgers University Press.

Lee, Craig. 1983. "Los Angeles," In *Hardcore California: A History of Punk and New Wave*, ed. Peter Belsito and Bob Davis, 10–40. San Francisco: Last Gasp.

Lee, Steve S., and Richard A. Peterson. 2004. "Internet-based Virtual Music Scenes: The Case of P2 in Alt.Country Music." In *Music Scenes: Local, Translocal, and Virtual*, ed. Andy Bennett and Richard A. Peterson. Nashville: Vanderbilt University Press.

Leonard, M. 1998. "Paper Planes: Traveling the New Grrrl Geographies." In *Cool Places: Geographies of Youth Cultures*, ed. T. Skelton and G. Valentine. New York: Routledge.

Lichbach, Mark Irving. 1996. *The Cooperator's Dilemma*. Ann Arbor, Mich.: University of Michigan Press.

Liebman, Robert C. and Robert Wuthnow, eds. 1983. *The New Christian Right: Mobilization and Legitimation*. Hawthorne, N.Y.: Aldine.

Locher, David A. 2002. *Collective Behavior*. Upper Saddle River, N.J.: Prentice-Hall.

Lockhart, William H. 2000. "'We Are One Life' But Not of One Gender Ideology: Unity, Ambiguity, and the Promise Keepers." *Sociology of Religion* 61, 1:73–92.

Lofland, John, and Lyn Lofland. 1995. *Analyzing Social Settings: A Guide to Qualitative Observation and Analysis*. 3rd ed. Belmont, Calif.: Wadsworth Publishing.

Lowe, Melanie. 2004. "'Tween' Scene: Resistance within the Mainstream." In *After Subculture: Critical Studies in Contemporary Youth Culture*, ed. Andy Bennett and Keith Kahn-Harris. New York: Palgrave Macmillan.

Luckenbill, David E., and Joel Best. 1981. "Careers in Deviance and Respectability: The Analogy's Limitations." *Social Problems* 29, 2:197–206.

Lunbeck, Elizabeth. 1994. *The Psychiatric Persuasion: Knowledge, Gender, and Power in Modern America*. Princeton, N.J.: Princeton University Press.

Lyman, Peter. 1987. "The Fraternal Bond as a Joking Relationship: A Case Study of the Role of Sexist Jokes in Male Group Bonding." In *Changing Men: New Directions in Research on Men and Masculinity*, ed. Michael Kimmel. Newbury Park, Calif.: Sage Publications.

Madhubuti, Haki R., and Maulana Karenga, eds. 1996. *Million Man March/Day of Absence: A Commemorative Anthology: Speeches, Commentary, Photogra-*

phy, Poetry, Illustrations, Documents. Chicago: Third World Press; Los Angeles: University of Sankore Press.

Maffesoli, Michel. 1996. *The Time of the Tribes: The Decline of Individualism in Mass Society*. London: Sage Publications.

Marcuse, Herbert. 1964. *One-Dimensional Man*. Boston: Beacon Press.

Martin, Greg. 2002. "Conceptualizing Cultural Politics in Subcultural and Social Movement Studies." *Social Movement Studies* 1, 1: 73–88.

Marty, Martin E., and R. Scott Appleby, eds. 1993. *Fundamentalism and the State*. Chicago: University of Chicago Press.

Marx, Karl. 1964 [1932]. *The Economic and Philosophic Manuscripts of 1844*. New York: International Publishers.

McAdam, Doug. 1982. *Political Process and the Development of Black Insurgency, 1930-1970*. Chicago: University of Chicago Press.

———. 1988. *Freedom Summer: The Idealists Revisited*. New York: Oxford University Press.

———. 1994. "Culture and Social Movements." In *New Social Movements: From Ideology to Identity*, ed. Hank Johnston, Enrique Larana, and Joseph R. Gusfield. Philadelphia: Temple University Press.

———. 1996. "Conceptual Origins, Current Problems, Future Directions." In *Comparative Perspectives on Social Movements*, ed. Douglas McAdam, John McCarthy, and Mayer Zald. Cambridge: Cambridge University Press.

McAdam, Doug, and Ronnelle Paulsen. 1997. "Specifying the Relationship Between Social Ties and Activism." In *Social Movements: Readings on Their Emergence, Mobilization, and Dynamics*, ed. Doug McAdam and David A. Snow. Los Angeles: Roxbury Publishing Company.

McAdam, Doug, and David A. Snow, eds. 1997. *Social Movements: Readings on Their Emergence, Mobilization, and Dynamics*. Los Angeles: Roxbury Publishing Company.

McAdam, Doug, Sidney Tarrow, and Charles Tilly. 2001. *Dynamics of Contention*. New York: Cambridge University Press.

McCarthy, John, and Mayer Zald. 1977. "Resource Mobilization and Social Movements: A Partial Theory." *American Journal of Sociology* 82:1212–1241.

McRobbie, Angela. 2000. *Feminism and Youth Culture*. 2nd ed. New York: Routledge.

McRobbie, Angela, and Jenny Garber. 1976. "Girls and Subcultures." In *Feminism and Youth Culture*, ed. Angela McRobbie. 2nd ed. New York: Routledge.

Melucci, Alberto. 1985. "The Symbolic Challenge of Contemporary Movements." *Social Research* 52:789–816.

———. 1988. "Getting Involved: Identity and Mobilization in Social Movements." In *From Structure to Action: Comparing Social Movement Research Across Cultures*, Vol. 1 of *International Social Movement Research*, ed. Bert Klandermans, Hanspeter Kriesi, and Sidney Tarrow. Greenwich, Conn.: JAI Press.

———. 1989. *Nomads of the Present: Social Movements and Individual Needs in Contemporary Society*. Philadelphia: Temple University Press.

———. 1994. "A Strange Kind of Newness: What's 'New' in New Social Movements?" In *New Social Movements: From Ideology to Identity*, ed. Hank

Johnston, Enrique Larana, and Joseph R. Gusfield. Philadelphia: Temple University Press.

Melucci, Alberto. 1996. *Challenging Codes: Collective Action in the Information Age*. Cambridge: Cambridge University Press.

Merton, Robert. 1968 [1949]. *Social Theory and Social Structure*. 3rd ed. New York: Free Press.

Messner, Michael. 1997. *Politics of Masculinities: Men in Movements*. Thousand Oaks, Calif.: Sage Publications.

Messner, Michael, and Don F. Sabo. 1990. *Sport, Men, and the Gender Order: Critical Feminist Perspectives*. Champaign, Ill.: Human Kinetics Books.

Miller, Timothy. 1991. *The Hippies and American Values*. Knoxville: University of Tennessee Press.

——. 1999. *The Sixties Communes: Hippies and Beyond*. Syracuse, N.Y.: Syracuse University Press.

Moore, David. 1994. *The Lads in Action: Social Process in an Urban Youth Subculture*. Aldershot, UK: Arena.

Moore, Ryan. 2005. "Alternative to What? Subcultural Capital and the Commercialization of a Music Scene." *Deviant Behavior* 26:229–252.

Morrison, Denton E. 1971. "Some Notes toward Theory on Relative Deprivation, Social Movements, and Social Change." *American Behavioral Scientist* May-June: 675–690.

Mueller, Carol. 1994. "Conflict Networks and the Origins of Women's Liberation." In *New Social Movements: From Ideology to Identity*, ed. Hank Johnston, Enrique Larana, and Joseph R. Gusfield. Philadelphia: Temple University Press.

Muggleton, David. 2000. *Inside Subculture: The Postmodern Meaning of Style*. Oxford: Berg.

Muggleton, David. 1997. "The Post-Subculturist." In *The Clubcultures Reader: Readings in Popular Cultural Studies*, ed. Steve Redhead, Derek Wynne, and Justin O'Connor. Oxford: Blackwell.

Muggleton, David, and Rupert Weinzierl, eds. 2003 . *The Post-Subcultures Reader*. Oxford: Berg.

Mungham, Geoff, and Geoff Pearson. 1976. *Working Class Youth Cultures*. London: Routledge and Kegan Paul.

Oberschall, Anthony. 1973. *Social Conflict and Social Movements*. Englewood Cliffs, N.J.: Prentice-Hall.

O'Hara, Craig. 1999. *The Philosophy of Punk: More Than Noise*. London and San Fransisco: AK Press.

O'Malley, Jaclyn. 2005. "Reno Police Classify Straight Edge as a Gang." *Reno Gazette-Journal* May 5, 2005.

Olson, Mancur. 1965. *The Logic of Collective Action*. New York: Schocken.

Opp, Karl-Dieter, and Wolfgang Roehl. 1990. "Repression, Micromobilization, and Political Protest." *Social Forces* 69:521–547.

Osgerby, Bill. 1998. *Youth in Britain Since 1945*. Oxford: Blackwell.

Parkin, Frank. 1968. *Middle Class Radicalism; The Social Bases of the British Campaign for Nuclear Disarmament*. New York: F. A. Praeger.

Parsons, Talcott, and Robert F. Bales. 1956. *Family, Socialization and Interactions Process*. London: Routledge and Kegan Paul.

Pfaff, Steven. 1996. "Collective Identity and Informal Groups in Revolutionary Mobilization: East Germany in 1989." *Social Forces* 75, 1:91–118.

Piano, Doreen. 2003. "Resisting Subjects: DIY Feminism and the Politics of Style in Subcultural Production." In *The Post-Subcultures Reader*, ed. David Muggleton and Rupert Weinzierl. Oxford: Berg.

Pileggi, Mary S. 1998. "No Sex, No Drugs, Just Hardcore Rock: Using Bourdieu to Understand Straight-Edge Kids and Their Practices." Ph.D. diss., Temple University.

Pinn, Anthony B. 1998. "Keep on Keepin' On: Reflections on "Get on the Bus" and the Language of the Movement." In *Black Religion after the Million Man March: Voices on the Future*, ed. Garth Kasimu Baker-Fletcher. Maryknoll, N.Y.: Orbis Books.

Polhemus, Ted. 1994. *Streetstyle: From Sidewalk to Catwalk*. New York: Thames and Hudson.

Polletta, Francesca. 1997. "Culture and Its Discontents: Recent Theorizing on the Cultural Dimensions of Protest." *Sociological Inquiry* 67, 4:431–450.

———. 1998. "'It Was Like a Fever . . .': Narrative and Identity in Social Protest." *Social Problems* 45:137–159.

Prus, Robert. 1996. *Symbolic Interaction and Ethnographic Research: Intersubjectivity and the Study of Human Lived Experience*. Albany: State University of New York Press.

Punch, Maurice. 1986. *The Politics and Ethics of Fieldwork*. Beverly Hills, Calif.: Sage Publications.

———. 1994. "Politics and Ethics in Qualitative Research." In *Handbook of Qualitative Research*, ed. Norman K. Denzin and Yvonna S. Lincoln. Thousand Oaks, Calif.: Sage Publications.

Redhead, Steve. 1990. *The End of the Century Party: Youth and Pop towards 2000*. Manchester, UK: Manchester University Press.

———. 1993. *Rave Off: Politics and Deviance in Contemporary Youth Culture*. Aldershot, UK: Avebury.

———. 1997. *Subculture to Clubculture: An Introduction to Popular Culture Studies*. Oxford: Blackwell.

Reinharz, Shulamit. 1992. *Feminist Methods in Social Research*. New York: Oxford University Press.

Rich, Adrienne. 1980. "Compulsory Heterosexuality and Lesbian Existence." *Signs* 5 (4):631–660.

Riemer, Jeffrey. 1977. "Varieties of Opportunistic Research." *Urban Life* 5, 4:467–477.

Robnett, Belinda. 1997. *How Long? African American Women and the Struggle for Freedom and Justice*. New York: Oxford University Press.

Rose, Tricia. 1994. *Black Noise: Rap Music and Black Culture in Contemporary America*. New York: Routledge.

Ross, Andrew. 2000. "Hacking Away at the Counter Culture." In *The Cybercultures Reader*, ed. David Bell and Barbara Kennedy. New York: Routledge.

Roszak , Betty, and Theodore Roszak, eds. 1969. *Masculine / Feminine: Readings in Sexual Mythology and the Liberation of Women*. New York: Harper and Row.

Rozell, Mark J., Clyde Wilcox, and John Green. 1998. "Religious Constituencies and Support for the Christian Right in the 1990s." *Social Science Quarterly* 79, 4:815–827.

Sabo, Donald F. 1994. "Pigskin, Patriarchy, and Pain." In *Sex, Violence, and Power in Sports: Rethinking Masculinity*, ed. Michael A. Messner and Donald F. Sabo. Freedom, Calif.: Crossing Press.

Sabo, Donald F., and David F. Gordon, eds. 1995. *Men's Health and Illness: Gender, Power, and the Body*. Thousand Oaks, Calif.: Sage Publications.

Sanders, Clinton. 1989. *Customizing the Body: The Art and Culture of Tattooing*. Philadelphia: Temple University Press.

Schacht, Steven P., and Doris W. Ewing, eds. 1997. "Feminism and Men: Toward a Relational Understanding of Patriarchy and Cooperative Social Change." *International Journal of Sociology and Social Policy*, 17:1/2.

Schawble, Michael L. 1996. *Unlocking the Iron Cage: The Men's Movement, Gender Politics, and American Culture*. New York: Oxford University Press.

Schilt, Kristin. 2003. "'I'll Resist with Every Inch and Every Breath': Girls and Zine Making as a Form of Resistance." *Youth and Society* 35, 1:71–97.

——. 2004. "'Riot Grrrl Is . . .': Contestation Over Meaning in a Music Scene." In *After Subculture: Critical Studies in Contemporary Youth Culture*, ed. Andy Bennett and Keith Kahn-Harris. New York: Palgrave Macmillan.

Schor, Juliet B. 1998. *The Overspent American: Upscaling, Downshifting, and the New Consumer*. New York: Basic Books.

Scott, Alan. 1990. *Ideology and the New Social Movements*. London: Unwin Hyman Ltd.

Scott, James. 1985. *Weapons of the Weak: Everyday Forms of Peasant Resistance*. New Haven: Yale University Press.

Sersen, Brent. Producer and director. 1999. *Release* [Film]. (Available from Victory Records, PO Box 146546, Chicago, Ill., 60614)

Shamir, Boas. 1990. "Calculations, Values, and Identities: The Sources of Collectivistic Work Motivation." *Human Relations* 43:313–332.

Shields, Rob. 2003. *The Virtual*. New York: Routledge.

Smelser, Neil. 1962. *Theory of Collective Behavior*. New York: Free Press.

Smith, M., and P. Kollack. 1999. *Communities in Cyberspace*. London: Routledge.

Snow, David A., E. Burke Rochford, Jr., Steven K. Worden, and Robert B. Benford. 1986. "Frame Alignment Processes, Micromobilization, and Movement Participation." *American Sociological Review* 51: 464–481.

Snow, David A., Daniel M. Cress, Liam Downey, and Andrew W. Jones. 1998. "Disrupting the 'Quotidian': Reconceptualizing the Relationship between Breakdown and the Emergence of Collective Action." *Mobilization* 3, 1:1–22.

Snow, David A., and Doug McAdam. 2000. "Identity Work Processes in the Context of Social Movements: Clarifying the Identity/Movement Nexus." In *Self, Identity, and Social Movements*, ed. Sheldon Stryker, Timothy Owens, and Robert W. White. Minneapolis: University of Minnesota Press.

Stacey, Judith, and Barrie Thorne. 1985. "The Missing Feminist Revolution in Sociology." *Social Problems* 32:301–316.

Stacey, Judith, and Susan Elizabeth Gerard. 1990. "We Are Not Doormats: The Influence of Feminism on Contemporary Evangelicals in the United States." In *Uncertain Terms: Negotiating Gender in American Culture*, ed. Faye Ginsburg and Anna Lowenhaupt Tsing. Boston: Beacon Press.

Stepnick, Andrea. 2000. "Making Godly Men: The Social Construction of Masculinities in Promise Keepers." Ph.D. diss. Florida State University.

Stewart, Alex. 1998. *The Ethnographer's Method*. Thousand Oaks, Calif.: Sage Publications.

Strife. 1997. "Force of Change." and "To An End." On *In This Defiance* [CD]. Chicago, Ill.: Victory Records.

Styker, Sheldon. 1968. "Identity Salience and Role Performance: The Relevance of Symbolic Interaction Theory for Family Research." *Journal of Marriage and the Family* 30, 4:588–564.

——. 1981. "Symbolic Interactionism: Themes and Variations In *Social Psychology: Sociological Perspectives*, ed. Morris Rosenburg and Ralph H. Turner. New York: Basic Books.

Tarrow, Sidney. 1994. *Power in Movement: Social Movements, Collective Action and Politics*. Cambridge: Cambridge University Press.

Taylor, Verta. 1989. "Sources of Continuity in Social Movements: The Women's Movement in Abeyance." *American Sociological Review* 54:761–775.

——. 1996. *Rock-a-By Baby: Feminism, Self-Help, and Postpartum Depression*. New York: Routledge.

——. 2000. "Emotions and Identity in Women's Self-Help Movements." In *Self, Identity, and Social Movements*, ed. Sheldon Stryker, Timothy Owens, and Robert W. White. Minneapolis: University of Minnesota Press.

Taylor, Verta, and Nicole Raeburn. 1995. "Identity Politics as High Risk Activism: Career Consequences for Lesbian, Gay, and Bisexual Sociologists." *Social Problems* 42:252–273.

Taylor, Verta, and Leila Rupp. 1993. "Women's Culture and Lesbian Feminist Activism: A Reconsideration of Cultural Feminism." *Signs* 19, 1:32–61.

Taylor, Verta, and Nancy E. Whittier. 1992. "Collective Identity in Social Movement Communities: Lesbian Feminist Mobilization." In *Frontiers in Social Movement Theory*, ed. Aldon D. Morris and Carol McClurg Mueller. New Haven: Yale University Press.

Thomas, Douglas. 2002. *Hacker Culture*. Minneapolis: University of Minnesota Press.

Thornton, Sarah. 1995. *Club Cultures: Music, Media and Subcultural Capital*. Middletown, Conn.: Wesleyan University Press.

Tilly, Charles. 1978. *From Mobilization to Revolution*. Reading, Mass.: Addison-Wesley.

Touraine, Alain. 1985. "An Introduction to the Study of Social Movements." *Social Research* 52, 4:749–787.

Trial. 1997. *Through the Darkest Days* [CD]. Seattle, Wash.: Meltdown.

Turner, Ralph, and Lewis Killian. 1957. *Collective Behavior*. Englewood Cliffs, NJ: Prentice-Hall.

Vail, D. Angus. 1999. "Tattoos Are Like Potato Chips . . . You Can't Have Just One: The Process of Becoming and Being a Collector." *Deviant Behavior* 20:253–273.

Van Maanen, John. 1983. "The Moral Fix: On the Ethics of Fieldwork." In *Contemporary Field Research*, ed. Robert Emerson. Boston: Little, Brown.

Walker, Theodore Jr. 1998. "Can a Million Black Men Be Good News?" In *Black Religion after the Million Man March: Voices on the Future*, ed. Garth Kasimu Baker-Fletcher. Maryknoll, N.Y.: Orbis Books.

Walser, Robert. 1993. *Running with the Devil: Power, Gender and Madness in Heavy Metal Music*. Hanover, N.H.: Wesleyan University Press.

Warren, Carol A. B. 1988. *Gender Issues in Field Research*. Newbury Park, Calif.: Sage Publications.

Weber, Max. 1946. *From Max Weber: Essays in Sociology*, ed. H. H. Gerth and C. Wright Mills. New York: Oxford University Press.

West, Candace, and Don H. Zimmerman. 1987. "Doing Gender." *Gender and Society* 1, 2:125–151.

White, Robert W. 1989. "From Peaceful Protest to Guerilla War: Micromobilization of the Provisional Irish Republican Army." *American Journal of Sociology* 94:1277–1302.

Whittier, Nancy E. 1995. *Feminist Generations: The Persistence of the Radical Women's Movement*. Philadelphia: Temple University Press.

———. 1997. "Political Generations, Micro-Cohorts, and the Transformation of Social Movements." *American Sociological Review* 62, 5:760–778.

Whyte, William. 1943. *Street Corner Society: The Social Structure of an Italian Slum*. Chicago: University of Chicago Press.

Widdicombe, Sue, and Robin Wooffitt. 1995. *The Language of Youth Subcultures: Social Identity in Action*. London and New York: Harvester Wheatsheaf.

Williams, J. Patrick. 2003. "The Straightedge Subculture on the Internet: A Case Study of Style-Display Online." *Media International Australia Incorporating Culture and Policy* 107:61–74.

———. n.d. "Authentic Identities: Straightedge Subculture, Music, and the Internet." Unpublished paper.

Williams, J. Patrick, and Heith Copes. 2005. "'How Edge Are You?' Constructing Authentic Identities and Subcultural Boundaries in a Straightedge Internet Forum." *Symbolic Interaction* 28, 1:67–89.

Williams, Rhys H. 2000. "Introduction: Promise Keepers: A Comment on Religion and Social Movements." *Sociology of Religion* 61, 1:1–10.

Willis, Paul. 1977. *Learning to Labor: How Working Class Kids Get Working Class Jobs*. New York: Columbia University Press.

Wilson, Brian, and Michael Atkinson. 2005. "Rave and Straightedge, the Virtual and the Real: Exploring Online and Offline Experiences in Canadian Youth Subcultures." *Youth and Society* 36, 3:276–311.

Wood, Robert T. 1999. "'Nailed to the X': A Lyrical History of the Straightedge Youth Subculture." *Journal of Youth Studies* 2, 2: 133–152.

Wooden, Wayne S., and Randy Blazak. 2001. *Renegade Kids, Suburban Outlaws: From Youth Culture to Delinquency.* 2nd ed. Belmont, Calif.: Wadsworth.

Young, Kevin, and Laura Craig. 1997. "Beyond White Pride: Identity, Meaning and Contradiction in the Canadian Skinhead Subculture." *Canadian Review of Sociology and Anthropology.* 34, 2:175–206.

Youth of Today. 1986. "Youth Crew." On *Can't Close My Eyes* [LP]. Huntington Beach, Calif.: Revelation Records.

Zald, Mayer, and Roberta Ash. 1966. "Social Movement Organizations." *Social Forces* 44:327–341.

Zhou, Xueguang. 1993. "Unorganized Interests and Collective Action in Communist China." *American Sociological Review* 58:54–73.

Zinn, Maxine Baca, Lynn Weber Cannon, Elizabeth Higginbotham, and Bonnie Thornton Dill. 1986. "The Costs of Exclusionary Practices in Women's Studies." *Signs* 11, 2: 290–303.

Zirakzadeh, Cyrus Ernesto. 1997. *Social Movements in Politics: A Comparative Study.* London and New York: Longman.

INDEX

Ross Haenfler earned his Ph.D. in sociology from the University of Colorado, where he coauthored *The Better World Handbook: From Good Intentions to Everyday Actions* with his friends Ellis Jones and Brett Johnson. Haenfler loves teaching and has taught many courses, including Social Movements, Political Sociology, Self and Consciousness, Implementing Social Change, Men and Masculinities, and Deviant Youth Subcultures. He is currently an assistant professor at the University of Mississippi. His hobbies include hiking, traveling, and vegetarian cooking. Haenfler has been part of the straight edge movement for over seventeen years. He continues to write about subcultures, masculinity, and social movements.